Key Considerations for Successful Biotechnological and Pharmaceutical Product Launches

Schriften zur Gesundheitsökonomie 22

Key Considerations for Successful Biotechnological and Pharmaceutical Product Launches

Jana Wolf Sussman

Wolf Sussman, Jana

Universität Erlangen-Nürnberg
Lehrstuhl für Gesundheitsmanagement
Lange Gasse 20
90403 Nürnberg, Deutschland

Key Considerations for Successful Biotechnological and Pharmaceutical Product Launches
Schriften zur Gesundheitsökonomie 22, HERZ, Nürnberg 2013
Zugl. Erlangen, Nürnberg, Univ., Diss., 2013
Erstreferent: Prof. Dr. Oliver Schöffski, MPH;
Zweitreferent: Prof. Dr. Adelheid-Susanne Esslinger
Promotionstermin: 07.02.2012
ISBN 978-3-936863-21-5

Herstellung: Books on Demand GmbH, Norderstedt

Table of Contents

List of Figures

List of Tables

List of Abbreviations

4Ps	Product, Price, Place, Promotion
7Ps	Product, Price, Place, Promotion, Payer, Processes, Positioning
ABPI	Association of the British Pharmaceutical Industry
AE	Adverse Event
AIDS	Autoimmune Deficiency Syndrome
AMG	Arzneimittelgesetz
AMNOG	Arzneimittelneuordnungsgesetz
ATU	Awareness, Trial & Usage
AV	Audio Visual
AZN	AstraZeneca
BfArM	Bundesinstitut für Arzneimittel und Medizinprodukte
Bio / Pharm	Biotechnological and / or Pharmaceutical
BCG	Boston Consulting Group
BLA	Biologics License Applications
BMS	Bristol Myers Squibb
BRIC	Brazil, Russia, India, and China
CAGR	Cumulative Annual Growth Rate
CAM	Commercial Accommodation Monitor
CBER	Center for Biologics Evaluation and Research
CDER	Center for Drug Evaluation and Research
CEO	Chief Executive Officer
Cf.	compare
CHB	Chronic Hepatitis B
CHIMP	Commission for Health Improvement
CHMP	Committee for Medicinal Products for Human Use
CME	Continued Medical Education
CML	Chronic Myeloid Leukemia
CMS	Concerned Member States
CNS	Central Nervous System
COMP	Committee for Orphan Medicinal Products

CP	Centralized Procedure
CPM	Critical Path Method
CRM	Customer Relationship Management
DNA	Deoxyribonucleic Acid
DTC	Direct To Consumer
E7 countries	Brazil, China, India, Indonesia, Mexico, Russia, and Turkey
EC	European Commission
EconLit	American Economic Association's Electronic Bibliography
ed.	editors
ED	Erectile Dysfunction
e.g.	Exempli gratia (for example)
EGF	Epidermal Growth Factor
EMA	European Medicines Agency
et al.	et alli (and others)
etc.	et cetera (and so on)
EU	European Union
FDA	United States Food and Drug Administration
FDAMA	Food and Drug Administration Modernization Act
G7	Canada, France, Germany, Italy, Japan, United Kingdom, and United States
GATT	General Agreement on Tariffs and Trade
GDP	Gross Domestic Product
GMP	Good Manufacturing Practices
GP	General Practitioner
GSK	Glaxo-Smith Kline
hGh	Human Growth Hormone
HIV	Human Immunodeficiency Virus
HR	Human Resources
IDI	Individual in-depth interviews
i.e.	id est (that is)
IMP	Investigational Medicinal Product

IND	Investigational New Drug Application
INN	International Nonproprietary Name
IP	Intellectual Property
IPNI	iPhysiciansNet Initiative
IQWiG	Institut für Qualität und Wirtschaftlichkeit im Gesundheitswesen (Institute for Quality and Efficiency in Health Care, Germany)
IRR	Internal Rate of Return
IST	Investigator-Sponsored Trial
KGaA	Kommanditgesellschaft auf Aktien (Partnership Limited by Shares)
KOL	Key Opinion Leader
KPI	Key Performance Indicator
LDL	Low-Density Lipoprotein
LLY	Eli Lilly
MAA	Marketing Authorization Application
MHRA	Medicines and Healthcare Products Regulatory Agency
MOA	Mechanism of Action
MRP	Mutual Recognition Procedure
NBER	National Bureau of Economic Research
NCEs	New Chemical Entities
NDA	New Drug Application
NEJM	New England Journal of Medicine
NICE	National Institute for Health and Clinical Excellence
NHS	National Health System
NME	New Medical Entity
NPV	Net Present Value
NRTI	Nucleoside / tide Reverse Transcriptase Inhibitor
NSAID	Non-steroidal anti-inflammatory drug
OTC	Over-the-counter
P4P	Pay-for-performance
PAH	Pulmonary Artery Hypertension
PAP	Patient Access Program

PCT	Patent Cooperation Treaty
PDMA	Product Development and Management Association
PERT	Project Evaluation and Review Technique
PFE	Pfizer
PhRMA	Pharmaceutical Research and Manufacturers of America
PM	Product Manager
POC	Point of Care
POCA	Phonetic Orthographic Computer Analysis
PPRS	Pharmaceutical Price Regulation Scheme
PR	Public Relations
PubMed	Database of the National Center for Biotechnology Information
QALY	Quality-adjusted life years
QOL	Quality-of-life
RACI	Responsible, Accountable, Consulted, Informed
R&D	Research & Development
RMS	Reference Member State
ROI	Return on Investment
ROIC	Return on Invested Capital
ROW	Rest of World
Rx	Prescription
SAE	Serious Adverse Event
SARS	Severe Acute Respiratory Syndrome
SME	Small and Medium-sized Enterprises
SNY	Sanofi-Aventis
SWOT	Strengths, Weaknesses, Opportunities, Threats
TKD	Takeda
UK	United Kingdom
UN	United Nations
US(A)	United States (of America)
VFA	Verband der forschenden Pharma-Unternehmen
WHO	World Health Organization
WTO	World Trade Organization

1. Relevance of the Topic

In general terms, innovation, defined as the introduction of new products into the marketplace, is vitally important for the overall welfare of a country and its people. New products and services improve the customers' lives.[1]

From a corporate perspective, the launch of a product, defined as its first introduction into a marketplace, determines its overall success in the market. It is the most crucial part of a product's life cycle that decides the product's trajectory and future path. International pharmaceutical studies show that the first 6 months post-launch determine the life cycle potential of a product.[2] During this launch phase, the decision makers face many unknowns. Currently, only about ten new chemical entities (NCEs) make it to market each year. This low number is attributed to the high side-effect risk for pharmaceutical drugs, which often times outweighs the potential gain of a product launch.[3] Thus, every launch counts and needs to be carefully planned once the decision to pursue the drug has been made.

A longitudinal study, done by the National Bureau of Economic Research (NBER) in 2003, based on data from 52 countries, shows that new chemical entity (pharmaceutical) launches increase the life expectancy of an entire population by .056 years (nearly 3 weeks) annually.[4] This implies that launch delays reduce longevity in a country[5], which is another reason why launching the right product at the right time is so important not only for the companies involved, but also for the people and countries affected.

---

1 Cf. Hauser, Tellis, Griffin (2006), p. 687, 710
2 Cf. Corstjens, Demeire, Horowitz (2005), pp. 319-331; Robinson (2010), p. 4; Seiter, Holz (2009), p. 929
3 Cf. Ortwein (2001), pp. 18-19
4 Cf. Lichtenberg (2005), pp. 69-70
5 Cf. Lichtenberg (2005), p. 71

In general, there is a dearth of reliable empirical data and studies on product launch success and the reasons why they do – or do not – make it to market.[6] Partially this is due to the proprietary, company-internal status of this information, partially due to the fact that every launch is different due to manifold product-specific, company-specific, and market-specific factors.[7]

All these factors have to be taken into consideration to prepare the overall success of a biotechnological and / or pharmaceutical (short: bio / pharmaceutical) product in the marketplace. Since this industry is heavily regulated and necessitates extensive studies for each approval in each indication and use, preparing and getting the launch right is even more crucial in this industry than most others. While a lot of work has been done reviewing various areas, developments and factors within the bio / pharmaceutical industry, no literature exists pulling these factors together into one comprehensive review of these factors in preparation for and at the time of a launch. This dissertation is trying to fill this gap by taking a close look at external and internal factors that have to be addressed and decided upon to prepare for a product launch in this industry. Since the marketplace is constantly changing, mainly due to new regulatory and financial pressures as well as a more demanding and educated patient base, these emerging factors are also considered.

1.1 Overview of this Dissertation

This dissertation starts where general books on marketing and innovation leave off, focusing on the specifics and peculiarities of bio / pharmaceutical product launches. Due to the long-term planning needs and the in-depth clinical studies involved with the launch of a pharmaceutical or biotech product, launch-relevant decisions are made years before the actual product launch and outside of the

6 Cf. Chandy, Hopstaken, Narasimhan, Prabhu (2006), p. 495; N. a. (1992), p. 6 ; Johne, Snelson (1988), pp. 120-121 ; Scott Morton (1999), pp. 421-440; Thölke, Hultink, Robben (2001), pp. 3-14

7 Cf. Chandy, et al. (2006), pp. 494-495; Simon, Kotler (2003)

commercial realm.[8] Due to the highly-regulated nature of this marketplace, many factors have to be aligned and considered to take into account current market conditions while addressing customer and stakeholder needs. Thus this dissertation pays tribute to the launch-relevant decisions that are made in the research and development world.

In Chapter 2, the products in the bio / pharmaceutical marketplace are defined, followed by an outline of the current and worldwide marketplace overview, including the idiosyncrasies of this market, particularly the regulatory landscape. To provide a better understanding of current launch environment, the key challenges in today's bio / pharmaceutical market are outlined.

Following this up-to-date market overview, the critical importance of the product launch in today's market is reviewed in Chapter 3: First, this is done based on the temporal view of a product launch, analyzing its role in the product life cycle. Subsequently, it is looked at on a content-driven basis, segmenting the key success factors previously established in a variety of studies and meta-analyses based on their origin:

- market-driven,
- product-driven, and
- company-driven

key considerations for a product launch.

In the market-driven section (chapter 4), the launch market (blockbuster or niche market), the product's launch position in it (first-to-market or follow-on product) as well as its position in the treatment paradigm (first- or second-line) are assessed and key launch considerations discussed. This includes competitive as-

8 One good example of this are the primary and secondary endpoints of a study, as they form the basis of the product's marketable benefits at launch. Thus, it is imperative to consider the market-relevance of these decisions a long time before the launch, as course corrections are pricey, time intensive, and thus might even be impossible.

sessments, intellectual property (IP) strategy and market selection, as well as launch timing based on factors such as reference pricing.

In the product-driven section (chapter 5), the product is taken through the launch-relevant considerations of the research & development process, such as trial design, patient selection, and how to deal with side effects. The value of strategic partnerships and alliances to offer more comprehensive customer solutions, instead of 'just' a product, is also touched upon. Subsequently, the marketing aspects of the launch preparation process are discussed. Here the focus lies on the relevant market research steps before discussing the 7Ps of Bio / Pharmaceutical marketing, relevant decisions such as branding and packaging. The final part of this section focuses on the stakeholders already outlined in the introduction and how these and their needs are to be specifically addressed in preparation for the launch.

In the third and final section (chapter 6), the company-driven organizational considerations get the necessary attention by providing insights and tools on how to align the company behind a product, pull the right people into the launch team, and how to coordinate internationally and cross-functionally. Last but not least, sales team requirements as well as control mechanisms and launch trackers to adjust the course after take-off, if possible, are presented.

Chapter 7 summarizes the findings of this dissertation while giving an outlook on potential future investigations.

1.2 Aim of this Dissertation

The aim is to help business professional to better understand the bio / pharmaceutical marketplace and thus be able to effectively plan for and execute a product launch.

To ensure practical relevance and to clarify some key points, market-specific cases and details as well as graphics are included to provide a quick reference guide and potentially a (mental) check list as they are going through the everyday craziness of a product launch.

In the current literature, a reference book that provides an overview of the factors that play a role in the launch process is missing. In this way, this dissertation aims to support future strategists, marketers, and business planners in mastering their launch processes, asking and answering the right questions at the right time – and ultimately delivering the best product possible to their customers. Research has shown that for a product's success process and execution are absolutely vital.[9]

1.3 Methodology of this Dissertation

After a series of confidential interviews with industry leaders, followed by literature research in various libraries and online databases in the United States (US) and Europe, a methodological review of available articles was carried out.

The four databases queried were Business Source Complete, EconLit (the American Economic Association's electronic bibliography), PubMed (the database of the National Center for Biotechnology Information), and Scopus. The key words were searched in two areas of relevance and combined with an 'AND' to ensure that the overlap of the two areas leads to relevant, substantial findings: "launch" OR "product introduction" OR "new product" OR "market entry" OR "market introduction" OR "product entry" AND "excellence" OR "key success factor" OR "key performance indicator" OR "KPI" OR "KSF" or "success indicator" OR "considerations" OR "important factor". No further restrictions were entered in the query.

[9] Cf. Cooper, Kleinschmidt (1993), p. 77

That the more specifically scientific databases, such as EconLit, PubMed and Scopus, only showed a low number of potential hits, 106, 93, and 370 respectively, shows how infrequently these issues are handled in this scientific space. The fact that the more general business database Business Source Complete came up with 2467 potential hits, on the other hand, proves that the selected key words are relevant.

All 3111 potential hits were searched, providing 7 relevant and 128 potentially relevant hits. The potentially relevant and relevant hits also included articles regarding general business launch success factors to ensure that these are factored in and taken into account for the more specific realm of pharmaceutical and biotechnological launches.
After further review of the 128 potentially relevant hits, 59 ultimately proved to be relevant for the purpose of this publication. All of their findings, in addition to the previously done library and database research were included in the following. It is important to note that, while the relevant hits were important for specific aspects of the bio / pharmaceutical product launch, few of them covered multiple aspects thereof: Thus, this dissertation is an attempt to fuse together the various findings of researchers and authors to a more holistic picture regarding launches in the bio / pharmaceutical realm.

2. Product Launches and the Current Bio / Pharmaceutical Marketplace

2.1 Definition of a Product Launch

The product launch can be defined from two perspectives:

- temporally, in the context of the overall innovation and the product life cycle, as a well
- content-driven, by its managerial content, such as the need to present the product to the target market in order to generate income.

Table 2-1 depicts definitions for product launches in current literature and categorizes them according to the temporal and content-driven perspective.

Table 2- 1: Product launch definitions

Source	Definition	Perspective
Call (1997), p. 10	The market introduction of new products is part of the product development process and contains all marketing-strategic and -operative planning and decision actions, that have to be turned into customer, competitive and company specific measures, so that the desired physical time point of market entry can be realized.	Temporal content-driven

Hultink, Robben (1999), p. 547	A launch strategy consists of those marketing decisions that are necessary to present a product to its target market and begin to generate income from sales of the new product (…)	Temporal content-driven
Lach (2001), p. 32	(…) the product launch is the comprehensive task of all phases of the innovation process for a new product, with the objective to optimally satisfy the needs of the target customers with the new product.	Temporal content-driven
Pleschak, Sabisch (1996), p. 241	The product launch is the last, concluding, and at the same time most critical phase of the innovation process.	Temporal
Vahs, Burmester (2005), p. 256	The market introduction of a new product contains the time from the beginning of the preparatory measures for the market entry until the successful assertion of the problem solution in the marketplace or until a stable sales growth has been reached.	Temporal

Source: Based on Kuhn (2007), p. 9

Both aspects will be discussed in this dissertation. The temporal view will be examined in chapter 3.1, while the content-driven view will be added in the subsequent part (chapter 3.2).

2.2 Products in the Bio / Pharmaceutical Market

The products to be launched within the pharmaceutical and biologics marketplace can be distinguished based on their building blocks, usage of the products, their patent status, and their prescription requirements, as visualized in table 2-2.

Table 2- 2: Distinguishing factors in the Bio / Pharmaceutical field

Building blocks	Pharmaceuticals	Biologics
Usage	Therapeutic	Prophylactic
Patent status	Originator	Generic/biosimilars
Prescription need	Ethical	OTC

Source: Own depiction

2.2.1 Pharmaceuticals and Biologics

Regarding the products' building blocks, one distinguishes between pharmaceutical, small-molecule based, and biologic, protein-based drugs. Table 2-3 breaks down the various distinguishing factors between these two types of drugs.

Table 2- 3: Distinguishing Pharmaceutical and Biotechnology products

Pharmaceutical Drugs	Biotechnology Drugs
Manufactured by chemical synthesis	Originates from a specific cell line
Simple, clearly defined structure	Complex, at times glycolyzed proteins/polypeptides
Relatively uncomplicated production process due to simplicity of product and process	Complicated and complex production process, sensitive to minute changes
Low molecular weight	High molecular weight
After patent expiration generics enter the market (copy of product)	After patent expiration biosimilars enter the market (copy not possible)

Source: Based on Boston Consulting Group (BCG) (2006), p. 13

While pharmaceuticals are the traditional drugs we envision as we are talking about medicines, biotechnology drugs have been up and coming over the past decades and thus warrant a small excursion into more details: Biotechnology products can be distinguished between so-called red (medicine), green (agriculture), and white (manufacturing process enhancing) biotechnology products. Due to its nature, this dissertation will focus on 'red' biotechnology products that are used in the same context as pharmaceutical drugs: to enhance life and cure diseases.[10]

Biotechnological products are protein-based and are usually produced in the cell lining of animal cells.[11] Various proteins that are usually produced by the body, such as insulin, can also be produced in specific clone cells. The advantage is that this causes fewer immune reactions and can be produced more readily.[12]

The idea of biological products is not new: As early as in the Middle Ages, leeches were used as a blood thinner. Leeches secrete the protein hirudine to keep the

[10] Cf. Boston Consulting Group(BCG) (2006), p. 7
[11] Cf. Ortwein (2001), p. 18; Ropp (1993)
[12] Cf. Ortwein (2001), p. 28

blood liquid at the bite site and inside its body. Using gene technology, it is now possible to produce hirudine biosynthetically.[13] The U.S. Code of Federal Regulations first defined biologic products as early as 1902.[14]

At times, the term biotechnology is also (mis)used to simply describe the smaller-size pharmaceutical companies. Gilead Sciences, for example, that is basing its success on mainly chemical compounds for the treatment of Human Immunodeficiency Virus (HIV) / Autoimmune Deficiency Syndrome (AIDS), is officially listed as the 'fifth largest biotech company'[15], even though from a product standpoint this is incorrect. In this work, all specifications of biotechnology and pharmaceuticals will be based on the ingredients of the drug instead of its parent company's size and nomenclature.

Due to the current dominance of pharmaceuticals and the growing importance of biologics, both pharmaceuticals and biologics will be discussed. Since the launch process and requirements for both types of products are rather similar, this does not result in an issue for this dissertation. In case of specific differences, these will be called out.

2.2.2 Therapeutic and Prophylactic Drugs

In the larger realm of medical care, one can distinguish between diagnostics and therapeutics. The first one diagnoses the disease (usually some kind of a test involving a bodily substance or fluid, such as a tissue sample or blood). The latter treats the disease diagnosed by the healthcare provider, at times determined by the previously mentioned diagnostic.

Within the realm of actual treatment of a disease, another distinction can be made between therapeutics and prophylactic drugs. The former cure or treat a disease

---

[13] Cf. Ortwein (2001), p. 28
[14] Cf. Ropp (1993)
[15] Cf. PriceWaterhouseCoopers (2010), p. 7

that has already manifested the latter aim to prevent this disease from manifesting itself, usually in form of a vaccination. Due to their nature, clinical trials for vaccines require large numbers of safety and efficacy data from healthy volunteers. It also carries a higher risk as it is intended for healthy people and not to treat an already sick individual. This means that at times the manufacturer might have to offer a 'money back guarantee' for someone who gets the disease s/he was vaccinated against.[16]

Since the market for therapeutics is larger and thus more important today, the main focus of this dissertation lies on this market space. Nonetheless, as prophylactic drugs shed additional light to the launch process success factors, they are also included.

2.2.3 Originator and Generic Drugs

In regard to a products' patent status, patent-protected, originator drugs and unprotected, generic drugs exist.[17] Patents secure the patent owner an exclusive right to the patented structure and manufacturing process (to be discussed in detail in chapter 4.3.1). In an innovation-driven field like bio / pharmaceuticals, patents are the key to protecting the market space and, by virtue of the exclusivity rights granted, to recover the immense development costs.[18]

---

[16] Cf. PriceWaterhouseCoopers (2008), pp. 20-21

[17] For completeness sake, here is to be mentioned that in the case of authorized generics, originator drug manufacturers allow certain generic manufacturers to produce and sell their products while they are still patented. This usually happens at the end of the patented period, allowing the original manufacturer to make some additional income prior to the patent expiration by selling this right to a generics manufacturer. The generics manufacturer in turn has the competitive advantage over his generic competitors.

[18] Cf. Grabowski (2002)

2.2.3.1 Originator Drugs

Originator drugs, also known as innovative drugs, are the result of original research and development, patent-protected, and thus have market exclusivity for a pre-determined period of time.

On a competitive level, bio / pharmaceutical companies that offer originator drugs with distinctive medical benefits have a higher degree of influence on the payers and buyers than its generic, me-too counterparts.[19] These patented originator drugs face increasingly strong competition from generics, which will only intensify as pricing and reimbursement are scrutinized in light of cost pressures in an the aging patient population.[20] The United Nations (UN) estimate that 2 billion people will be over the age of 60 by 2050.[21] This necessitates a growing, yet affordable supply of drugs, which is most easily, and cost-effectively, met by generics.

2.2.3.2 Generics and Biosimilars

Both pharmaceutical and biotech products are copied as their patents expire. Generic drugs make out about 65% percent of products dispersed in the US, and up to 70% in European countries.[22]

Generics are defined as an equivalent to the originator drug approved by the authorities whose patent has expired.[23] Bioequivalence studies prove clinical equivalence of products that have the same ingredients and dosage, but different galenics.[24] Generic drugs have to adhere to the same safety standards as branded drugs, with the same consequences. Thus the US Food and Drug Administration (FDA)

---

[19] Cf. Porter (2008), p. 7
[20] Cf. Datamonitor (2008), p. 24; Pfister (2010), p. 2
[21] Cf. Ng (2004), p. 291
[22] Cf. PriceWaterhouseCoopers (2009), p. 13
[23] Cf. Ng (2004), p. 191
[24] Cf. Ortwein (2001), p. 42

banned 30 generics by Ranbaxy, the Indian manufacturer of generics, in 2008 due to concerns about the manufacturing standards at two of their Indian plants.[25]

In case of pharmaceuticals, these are called generics, in case of biotechnology drugs, they are called biosimilars (and, by some, biogenerics or follow-on biologics). The distinction is made as pharmaceuticals can be copied 100% and generics are identical to the patented product. Since biotechnology products are won out of a highly complex production process with unique living cells or organisms, biosimilars are merely similar to the original product, but never identical.[26] Thus far, few biosimilars have been approved, due to the costly and difficult manufacturing and approval process.[27]
For the purpose of this dissertation, the focus lies on originator drugs, as this poses the most complex circumstances for a product launch due to novelty of the active ingredients and thus the regulatory requirements.

From an originator drug's point-of-view, it is also important to clearly position and brand itself to clearly establish its benefits versus other available drugs. Additionally, originator drugs might be relegated to a second line position, after the cheaper, generic option has failed.[28] As this dissertation focuses on originator drugs, these factors have to be taken into account and will be further discussed in chapters 3.1 (Life Cycle Planning) and 4.2 (Implications of market entry and treatment lines). Also, while this is beyond the scope of this dissertation to go into further details, it needs to be stated at this point that the launch product has to be aligned with the overall business strategy, fit into the corporate portfolio and be feasible within the resource constraints.[29]

---

[25] Cf. Favole, Mundy (2008)
[26] Cf. BCG (2006), p. 13; European Medicines Agency (EMA) (2005)
[27] Note: From a legislative perspective, the EMA released guidelines for biosimilars as early as 2005 (Ernst & Young (2005), p. 63), and US President Obama signed off on a simplified biosimilar approval pathway in the Patient Protection and Affordable Care Act on March 23, 2010. Prior to the 2010 Act, biologics have been approved using comparability, such as Omnitrope, a human growth hormone, which is comparable to Genotropin.
[28] Cf. Seiter, Holz (2009), pp. 924-930
[29] Cf. Khurana, Rosenthal (1998), p. 72

2.2.4 Prescription and Non-prescription Drugs

Based on the necessary steps to procure the drug, one distinguishes between prescription (Rx, also called 'ethical') drugs and over-the-counter (OTC) drugs.[30]

Ethical drugs are prescription drugs requiring a healthcare provider's prescription.[31] Thus, as shown in figure 2-1, the person making the product decision, the physician, is not the ultimate consumer, the patient. This means the physician holds a gatekeeper position in case of ethical drugs, complicating the overall buying process by turning it into a complex triangle between the patient (recipient of the drug), the prescriber (decision maker) and the health insurance (payer).

Figure 2- 1: Purchasing triangle for ethical Bio / Pharmaceutical drugs

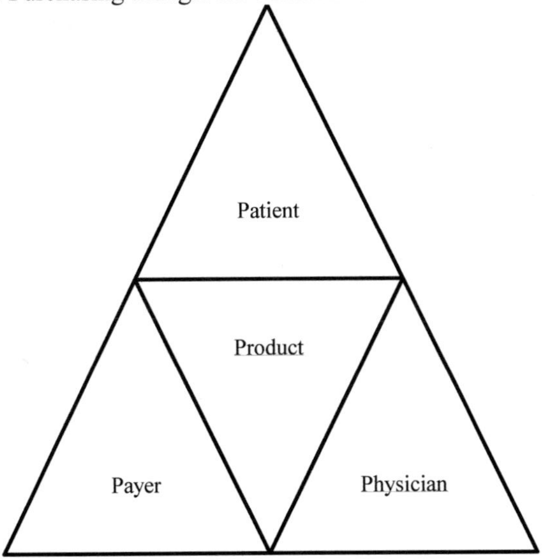

Source: Own depiction

---

[30] Note that in many countries even non-prescription drugs need to be distributed through special channels, such as pharmacies in Germany.

[31] Cf. Ng (2004), p. 1, Note that in some countries, such as the US, other healthcare providers, such as nurse practitioners and physician assistants are also allowed to prescribe drugs. These need to be addressed just like physician prescribers in the overall context of a product launch.

OTC drugs thus are deemed safe enough to be purchased directly by the patient or consumer at a pharmacy or drug store. They are usually well established in the marketplace already.[32] OTC medication does not necessitate a physician's prescription and is usually paid for by the patient, thus turning this transaction into a simple consumer buying process.[33] Since ethical drugs pose the more complex and bio / pharm-specific buying situation, this dissertation focuses on this type of drug.

In summary, the gray-shaded areas in table 2-4 constitute the focus of this dissertation:

Table 2- 4: Focus of this dissertation

Building blocks	Pharmaceuticals	Biologics
Usage	Therapeutic	Prophylactic
Patent status	Originator	Generic/biosimilars
Prescription need	Ethical	OTC

Source: Own depiction

To quantify the bio / pharmaceutical marketplace and to substantiate the inclusion and exclusion criteria made in the previous section with numbers, the overall marketplace will be reviewed in the following.

2.3 Bio / Pharmaceutical Market Size and Growth

As depicted in figure 2-2, worldwide prescription drug sales experienced consistent growth over the past year. In 2009, the worldwide bio / pharmaceutical sales were at $671 billion, out of which $644 billion (96%) are accounted for by prescription drugs with an estimated Cumulative Annual Growth Rate (CAGR) of 2.9% over the next 7 years.[34]

---

[32] Cf. Ng (2004), pp. 1-2; Weißbäcker, Müller (2005), pp. 204-205
[33] Cf. PriceWaterhouseCoopers (2008), p. 14-15
[34] Cf. EvaluatePharma (2011), pp. 6-8

Figure 2- 2: Worldwide prescription drug sales

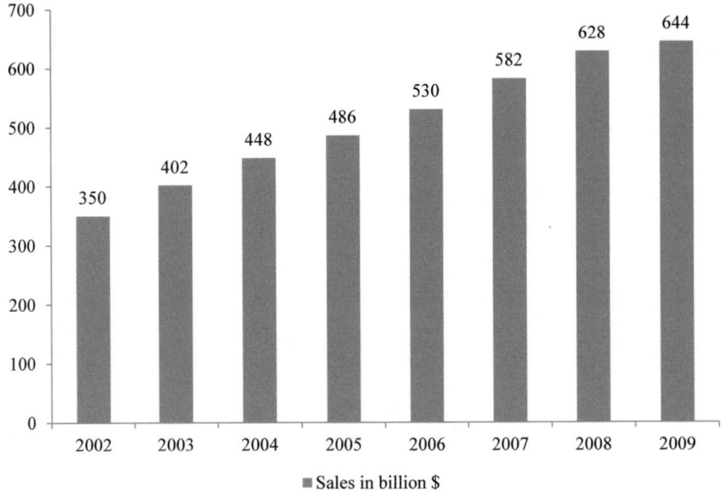

Source: EvaluatePharma (2011), p. 6

As the graph above shows, worldwide prescription drug sales were on the rise over the past years. Health is the most important good, or – as they say: 'Health isn't everything, but without health, everything is nothing'. Even in times of economic downturn, the healthcare market, and thus the bio / pharmaceutical market, continues to expand.[35]

Looking at the growth rate depicted in figure 2-3, though, it becomes clear that the year-over-year growth has slowed down over time.

---

[35] Cf. Ng (2004), p. 301

Figure 2- 3: Year-over-year sales growth of prescription drugs worldwide

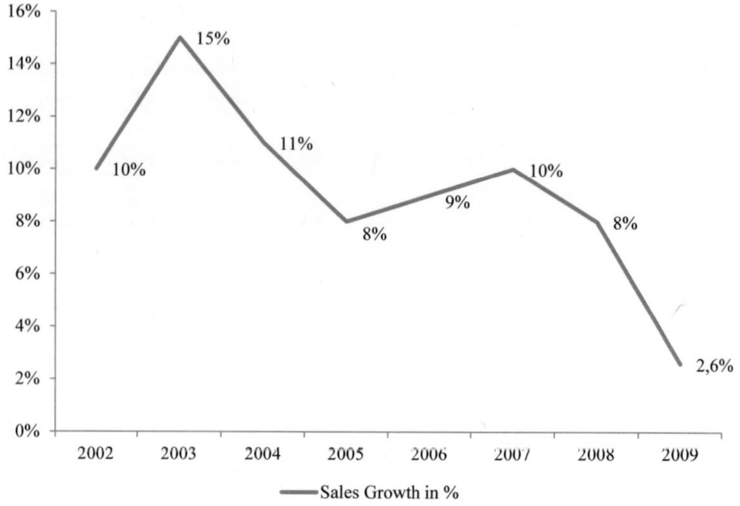

Source: EvaluatePharma (2011), p. 6

Of the overall drug market, only $27 billion (4%) are accounted for by OTC drugs, giving prescription drugs a predominant role in the overall marketplace, as shown in figure 2-4. This fact also explains why the focus of this dissertation lies in the complex, but lucrative prescription drug segment.

Figure 2- 4: Worldwide market share of prescription vs. OTC drugs

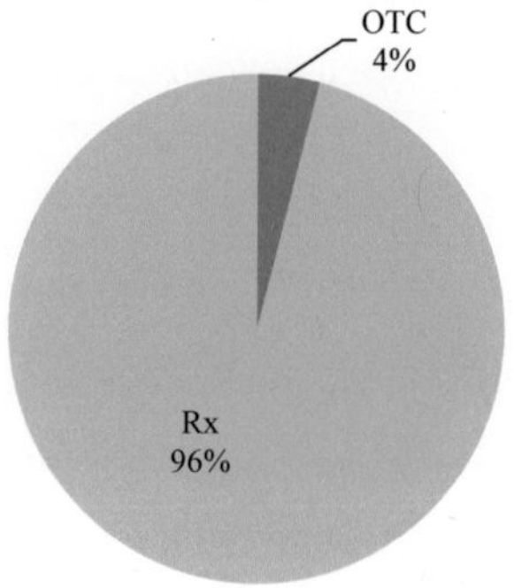

Source: Based on EvaluatePharma (2011)

The same is true for originator drugs versus generic drugs, here the monetary value of originator market is more than 11 times higher than the generic one, as depicted in figure 2-5. This is mainly due to the fact that generic drugs, despite being sold in large volumes, cost a fraction of originator drugs. This is the other reason why this dissertation focuses on prescription drugs.

Figure 2- 5: Worldwide market share of generic vs. originator drugs

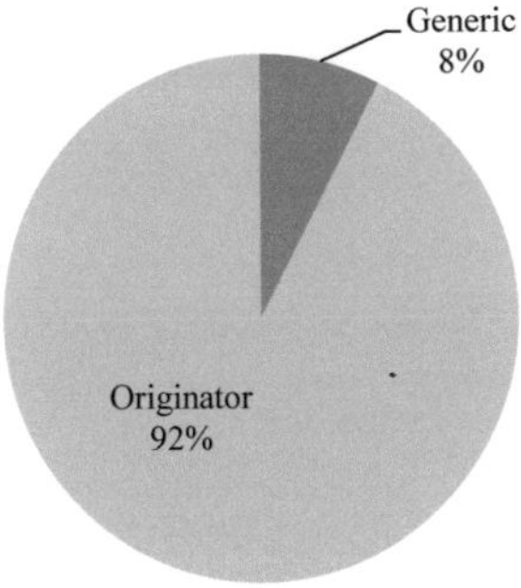

Source: Based on data from EvaluatePharma (2011)

As shown in figure 2-6, the US market still makes up 42% of global pharmaceutical sales followed by Europe and Japan36, but the BRIC countries (Brazil, Russia, India, and China), especially China are catching up fast and subsequently will be of increased importance over the next decades.[37] In the ROW (rest of world) region sales increased in double-digits between 2009 and 2010 (Asia- Africa- Australia (+13.3%), Latin America (+16.3%)), versus single-digit growth in North America (+3.2%), Europe (+1.8%) and Japan (.4%), also visualized in figure 4-5 later on.[38]

[36] Cf. Cacciotti, Clinton (2011) based on IMS data audit, p. 6

[37] Cf. Note: In the Asian markets, and to a growing extent in other markets as well, traditional Chinese medicine and alternative, herbal treatments are highly relevant and pose a serious competition

[38] Cf. Cacciotti, Clinton (2011), p. 6

Figure 2- 6: Global pharmaceutical sales by region

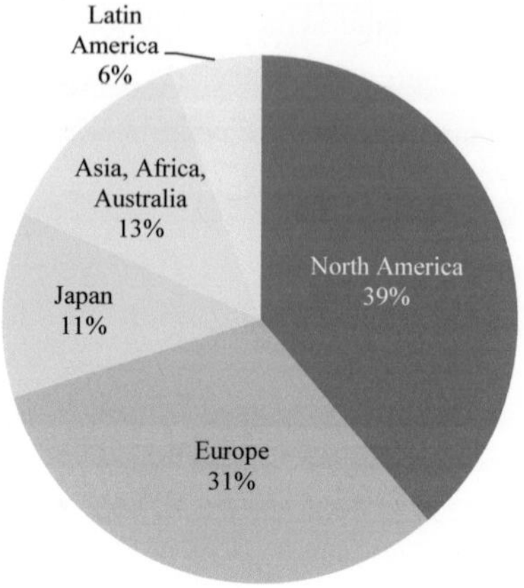

Source: Cacciotti, Clinton (2011) based on IMS data audit, p. 6

From a corporate perspective, and as shown in figure 2-7, the global players remain European and US-American at this point. The Top 10 is fully dominated by US-American and European companies, in the Top 10 to 20, Teva, Astellas, Daiichi-Sankyo, Eisai and Takeda (TKD) add one Israeli and four Japanese companies into the mix, respectively. Important to note is here, that Teva is a purely generic manufacturer[39] and does not play a role in the originator market, which is the focus of this work.

[39] Cf. Teva Pharmaceuticals (2011)

Figure 2- 7: Top 20 Bio / Pharmaceutical companies based on worldwide sales

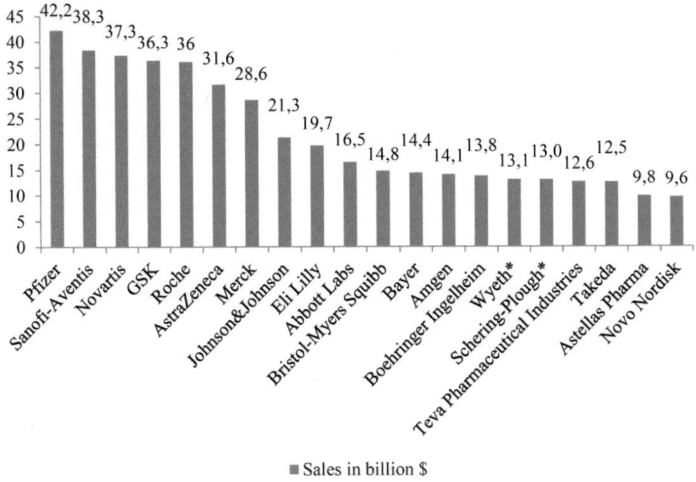

Source: Based on MedTRACK (2011)

At this point, the most successful drugs in terms of global sales are shown in figure 2-8:

Figure 2- 8: Top 20 Bio / Pharmaceutical products based on worldwide sales

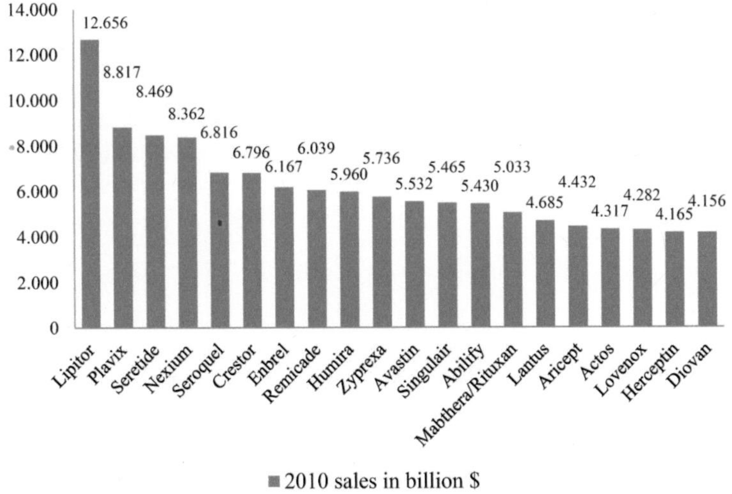

Source: Cacciotti, Clinton (2011) based on IMS data audit, p. 12

Biotechnology has become more important over the course of the past decades is considered to be a key technology for the future of medical research and practice. Especially in the fields of oncology (Avastin (bevacizumab), Herceptin (trastuzumab), Mabthera / Rituxan (rituximab), immunology (Enbrel (eternercept), Humira (adalimumab), Remicade (infliximab)) and metabolic diseases (various growth hormones), biotechnology has provided significant therapeutic advances already.[40]

While biotech drugs accounted for only 4% of worldwide introductions between 1982 and 1992, they already accounted for 16% in the time period between 1993-2003[41], 17% in 2009 and is expected to be up to 23% in 2016.[42] Due to the fact that biologics are significantly more pricey than pharmaceuticals, in terms of sales they make up 31% of the overall bio / pharmaceutical market and, with the addition of new biotechnology drugs currently in development and the market growth of new biotech drugs, are expected to represent nearly half (48%) of the market in 2016.[43] It is also to be noted, that half of these introductions originated from US companies.[44]

[40] Cf. BCG (2006), p. 3-5; Cacciotti, Clinton (2011), p. 12; Trilling (2008b), pp. 235-236
[41] Cf. DiMasi, Grabowski (2007), p. 213
[42] Cf. EvaluatePharma (2011), p. 8
[43] Cf. EvaluatePharma (2011p. 8
[44] Cf. DiMasi, Grabowski (2007), p. 213

Figure 2- 9: Pharmaceuticals vs. biologics based on number of originator products currently on the market and worldwide sales – by sales and by volume

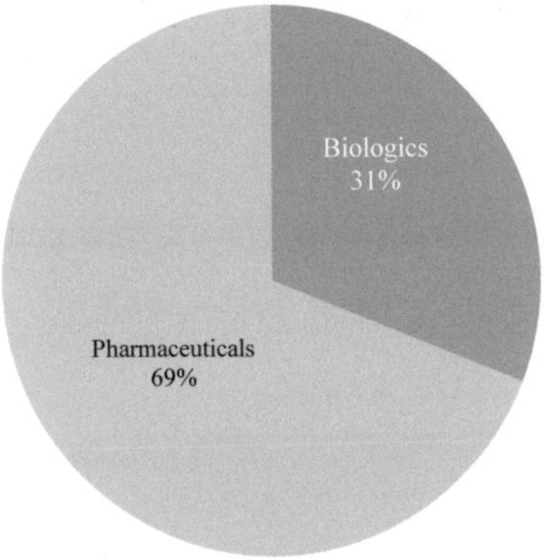

by sales

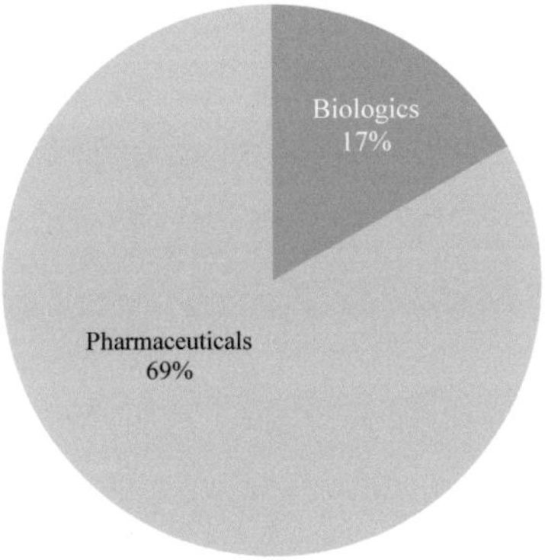

by volume

Source: Own depiction based on data from EvaluatePharma (2011)

Comparing the two pie charts in figure 2-9, it is obvious that while biotechnology products only make up 17% of patented products in the current marketplace, their sales value is significantly higher with 31% of the global market. This shows how lucrative the biotechnology sector is for small biotech companies and traditional pharma giants alike.

Over the course of the past 30 years, the red biotechnology sector has exploded. Over 4,000 start ups have been formed and annual revenues are at around $117 billion world-wide in 2009, and expected to grow 62% to 189 billion in 2016.[45] With a historically greater return rate, higher average peak sales, as well as slower sales decline (due to the complexities of developing biosimilars, as mentioned before), biologics are the current focus of many development pipelines.[46]

2.4 Therapeutic Areas

With $56 billion worldwide sales (~8% of the worldwide market share) in 2010, as depicted in figure 2-10, oncology remains the leading therapeutic area.[47]

[45] Cf. EvaluatePharma (2011), p. 8; Pisano (2006), p. 118
[46] Cf. Cacciotti, Clinton (2011), p. 12; David, Tramontin, Zemmel (2009), pp. 609-610
[47] Cf. Clinton, Mozeson (2010), p. 74, EvaluatePharma (2011), p. 21

Figure 2- 10: Key therapeutic areas based on worldwide sales

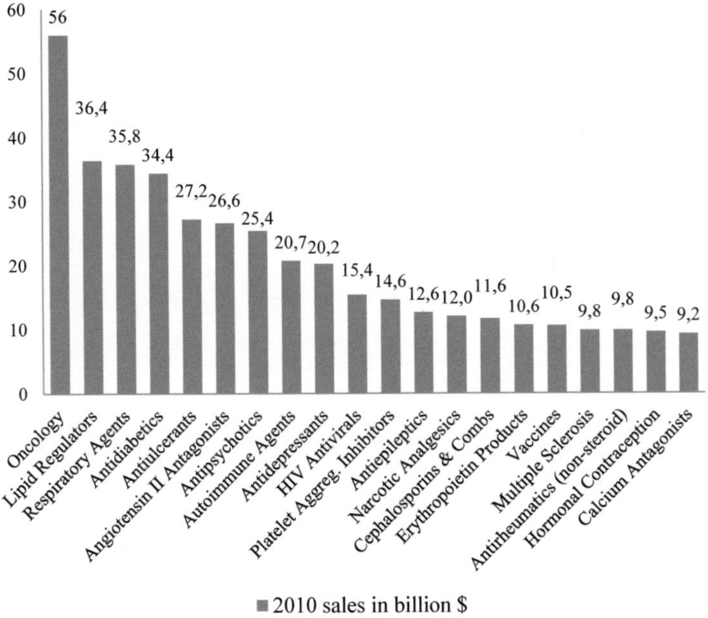

Source: Cacciotti, Clinton (2011) based on IMS data audit, p. 12

With the acquisition of Genentech and its top oncology products (Avastin Herceptin, and Mabthera / Rituxan) Roche is positioned to dominate this market for the coming years.[48] Oncology is estimated to continue to grow both in overall market share (+1%) and sales (+5%) until 2016. This is followed by anti-diabetics and anti-rheumatics.[49]

It is interesting to note that vaccines (prophylactic drugs) are expected to grow by 7% until 2016, to become the number 4 ranked area, with a market share increase of 1%. In the vaccine market, the top players are Glaxo-Smith Kline (GSK), Sanofi-Aventis (SNY), and Pfizer (PFE).[50]

---

[48] Cf. EvaluatePharma (2011), p. 14
[49] Cf. EvaluatePharma (2011), p. 13
[50] Cf. EvaluatePharma (2011), p. 13, 17

Market experts estimate that the existing trend towards integrated medicine, from prophylaxis to treatment, will continue to lead to a closer collaboration of bio / pharmaceutical companies with the entire spectrum of healthcare providers, products and services to create perceived value and effectively distinguish one's offer from the competition.[51]

2.5 Particularities of the Bio / Pharmaceutical Market Structure

The bio / pharmaceutical mainly differs from other industries in the following two points.

First, since drugs have the potential to harm as much as they do good, the industry and their product testing and approvals are highly regulated. This leads to a complex, costly and time intensive approval process for every drug.[52]

Secondly, as previously mentioned, a higher than usual number of stakeholders is involved in the buying process for prescription drugs: This leads to tensions between the manufacturer and provider of goods (the bio / pharmaceutical company), the ultimate customer (the patient), the decision maker (the physician) and the payer (government or private health insurance). Since the person deciding on, using, and paying for the product are not identical in this industry (the way they are when we go out and buy a coke), interests vary and tensions arise. This is regulated, yet also complicated for the participants, by the regulatory framework that governs the use of these drugs, depicted as the circle around the purchasing triangle in figure 2-11.

---

[51] Cf. Hilleke-Daniel (1989), pp. 25-27; PriceWaterhouseCoopers (2009), pp. 8-12
[52] Cf. Terblanche (2008), p. 202

Figure 2- 11: Regulatory framework shapes the purchasing triangle

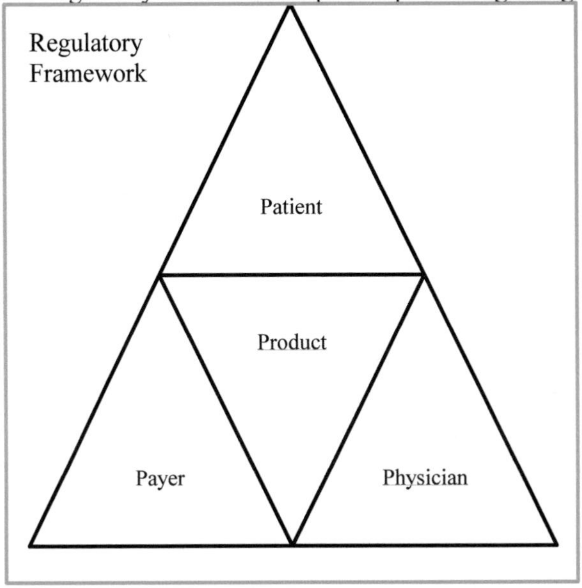

Source: Own depiction

To give an understanding of the complexities of this market, these specific aspects of the bio / pharmaceutical industry are to be outlined briefly in the following.

2.5.1 The Research & Clinical Development Process

In the bio / pharmaceutical field, product development is lengthy, complex and highly expensive due to regulatory requirements. It takes about 10-12 years from initial research until the launch of a bio / pharmaceutical product and is estimated to cost between $800 million to $1.2 billion.[53]

---

[53] Cf. Ng (2004), pp. 1-2; Datamonitor (2008), p. 24; PriceWaterhouseCoopers (2009), p. 13; for more information please see section 2.5.3

The clinical pre-launch development of all bio / pharmaceutical products can be broken into three phases:

- Phase I to collect safety data with healthy individuals,
- Phase II to test drug safety on potential patients and establish dose ranging, and
- Phase III to fully test the drug's safety and efficacy in established doses on potential patients

These phases each have a specific purpose in clinical trials, involving various groups of participants, vary in duration and cost, while the likelihood of the product's launch increases from phase to phase, as depicted in table 2-5.

Table 2- 5: Key facts about the phases of clinical development

	Pre-Clinical	Phase I	Phase II	Phase III	Approval	Phase IV
Main purpose / task		Safety Data	Drug safety and dose ranging	Drug safety and efficacy		Post-Marketing Surveillance of population at large
Participants		Healthy Persons	Potential Patients			Actual Patients
Duration (years)	4-6.5	1-1.5	2	3-3.5	.5-2.5	
Cost (in million €)	200-300	200-400			20-40	30-60
Likelihood to reach the next phase*	50%	70%	60%	70%		
Likelihood to launch*	10%	20%	30%	65%		

*approximation based on historical data

Sources: Based on DiMasi, Grabowski (2007), p. 213; Fischer, Breitenbach, (2010a), pp. 35-36; Ng (2004), p. 144

2.5.2 Regulatory Authorities

Irrespective of the country one is seeking approval in, there is a state authority that needs to authorize the product in question to be distributed in the respective market space. The two most important authorities for bio / pharmaceutical product approvals are the European Medicines Agency (EMA) [54] in the European Union (EU), and the in the USA.

Within Europe, Switzerland, as a non-EU member has its own regulatory agency, SwissMedic.[55] While it is a small marketplace, it is important, as some major companies (namely Roche and Novartis) are Swiss-based and oftentimes are able to receive early approval with favorable labeling in their home country.[56]

Failing to gain approval in the US does not only exclude a company from selling its product in the most lucrative marketplace in the world, but also sends a signal to countries whose approval is referencing the FDA, such as Mexico, Canada, and some others.[57]

Other countries built their regulatory body based on the FDA model, such as the State Drug and Food Administration in China.[58] Over the next decade, the E7 countries (Brazil, China, India, Indonesia, Mexico, Russia, and Turkey) will become an increasingly important market for the bio / pharmaceutical industry.[59] The same is true for their regulating authorities.[60] Thus, keeping a close eye on these markets is going to be crucial for all global players. Since the EU and the USA are the two leading markets for pharmaceutical and biotechnology drugs,

---

54 Cf. At the end of 2009, the EMEA changed its name to EMA
55 Cf. Swissmedic (2011)
56 Cf. Danzon, Epstein (2009), pp. 28-30
57 Cf. Datamonitor (2008), p. 24
58 Cf. FDA (2011)
59 Cf. PriceWaterhouseCoopers (2008), pp. 1-5
60 Cf. PriceWaterhouseCoopers (2008), p. 36

this dissertation is going to focus on these in its description of regulatory considerations for launch strategies.[61]

The Japanese pharmaceutical market is only touched on marginally in this dissertation. This is due to its unusual structure and lack of multinationalism: Japanese Research & Development (R&D) tends to focus on imitative (not innovative) research and their drugs are usually licensed to and marketed by non-Japanese firms in the rest of the world, while Japanese firms in-license international products for domestic usage.[62] While Japan has been loosening its regulations for international business over the past years[63], the US and EU markets still provide the most useful global launch perspective.

While the specific approval processes differ, both thc US and the EU require the manufacturers to work with the agency to design appropriate clinical trials that allow them to submit clinical data that give a substantial enough insight into the products efficacy and safety data to allow for an educated approval decision.

In this dissertation, some key points of the approval processes are highlighted, for detailed information on the documentation requirements and timelines, it is necessary to visit the respective authorities' websites for the latest and most comprehensive information.

2.5.2.1 United States Food and Drug Administration (FDA)

The FDA has an Office of Regulatory Affairs and four centers, out of which the Center for Drug Evaluation and Research (CDER) and the Center for Biologics Evaluation and Research (CBER) are the relevant ones for the review and approval pharmaceuticals and biologics, respectively.[64]

---

[61] Cf. For additional information on other countries regulatory set up, please refer to Ng (2004), Chapters 7 and 8, as well as the respective authorities' websites for latest updates and details.

[62] Cf. Grabowski (1989), pp. 19-20; Mahlich (2007), pp. 75-77; Simon (1989), pp. 241-252

[63] Cf. Mahlich (2007), pp. 77-92

[64] Cf. Ng (2004), pp. 161-163

The FDA in its current form was founded in 1930, having grown out of the 'Important Drugs Act' in 1848 (allowing for customs checks of medical entities from abroad) and the 'Food, Drug and Insecticide Administration' founded in 1927.[65]

The US drug approval process can be broken into two phases:

1. The clinical phase, that is defined as the time from the investigational new drug application (IND) filing, which usually takes 30 days, until the new drug application (NDA) for pharmaceuticals, or the Biologics License Applications (BLA) for biologics (for details see figure 2-12).[66]

2. The approval phase, defined as the time from the NDA or BLA until the FDA's approval of application for marketing (for details see figure 2-13).[67]

[65] Cf. Fischer, Breitenbach (2010a), pp. 19-20
[66] Cf. DiMasi, Grabowski (2007), p. 210; Ng (2004), pp. 176-181
[67] Cf. DiMasi, Grabowski (2007), p. 210

Figure 2- 12: The IND review process

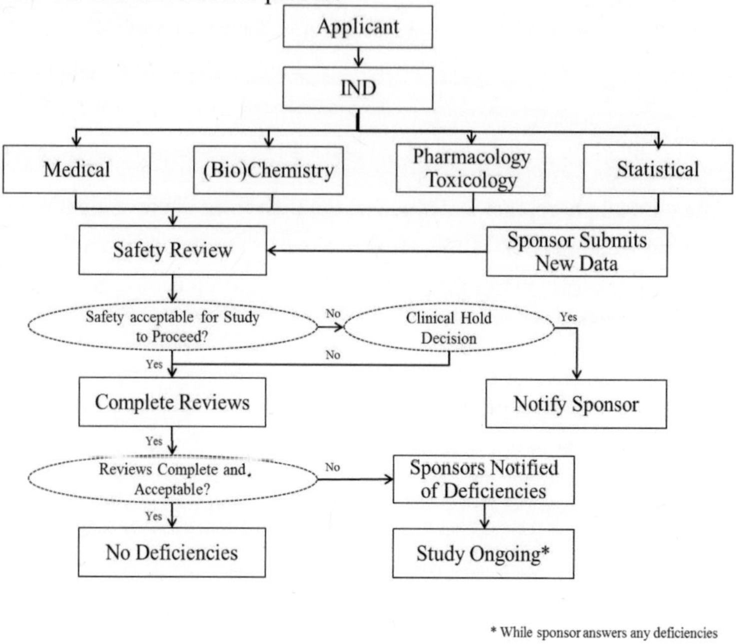

Source: CDER Handbook (1998), p. 12

Before the IND, as well as at the end of each clinical trial phase, and before the NDA / BLA submission, the FDA meets with the company to discuss results and prepare filings. The FDA has the right to stop clinical trials at any point to ensure that safety issues and other deficiencies in the trials are resolved.[68]

[68] Cf. Ng (2004), pp. 180-181; FDA (2011)

Figure 2- 13: The NDA / BLA review process

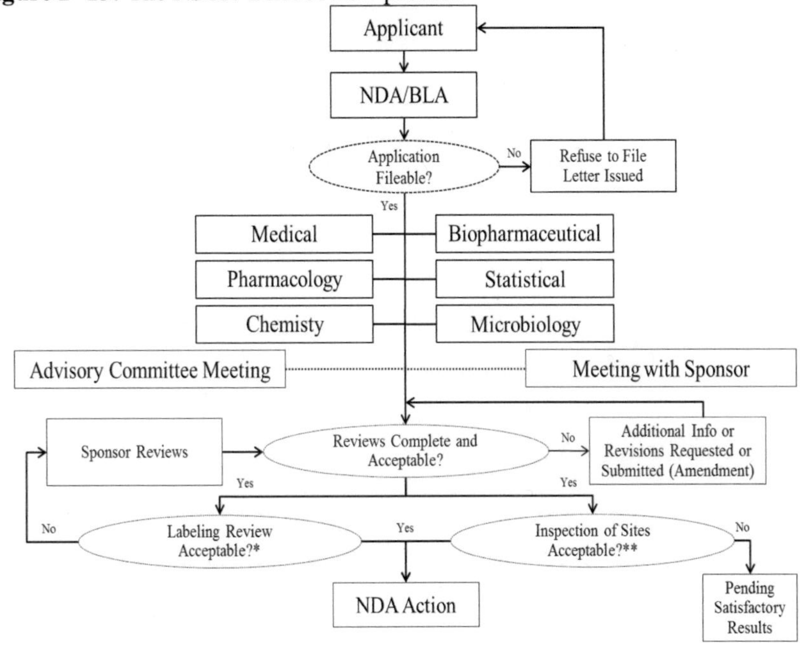

Source: CDER Handbook (1998), p. 19

Due to an earlier developed and thus larger biotechnology sector with higher R&D expenditures, the US has approved significantly more biotechnology products in the past years than Europe.[69]

Because of the previously mentioned safety concerns, the approval rates have been rather low over the past years (between 18 and 25 per annum), as shown in the FDA approval numbers in figure 2-14.[70]

---

[69] Cf. Ernst & Young (2005), p. 57

[70] Cf. Carroll (2011); Dooren (2010); FDA (2011); Larkin (2010)

Figure 2- 14: FDA drug approvals 2007-2010

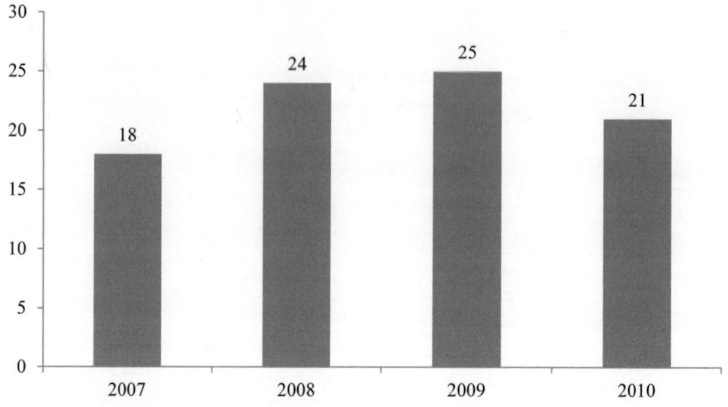

Sources: Based on Carroll (2011), Dooren (2010)

As a side note demonstrating the importance of biotechnology, about 1/3 to 1/2 of all FDA drug approvals are currently biotechnology products.[71]

2.5.2.2 European Medicines Agency (EMA)

While European countries used to have their own authorities for drug approval, such as the German BfArM (Bundesinstitut für Arzneimittel und Medizinprodukte) founded in 1975,[72] it is always possible – and mostly required for innovative products - to apply for a centralized, EU-wide drug approval at the EMA in London since January 1995.[73]
Just like the FDA approval process, the EMA process can be broken into two steps:

1. The clinical trials application, which only differs one major point from the FDA's IND process, as a Qualified Person has to testify that the investigational medicinal product (IMP) is manufactured according to Good Manu-

---

[71] Cf. BCG (2006), p. 12; Carroll (2011)
[72] Cf. Fischer, Breitenbach (2010a), pp. 15-17
[73] Cf. Fischer, Breitenbach (2010a), p. 44; Ortwein (2001), p. 57; Schlemminger (2010), pp. 142-144

facturing Practices (GMP). These applications are approved on a member state level.[74]

2. The Pharmaceutical Marketing Authorization Application (MAA), which is the rough equivalent to the FDA's NDA.[75]

Figure 2-15 shows the overall flow of a centralized EMA approval process, including the estimated times for each phase, which will be described further in the following.

Figure 2- 15: EMA approval process

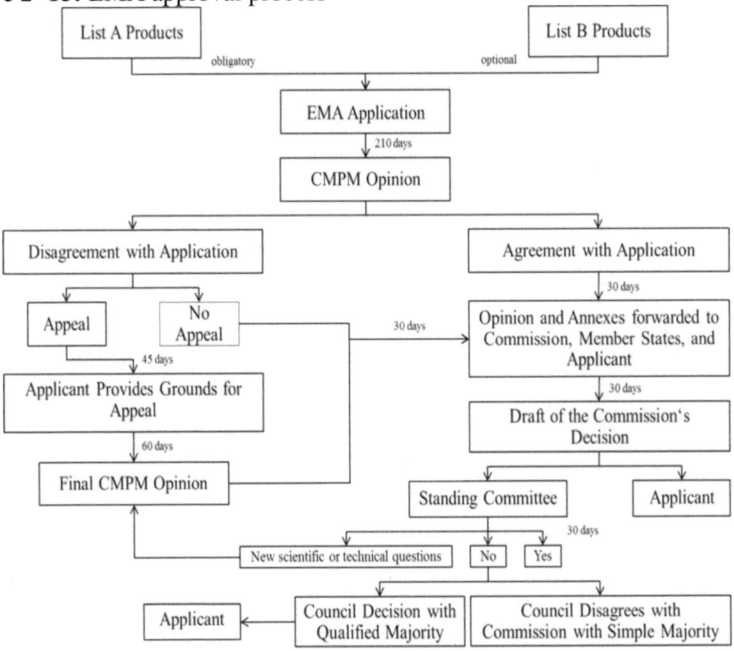

Sources: Based on Council of the European Communities (1993); Ortwein (2001), p. 59

[74] Cf. Ng (2004), p. 193
[75] Cf. Fischer, Breitenbach (2010a), pp. 44-45; Ng (2004), p. 193

According to the Regulation No. 726 / 2004 (known as the 'new pharmaceutical directive')[76] in the EU, companies can either follow the approval process through a specific member state and then go through a 'mutual recognition' (MR) process, or pursue a 'centralized procedure' (CP) by working directly with the EMA. This centralized procedure has been mandatory for biotechnology products, as well as medicines for the treatment of diabetes, cancer, HIV / AIDS, neurodegenerative diseases and all orphan drugs since October 2005. As of May 2008, this also includes drugs for viral and autoimmune diseases (so-called 'List A' products).[77] For conventional pharmaceuticals, it is still optional to pursue the 'mutual recognition procedure' ('List B' products).[78]

Choosing the mutual recognition procedure (MRP), the originator submits the NCEs in one country and files for mutual recognition in the other countries. Once the rapporteur country has approved the drug, it is automatically approved in all other countries within 90 days, unless the other countries object.[79]

The MAA approval process in which the EMA forwards its opinion to the European Commission (EC) for the final decision, takes about 300 days if no objections are raised, twice as long, if there are objections.[80] Thus, it behooves the applying company to work closely with the EMA and provide all necessary information in the adequate format, doing its part to facilitate a quick approval and ultimate launch. In general, the EMA centralized procedure leads to an average approval time of 15 months.[81]

The approval times for MRPs are a lot more volatile than the ones with Central Procedure, at times leading to double the recommended best practice time for approvals of 240 days. This is mainly due to the fact that the Concerned Member States (CMS) are reluctant to accept the initial assessment of the Reference Mem-

---

[76] Cf. European Parliament (2004)
[77] Cf. Ernst & Young (2005), p. 63
[78] Cf. Danzon, Wang, Wang (2005), p. 270; Ng (2004), p. 166, pp. 196-200
[79] Cf. Danzon, et al. (2005), p. 270
[80] Cf. Ng (2004), p. 198
[81] Cf. CMR International (2001), pp. 1-6; Danzon, et al. (2005), p. 270

ber States (RMS).[82] Since most innovative new pharmaceutical products and all biologics are List A products, the central procedure can be seen as the most important one for upcoming launches.

While studies show that the mean approval times between FDA and EMA are rather similar, individual differences are rather significant and have to be factored into the overall launch plan, as is shown on a few real-life examples in figure 2-16.[83]

Figure 2- 16: Exemplary FDA and EMA approval times

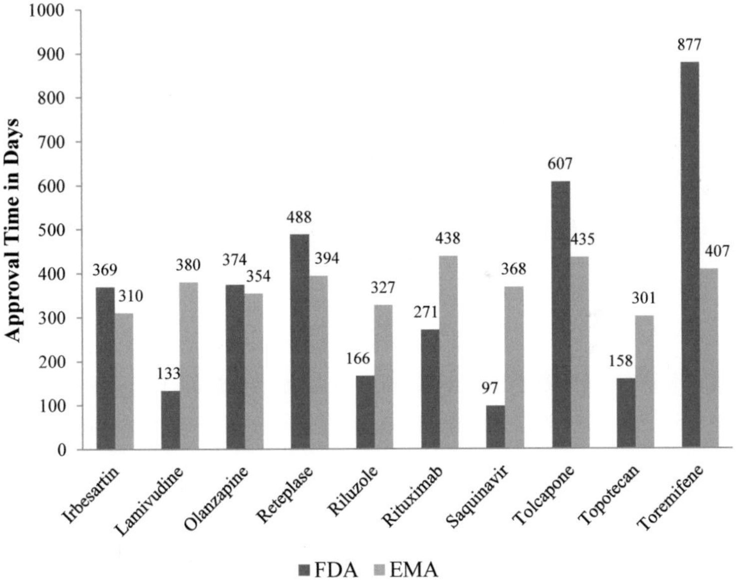

Source: Based on Healy, Kaitin (1999), p. 976

---

[82] Cf. CMR International (2001), pp. 2-5
[83] Cf. Healy, Kaitin (1999), pp. 969-978

2.5.3 Additional Stakeholders

In addition to the regulatory authorities outlined above, additional key stakeholders exist in the bio / pharmaceutical marketplace and need to be considered in preparation for a product launch. Stakeholders can be defined as “any group or individual who can affect or is affected by the achievement of the organization’s objectives”[84], in this case, the product launch.

Over the past years, payers and patients have increasingly important in the bio / pharmaceutical marketplace. With an aging population and increasing healthcare costs, payers are taking a close look at cutting costs and thus are scrutinizing the drug manufacturers accordingly. Governments and payers are more closely involved in the pricing decisions for new drugs (see Chapter 5.3.2.1), consequently healthcare cost effectiveness entities such as National Institute for Health and Clinical Excellence (NICE) and Institute for Quality and Cost Effectiveness in the Healthcare System (IQWiG) have been established (further details in Chapter 5.3.3).[85]

With increasingly available health information through online resources and a generally increasing independence and responsibility of the patient, patients are playing an increasing role in the marketplace as well.[86] Especially in high-risk and chronic disease states (cancer, diabetes, osteoporosis etc.) they are organized in patient organizations. Overall, patients are a new force to be reckoned with and should not be underestimated, even though direct marketing to patients is limited or forbidden in most countries (see chapter 5.3.5.1).

Thus the stakeholders within the pharmaceutical marketplace are plenty (see figure 2-17):

---

[84] Freeman (1984), p. 46
[85] Cf. Terblanche (2008), p. 207
[86] Cf. Trilling (2008b), pp. 236-237

- Regulatory authorities in their capacity to allow drugs to enter the market and in controlling their use during and past the launch phase
- Payers, government or private insurance as they determine the effectual use of a drug based on their guidelines and payment provisions (tiering and capitations for prescriptions)
- Physicians, in their capacity as prescribers and influencers of payers
- Patients and their patient organizations as the ultimate consumer and benefitting party of new drugs as they become available
- The public and media, in their capacity to disseminate information and form opinions

These all need to be taken into consideration when establishing a launch plan and determining the success factors of a product launch.

Figure 2- 17: Stakeholders for bio / pharm product launches

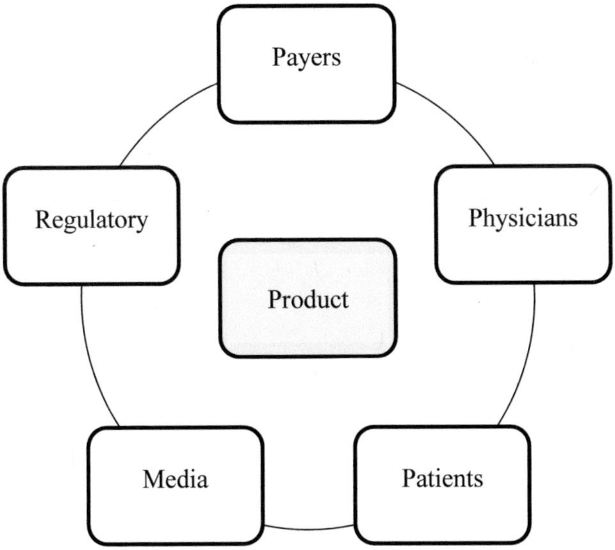

Figure: Own depiction

2.6 Special Considerations and Current Trends within the Bio / Pharmaceutical Market

To hone in on today's key considerations for product launches, current market trends need to be taken into account. It is estimated that it requires about 8,000 to 10,000 tested substances to eventually end up with one marketed product.[87] Thus the innovation pressure on the bio / pharmaceutical industry is particularly high.[88]

With a return on invested capital (ROIC) of 31.7%, the pharmaceutical industry has been one of the most profitable US industries between 1992 and 2006 (the average ROIC lying at 14.9%)[89], but this might be changing due to the issues outlined in the following, like drying up pipelines and higher regulations demands, especially on a product's safety profile.[90] On the marketing side, the return on investment (ROI) (sales per marketing dollar spent) has been steadily diminishing since the beginning of this millennium.[91]

Over the past years, major changes could be observed in the bio / pharmaceutical marketplace. These need to be carefully managed in everyday business and are particularly important in light of new product development and launches.[92] In the following, the current challenges players are facing as they are developing and trying to launch new products are described in some more detail.

[87] Cf. Note: Novel approaches to more targeted approaches in early–stage research are under discussion but far from being a common reality.
[88] Cf. Fischer, Breitenbach (2010a), pp. 23-25
[89] Cf. Porter (2008), p. 5
[90] Cf. Rao (2008), p. 95
[91] Cf. Vanderveer, Pines (2003a), p. 2
[92] Cf. Kesic, Bertoncelj (2008), p. 90

2.6.1 Patent Loss of Originator Drugs

Many patented drugs, estimated between $63 and $115 billion in sales, are expected to expire by 2012[93], leaving a big hole in the pockets of its manufacturers that have to be filled with innovative and successful launches.

In 2010, worldwide Lipitor (atrovastatin calcium / PFE, Astellas, Almirali) sales reached $12.7 billion which are rapidly diminishing in 2011 due to its patent loss. In the US statin market alone, patent expiries and subsequent generic uptake are estimated to slash the market by 80% within 10 years. [94] Other important originator drugs losing their patents in 2011 are Plavix (lopidogrel hydrogen sulfate / Bristol Myers Squibb (BMS), SNY), Advair (fluticasone propionate & salmeterol xinafoate / GSK, Almirali, others), Seroquel (quetiapine hexifumarate / AstraZeneca (AZN), Astellas), Actos (pioglitazone hydrochloride / TKD, Abbott), and Zyprexa (olanzapine / Eli Lilly (LLY)).[95] To quantify the impact of these patent expirations, expected sales at risk and actual losses are shown in figure 2-18.

Figure 2- 18: Patent expirations 2002-2016

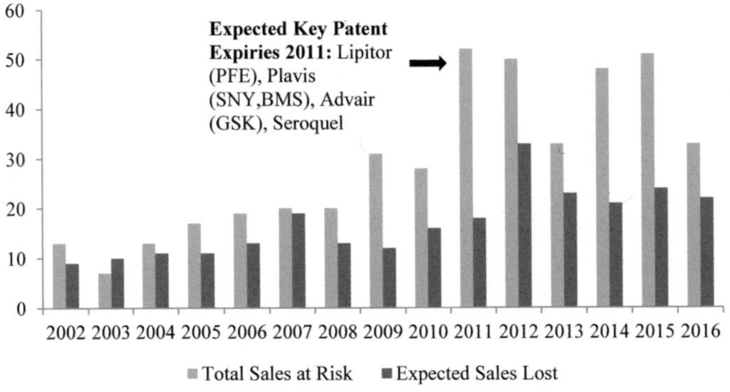

Source: EvaluatePharma (2011), p. 6

---

[93] Cf. Buono (2007), p. 36; Datamonitor (2008), p. 25
[94] Cf. Cacciotti, Clinton (2011), p. 12; Emerton (2006), pp. 73-78
[95] Cf. Cacciotti, Clinton (2011), p. 12; EvaluatePharma (2011), p. 6

Particularly small-cap companies in the specialty sector, with a rather limited portfolio, are particularly susceptible to serious threats by patent expirations.[96] The imminent patent losses necessitate top launches for each new drug and an even better life cycle plan for the entire portfolio (see chapter 3.1).

2.6.2 Pipeline Dearth

While current blockbusters are losing their patent status, fewer new compounds are discovered by the bio / pharmaceutical industry.[97] This is due to the fact that clinical trial requirements have become more complex[98], and despite the fact that R&D expenditures increase (see next point) the turn-out has been smaller than before.
Some pharmaceutical companies are fixing the dearth in the pipeline by acquiring smaller players or compounds from biotechnology companies.[99] According to Parexel, a US-based pharmaceutical services group, 32% of the pipeline of the top 10 pharmaceutical companies are in-licensed.[100]

While this trend towards mergers and acquisitions, including a significant portion of biologic and specialty products, is helping to fix the pipeline dearth, it brings along organizational changes and difficulties that might make the launch of the product more difficult (also see organizational chapter 6).[101]

According to some industry specialists, an overhaul of the entire value chain of the pharmaceutical industry will be necessary to improve and secure its financial performance.[102]

---

[96] Cf. Gal, Chou, Chari (2008), p. 111
[97] Cf. Gilbert, Henske, Singh (2003)
[98] Cf. Ng (2004), p. 282
[99] Cf. PriceWaterhouseCoopers (2008), pp. 27-28; Mirasol (2008)
[100] Cf. Mirasol (2008)
[101] Cf. Gudiksen, Fleming, Furstenthal, Ma (2008), p. 563
[102] Cf. Gudiksen, et al. (2008), p. 563

2.6.3 Increased Development Cost

The lack of viable development candidates and thus an all-too-lean pipeline, combined with additional regulatory requirements, lead to increased costs for the development of a drug.

While pharmaceutical companies spend large amounts on R&D (the cost for developing a drug is currently estimated at $800 million to $1 billion[103]), about 90% of products in development do not make it to market.[104] While R&D expenditures increased, the number of approved products has diminished over the past decade.[105] The cost for biotechnology R&D is at least equal to the cost of pharmaceutical R&D.[106] According to the Tufts Center for the Study of Drug Development, it is estimated to be even $1.2 billion, $400 million more than for small molecules.[107] Out of about 6,000 synthesized biotech compounds, only 10-20% have made it into clinical trials and only one has made it to market.[108] Thus the approved products do have to make up for the failed products and render the entire organization profitable.[109]

2.6.4 Increased Safety Concerns

Safety requirements first were dramatically increased after the thalidomide (Contergan / Gruenenthal) scandal in the 1950s, which caused severe deformations in unborn children whose mothers were taking this sedative during the first trimester of their pregnancy. After long political discussions in Germany, this scandal led to

---

[103] Cf. Datamonitor (2008), p. 24; some sources claim that this is an overestimate, which is a matter not to be discussed in this dissertation. For further information on this please refer to: Light (2007), pp. 895-Other sources come up with even higher numbers: Gilbert, et al. (2003)
[104] Cf. Kucher, Janssen (2004), p. 1
[105] Cf. PriceWaterhouseCoopers (2008), pp. 5-6
[106] Cf. Pisano (2006), p. 118
[107] Cf. PriceWaterhouseCoopers (2009), p. 13
[108] Cf. Pisano (2006), p. 119
[109] Cf. Kucher, Janssen (2004), p. 1

an update of the pharmaceutical legislature in the Arzneimittelgesetz (AMG) that is in effect since January 1, 1978, with 14 updates to date.[110]

The recent Vioxx scandal in the US had a signaling effect, making regulatory authorities around the globe increasingly vigilant regarding safety issues of drugs. Vioxx (rofecoxib) is a non-steroidal anti-inflammatory drug (NSAID), of the Cox-2 inhibitor class, that had 1.5% cardiovascular incidents in the treatment arm receiving Vioxx vs. .75% in the placebo arm. Even though this was determined to be a class effect of all Cox-2 inhibitors, Merck, the manufacturer of Vioxx, is facing class action lawsuits. Merck has paid millions in damages so far, including a 77-year-old retiree from Atlantic City who received 4.5 million in damages for not having received sufficient information on the cardiovascular risk of Vioxx in April 2005.[111]

One competitive drug, Bextra (valdecoxib / Searle, PFE) was also voluntarily withdrawn due to concerns about heart issues in 2005. Celebrex (celecoxib/ PFE) is the only Cox-2 inhibitor remaining on the market today.[112] The EMA issues a warning to use caution when prescribing Cox-2 inhibitors and not to provide it to patients with stroke or ischemic heart disease.[113]
After the Vioxx controversy in 2004, the FDA passed the FDA Amendments Act of 2007, increasing the influence of the FDA on drug manufacturers in the US by giving it the right to demand additional safety studies prior and post drug approval.[114]

In Europe, the EMA has added a risk management plan section to the application process for all future drugs.[115] The FDA is also reviewing already approved prod-

[110] Cf. Aigner, Czubayko, Klebe, Stubbs (2010), p. 89; Ng (2004), p. 144; Ortwein (2001), p. 33, Note: In the US, thalidomide (marketed by Celgene) was given orphan status for the treatment of leprosy in 1995 and received approval in 1998 (Grabowski, H. (2005), p. 471; Raje, Anderson (1999), pp. 1606-1609). In the EU it also received marketing authorization for the treatment of multiple myeloma in elderly patients (Medical News Today (2008)).
[111] Cf. Fischer, Breitenbach (2010a), pp. 20-21
[112] Cf. Drugs.com (2011); Drugs.com (2011a)
[113] Cf. Ernst & Young (2005), p. 65
[114] Cf. Datamonitor (2008), p. 24
[115] Cf. Ernst & Young (2005), p. 65

ucts for potential safety concerns, adding Black Box warnings, their strongest safety warning, to various product inserts. For example Xolair (omalizumab, Tanox / Novartis / Roche) received a black box warning, a full four years after its initial approval.[116]

Since authorities become increasingly cautious about product approvals, it is imperative to have a fully reviewed and valid set of clinical data available to facilitate and positively influence the outcome of the application process.

2.6.5 Price Pressures

With an aging population and increasing healthcare demands from the patient side, governments and health insurances are looking to cut down the cost of healthcare, including the cost of drugs.[117]

The nature of price pressures differs in every country and is becoming increasingly strong. The United Kingdom (UK) and Germany have set up cost effectiveness agencies, such as NICE[118] and IQWiG, respectively, to be discussed later. Other countries such as France, Australia, and Canada - to name a few that will not be further discussed in detail - have set up similar hurdles.[119] More and more, payers and legislators determine which products establish themselves on a market by translating research evidence into clinical guidance.[120] Basis for their assessment are health-economic studies that provide the necessary economic arguments for the respective drug.[121] These specific hurdles need to be known, addressed and overcome to successfully launch internationally. In general, increased price pressures might lead to fewer approved drugs, as 'me-too' drugs do not make the health-economic cut anymore. Also, particularly in mature primary care markets,

---

[116] Cf. Waknine (2007); FDA (2007)
[117] Cf. Kotzian (2004), p. 192; Barnett (2009), p. 55
[118] Cf. Müller (2005), pp. 26-27
[119] Cf. Honig (2011), p. 154
[120] N.a. (2005), p. 1673
[121] Cf. Seiter, Holz (2009), p. 924

new products might be relegated to a 'second-line' position in respective guidelines, only coming into effect after a generic first-line product has failed.[122] This means, that these products will have to build a strong case for their second-line use, potentially improving the monitoring of first-line therapy and its failures, thus growing the market for second-line treatment.[123]

Figure 2-19 visualizes the current pressures affecting bio / pharmaceutical launches today. Increased development costs and a pipeline dearth necessitate good market performance to fuel the R&D efforts. New product launches are needed to feed the pipeline, particularly in light of the upcoming patent losses for many major players. Unfortunately, with price pressures from the marketplace and regulatory pressures and increased requirements from the respective authorities, product launches are taking increasingly longer, if they happen at all.

Figure 2- 19: Current pressures on bio / pharm launches

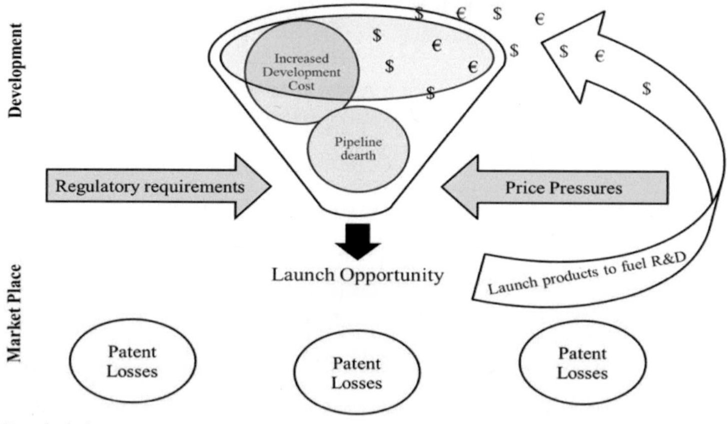

Source: Own depiction

[122] Cf. Bernard (2010), pp. 2-3; Wartenberg, Ziedman, Rickwood (2010)
[123] Cf. Wartenberg, Ziedman, Rickwood (2010), p. 7

3. Critical Importance of a Product Launch

The product launch, i.e. the introduction of a product into the marketplace, is known to be the decisive moment of a product's success and usually the most expensive part of product development. Under the watchful eye of the capital markets, and particularly due to the pipeline dearth of bio / pharmaceutical companies, the product launch becomes a 'great adventure'.[124]

In the bio / pharmaceutical industry, about 70% of drugs earn back their R&D cost, but only 40% manage to earn back their marketing expenses.[125]

A longitudinal 10-year study on launch excellence in this industry, executed by IMS Health from 1995-2004, yielded discouraging results: Out of 4225 launches done in eight countries[126], only 88 (2.1%) met the success criteria[127] in one single country, and 35 (.8%) managed to meet these criteria in more than one country. In 2010, the number dwindled to only eight launches (.6%).[128] The results of this particular IMS Health study clearly show that there is lots of room for improvement when it comes to bio / pharmaceutical launches. The specific success factors derived from this study[129] as well as others will be discussed later on.

To take a closer look at the product launch from a temporal perspective, its role in the product life cycle is discussed in the following, both from a general, strategic, as well as from an industry-specific point-of-view.

---

[124] Cf. Grabowski, Wang (2006), p. 453; Zeiner, Schiel (2007), p. 1396
[125] Cf. Grabowski, Vernon, DiMasi (2002), p. 22
[126] Cf. Countries included in this study were: USA, Canada, Japan, UK, France, Germany, Spain, and Italy
[127] Cf. Success criteria were: medical competency, promotional effectiveness, and market penetration
[128] Cf. Pfister (2010), p. 1; Zeiner, Schiel (2007), pp. 1396-1402
[129] Cf. Success factors derived were: Innovation & market expansion, market access, launch window management and monitoring, and operational process excellence (tabulated later in this dissertation).

3.1 Temporal View on a Product Launch: Life Cycle Planning

Every product and every market follows a certain life cycle pattern, commonly represented by the life cycle curve, shown in figure 3-1.

Figure 3- 1: The product life cycle

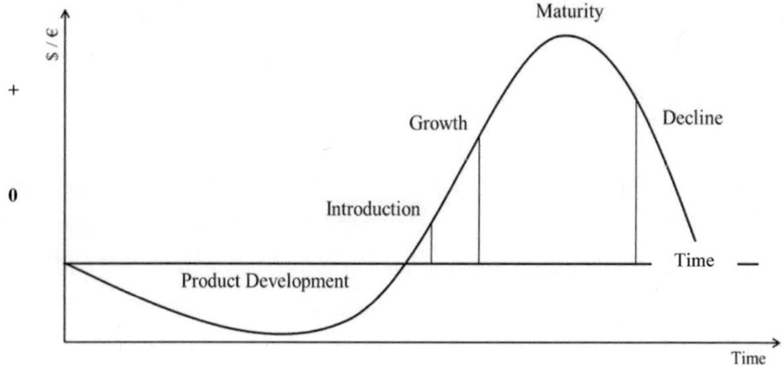

Source: Based on Kotler (1972), p. 430; Kotler, Armstrong (1989), p. 289

Due to a dearth in the late-stage pipeline, proper life cycle management will become increasingly important in the coming decades.[130]

The classic life cycle curve can be used both as a predictive curve, to provide a visual of the expected product success over time, as well as a comparative device, mirroring the product's success vs. the overall market development or the success of a competitive product. To build a relevant product life cycle projection, both the own products as well as competitive products can provide valuable data points and then have to be adjusted based on range possibilities and differences between the analogs used to model the life cycle curve and the new product launch.[131]

---

[130] Cf. Datamonitor (2008), p. 24; Dubey, Dubey (2009), p. 104; Ng (2004), pp. 299-300
[131] Cf. Foldes (2010), pp. 6-8

The goal of life cycle planning is to 'distort' the product's life cycle to the company's advantage.[132] During the launch phase this means to increase the slope of the launch curve and to shorten the time to peak sales as much as possible.[133] Here studies have shown that successful products gain the majority of their market share within the first 6 months after launch, which makes for a very short window of opportunity.[134]

Figure 3- 2: Market position change in the 18 months between 6 months post-launch and 2 years post-launch

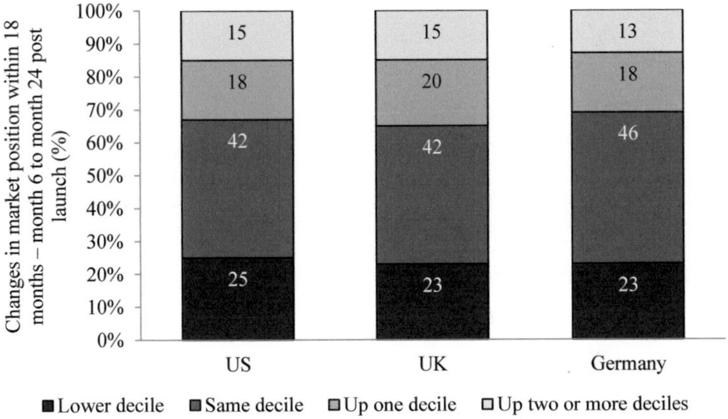

Source: Based on Wartenberg, Ziedman, Rickwood (2010), p. 7

As shown in figure 3-2 above, based on data accumulated by IMS in 2009, launch products tend to remain at or drop from their market position achieved at six months as time goes on. Thus getting the launch right is crucial for the future trajectory.[135]

Based on empirical data collected for 734 ethical products between 1955-1960, William Cox found that pharmaceutical drugs usually had a life cycle form with a

[132] Cf. Christopher, McDonald (1995), pp. 132-135
[133] Cf. Zeiner, Schiel, (2007), pp. 1400-1401
[134] Cf. Corstjens, et al. (2005), pp. 319-331; Pfister (2010), p. 3; Seiter, Holz (2009), p. 927; Zeiner, Schiel (2007), p. 1401
[135] Cf. Wartenberg, Ziedman, Rickwood (2010), p. 7

second cycle (recycle), as the companies used to promotionally push the product once more before the end of the life cycle, as depicted in figure 3-3.

Figure 3- 3: Cycle-recycle product life cycle

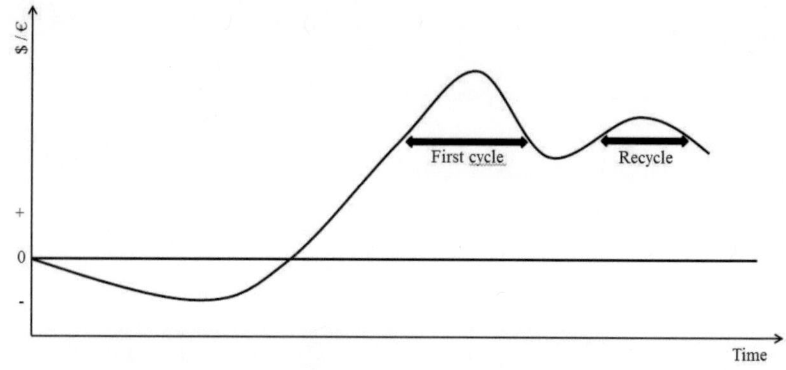

Source: Based on Cox (1967), pp. 375-384

Cox' studies also showed empirically that the introductory phase for pharmaceuticals usually lasted six months, followed by another 6 months of growth, a 15 month maturity phase, and a decline phase that was longer than the three previous stages combined.[136] While these data are rather old,[137] they point out the value of using existing data to learn about the product life cycles and make educated decisions of upcoming launches. E.g., is a promotional push in the decline phase the right way to spend money or should the funds not rather be spent in the introductory and growth phase to ensure a steeper trajectory for the product? How long are the individual phases for our product really and have we planned and budgeted accordingly (e.g. sales force, promotional activities etc.)? It is necessary to plan for the entire life cycle and to provide resources at risk for this purpose[138], which can be mitigated through early decision processes such as gating[139] and go / no go decisions (see chapter 5.3.1).

---

[136] Cf. Kotler (1972), pp. 430-431
[137] Cf. Data based on 754 ethical drugs in the US between 1955-1960 (Cox (1967), pp. 375-376)
[138] Cf. Cohen (2006), pp. 292-293
[139] Cf. Hart, Hultink, Tzokas, Commandeur (2003), pp. 22-36

To optimize a product's and its parent company's success in the marketplace, it is essential to keep in mind and plan for the product's entire life cycle at the time of launch.[140] One of the goals is to prevent generic competition (unless it is a friendly generic produced by the own corporation as large pharma giants like Novartis do it with its various subsidiaries) for the branded, patented product, which would lead to huge financial losses.[141] This is ideally done by extending the product range, developing the market, and eventually transitioning to the next product in the pipeline, if available, as shown in the following figure 3-4.[142]

Figure 3- 4: Product portfolio strategy based on the product life cycle

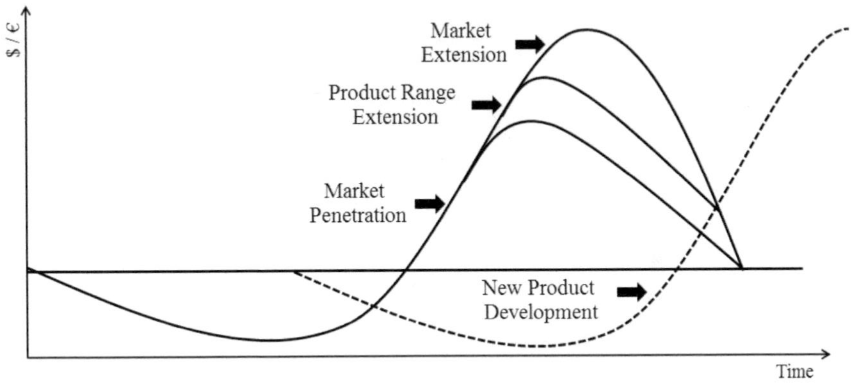

Source: Christopher, McDonald (1995), p. 134

Thus one product's mature and decline phase might just be another product's launch phase. One example for successful life cycle planning within one's own portfolio is the acquisition and subsequent launch of Valtrex (valacyclovir), a prodrug of the market leader Zovirax (acyclovir) that was launched prior to Zovirax going off patent, distinguished itself through improved bioavailability (oral rates were comparable to Zovirax' intravenous rates) and less frequent dosing.

---

[140] Cf. IBM (2006), p. 2
[141] Cf. Breitenbach, Lewis (2010), pp. 250-251; Fischer, Breitenbach (2010a), p. 13
[142] Cf. Christopher, McDonald (1995), pp. 132-135

This softened the financial blow to AZN as Zovirax became generic, and the company was even able to provide data to prospective payers that proved branded Valtrex to be more cost-effective than generic Zovirax (acyclovir).[143]

From a company's internal management and preparation point-of-view, a product's launch phase is usually described as the two years pre- and post-launch, thus starting in the development phase and reaching into the product's growth phase, as depicted in figure 3-5.[144]

Figure 3- 5: The classic launch phase

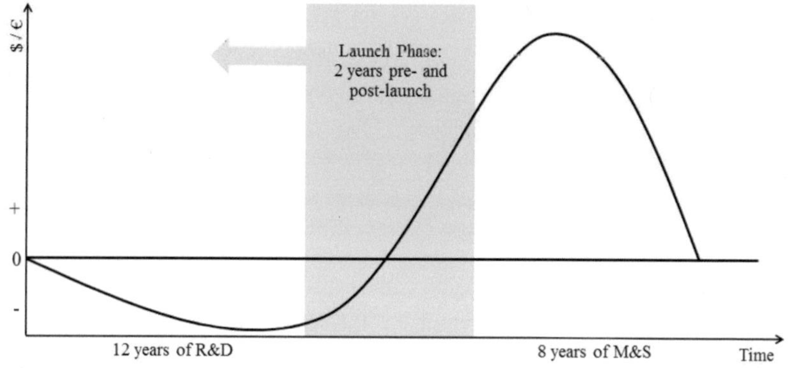

Source: Own depiction

It can be argued that for the highly regulated bio / pharmaceutical market, this launch phase might start earlier – or rather, that the usual players during the launch phase, such as the commercial team (marketing, sales etc.) need to be involved before the commonly used 2-year mark[145] prior to the intended launch to ensure that the product is brought into the market with the necessary attributes and data points (see chapter 5: Product-based considerations).

---

[143] Cf. Breitenbach, Lewis (2010), p. 251; Datamonitor (2005)
[144] Cf. Illert, Betz, Schlumberger (2007), p. 3; Zeiner, Schiel (2007), p. 1396
[145] Cf. Trilling (2008a), pp. 221-222

To optimize the launch product's life cycle, the three key levers are (see figure 3-6): Anticipating the launch earlier, accelerating penetration, and thus maximizing peak sales. For this to happen, the launch needs to be planned in time, taking into account both strategic and short-term priorities, and then executing the launch flawlessly, ensuring appropriate communication and effective collaboration.[146] Conflict is inevitable in the high-pressure environment of a new product development and launch. Here it is crucial to be prepared to handle conflict and to be able to remain collaborative over the long term. A study suggests that communication management is the most important factor in case of conflict management, followed by trust and commitment.[147] By accelerating the launch through optimized planning and preparation, higher sales will be realized earlier in the game, increasing the overall ROI of the product. This is particularly important since the patent life of an originator drug is limited and sales are unlikely to be realized past the patent expiration.[148]

Figure 3- 6: Product launch levers

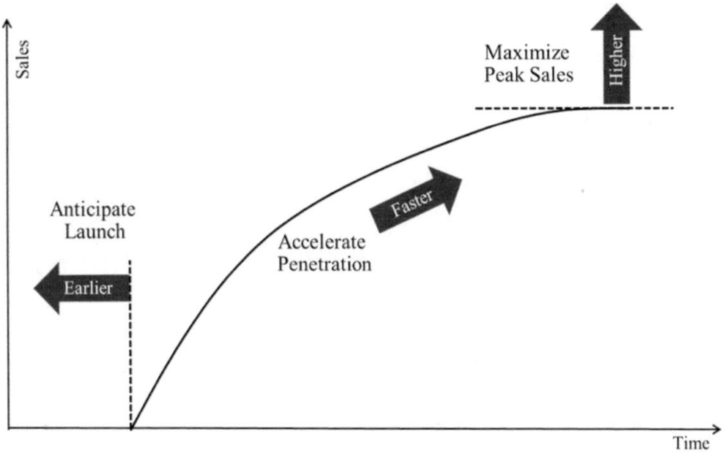

Source: Based on Illert, et al. (2007), p. 3; Zeiner (2008), p. 430

[146] Cf. Illert, et al. (2007), p. 3
[147] Cf. Lam, Chin (2005), p. 770
[148] Cf. Troll (1898), pp. 94-97

For all businesses, it is important to identify current and future key success factors, as well as emerging trends that influence these success factors.[149] Meta-analyses of success factor studies in the general business realm proved to come up with contradictory and unstable results.[150] In the pharmaceutical and biotechnology market in particular, no single market entry strategy template exists that fits all products, markets, and companies.[151] Thus the search for key success factors begins anew with every product launch, based on past data and experiences, as well as all new, currently available information. While there is little agreement within the literature how success is to be defined, profit-based and sales-based financial measures predominate, as this is the way companies and the financial markets value and measure their own success.[152]

3.2 Content Driven View on a Product Launch: Success Factors

Since every drug is different and the market is constantly changing, there is no 'one-size-fits-all' approach for successful product launches in general, and due its strictly regulated and fiercely competitive nature of the bio / pharmaceutical markets in particular.[153] Quite the contrary, assessments of key success factors through anecdotal case studies and expert interviews alone lead to information bias and methodical errors.[154] Thus this work captures the most relevant factors derived both from empirical data and meta-analyses, as well as some market expert opinions as a guideline throughout the process of this dissertation, touching upon each of the points without restricting itself to the methodology and findings of one respective study alone.

---

[149] Cf. Aaker (1995), pp. 100-102
[150] Astebro, Michela (2005), p. 324
[151] Cf. Kucher, Janssen (2004), p. 1
[152] N.a. (1992), p. 9
[153] Cf. Calantone, Griffith (2007), pp. 414-418
[154] Cf. Ernst (2002), pp. 33-34

To categorize the sparse data available in the literature, the three key success factor areas identified by Simon and Kotler (2003) are used to systematically sort these findings into the following categories:

- Market-based (external) success factors
- Product-based (internal) success factors
- Company-based (internal) success factors

While the general literature and studies mainly provide specific information regarding company-based success factors (probably due to the fact that market and product cannot be defined from a general perspective), bio / pharmaceutical literature and studies provide more additional market- and product-specific insights regarding these success factors.

The following table 3-1 is a comprehensive grid of available information and studies on launch success factors in general, and specific factors regarding bio / pharmaceutical launches in table 3-2, sorted by and tabulated in the three aforementioned categories.

Table 3- 1: General literature and studies regarding product launches

General Literature and Studies			
	Market-based success factors	**Product-based success factors**	**Company-based success factors**
	External factors	Internal factors	
Barclay (1992a), p. 262	• Good market knowledge and strategy	• Unique and superior product that meets customer wants and needs	• Open-minded and professional management • Good communication and coordination • Proficiency in technological activities
Brettel, Sattler (2009), pp. 217-257			• Dedication of internal resources • Proficiency in new product development process • Explicit knowledge management • Absorptive capacity • Top management support • Ability to deal with technical uncertainty
Di Benedetto (1999), pp. 530-544	• Launch timing relative to customers and competition	• Market testing process (conducting market research and analyzing results to modify product)	**Skills, Resources, and Strategic Launch Activities** • Cross-functional teams involvement in strategic decision making for manufacturing, distribution, marketing, and sales. • High skills, synergies, and resources in marketing and technical streams of the company **Tactical Launch Activities** • High quality of selling effort, advertising, service, and technical support • Good management of launch (marketing plans, launch direction and launch itself)

			• Good management of support program (distribution channels, sales force training, pricing, advertising program execution) **Market Information Gathering Activities** • Studying customer feedback during and after launch • Planning and testing advertising • Contracting out specialized research to research professionals
Ernst (2002), pp. 1-40	• Market orientation	• Customer integration in product development process	• Quality of planning prior to development • Continuous commercial assessment of the launch project
Henard, Szymanski (2001), pp. 362-375	• Market potential • Order of entry	• Product advantage • Product meets customer needs • Product technological sophistication	• Dedicated human resources (HR) • Dedicated R&D resources • Pre-development task proficiency • Marketing task proficiency • Technological proficiency
Kuhn (2007), pp. 122-134	• Market potential	• Novelty of product • Price advantage	**Marketing tools** • Intensity of marketing measures • Fit between brand and product • Communication of product advantage **Management** • Market orientation • Top management support

			• Incentives • Intensity of cooperation
Langerak, Hultink, Robben (2004), pp. 74-94	• Better new product performance	• Higher product advantage	• Greater proficiency in launch tactics

Note: Details on the specifics of the studies tabulated above can be found in the appendix

Table 3- 2 : Bio / Pharmaceutical literature and studies regarding product launches

Bio / Pharmaceutical Literature and Studies			
	Market-based success factors	**Product-based success factors**	**Company-based success factors**
	External factors	Internal factors	
Gudiksen, et al. (2008), pp. 563-567	• Market size at launch • 5-year market growth rate	Average differentiation relative to standard of care	
Illert, et al. (2007)	**Shape the Market:** • Broad clinical trials that give physicians experience with drug prior to launch • Scenario planning and war games	**Shape the Product:** • Excellent coordination between R&D and commercial functions early on • Health outcome analysis and compelling value story	**Shape the Organization:** • New infrastructure in case of new therapeu-tic area • Coordinated positioning and shared resource decisions • Conflict management • Synergy maximization
Seiter, Holz (2009), p. 925	**Early market leadership:** Excellent launches lead to a market leadership (or at least a number two position within the first two years post-launch). **Quick market penetration:** Excel-lent launches are on a top trajecto-ry, providing excellent speed to market.		**Optimal promotional investment:** Top product launches must lead to a higher than average sales return on the promotional investment, including the sales team.

Simon, Kotler (2003), p. 115	Physicians: • Opinion Leader capture • Physician Education Payers: • Reimbursement strategy, PharmacoEconomics Consumers: • Disease Awareness • Links with patient community	• Multiple Indications • Dosage/formulations • Speed-to-market • Price (first-in-class or comparator choice) • Early positioning (data-driven differentiation)	• Resource Allocation • Integrated brand teams • Speed to market (parallel R&D processes • Balance of central planning and local execution • Infrastructure for fast global rollout
Zeiner, Schiel (2007), pp. 1396-1402	• Market access • Market expansion • Market penetration	• Innovation	• Medical competency • Promotional effectiveness • Launch window management and monitoring • Operational process excellence

Note: Details on the specifics of the studies tabulated above can be found in the appendix

In all these studies and reviews, launch success is quantified by the product's sales and profitability.[155] Based on a recent study conducted by IMS, excellent launches - on average - realize incremental annual sales of $ 374 million versus suboptimal launches.[156]

A successful development and launch strategy necessitates both a viable product and a launch structure that is able to carry out a launch successfully (internal success factors) as well as favorable circumstances (external success factors), such as the current market needs based on demographics and socio-cultural needs[157], the legal environment and regulations, political situation, competitive environment, and new market developments.[158]

3.3 Key Considerations for a Product Launch

Taking into account the key success factors tabulated above, key considerations for the product launch will discussed in these three corresponding sections (see figure 3-7):

- The marketplace (Market-based, strategic considerations: chapter 4)
- The product itself and its role for the stakeholders (Marketing, operational considerations – chapter 5)
- The company (or companies, in case of an alliance) (Organizational Considerations – chapter 6)[159]

---

[155] Cf. Kuhn (2007), p. 27
[156] Cf. Bernhard (2010a), p. 2
[157] Note: socio-cultural needs play an increasingly important role for lifestyle drugs (e.g. erectile dysfunction, weight control, anti-aging etc.)
[158] Cf. Kotler, Armstrong (1989), pp. 48-49; Ortwein (2001), p. 20
[159] Cf. Falk (2005), p. 246

Figure 3- 7: Key areas of consideration in a product launch

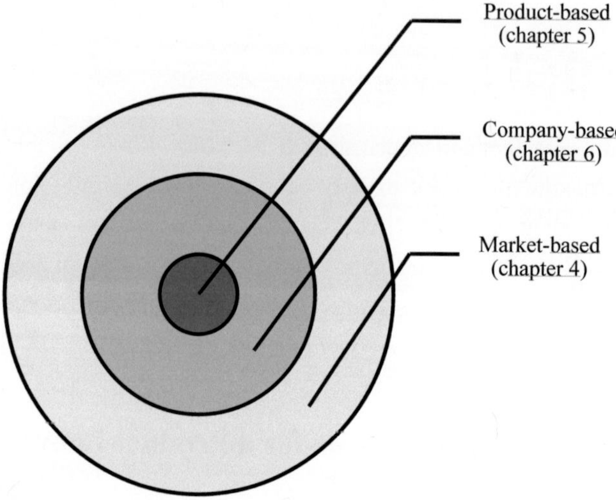

Source: Own depiction

The success factors in these respective areas are integrated in the discussion of these three key areas of consideration. They are substantiated by additional literature regarding the bio / pharmaceutical market and launch requirements, as well as specific industry examples to illustrate the impact of these considerations on everyday business. Wherever possible, these insights are visualized and tabulated to allow readers to use this information for their own impending launches and assessments.

4. Market-based Considerations

The first step to ensure a successful launch is to scope out the launch landscape and to understand the opportunities and threats within the marketplace. This can be achieved by assessing the market conditions and the potential product's position within this marketplace. Secondly, the competitive situation has to be scoped out. Last but not least, it is crucial to consider which of the potential markets assessed to enter into, which is described later on.

4.1 Marketplace Assessment

Market dynamics are to be considered as they need to influence the penetration strategies chosen for market entry, and ultimately shape the product's performance during the launch phase and beyond. A lack of vision, poor life cycle planning and /or poor positioning within the marketplace and regarding its competitors present barriers to success that cannot be overcome any more in later launch stages.[160] These market conditions need to be assessed pre-launch and reevaluated on an ongoing basis.[161]

One way to establish the launch product's starting position is by evaluating the following factors as listed in Table 4-1:

Table 4- 1: Market-related factors to consider for a product launch

Blockbuster market/product	**Niche market/product**
2nd line products	1st line product
First to market product	Follow on product

Source: Own depiction

[160] Cf. Illert, et al. (2007), p. 3
[161] Cf. Datamonitor (2004), p. 6

While these factors can be strategically decided upon in a long-term strategic business plan, for the purpose of this dissertation – focusing on the launch of a product – these factors can be seen as extrinsically given. Nevertheless, their assessment it is crucial to understand the market one is playing in and thus to successfully plan and execute the launch.

4.1.1. Mass Markets and Blockbusters

Usually occurring in mature, high-potential markets with large patient populations, also known as mass-markets, blockbusters are usually defined as drugs that make more than a billion dollars in sales, irrespective of the time period this happens in. Some, such as the marketers at AstraZeneca, distinguish Megabrands within the set of blockbusters as products that are able to reach one billion US dollars in sales every year. Examples for megabrands are: Celebrex (celecoxib / PFE), Viagra (sildenafil / PFE), and Lipitor (atrovastatin / PFE). Nonetheless, it is important to note that the market success can only be optimized if a timely and complete market penetration can be ensured.[162]

Building a blockbuster has become more cost-intensive and the competition is faster in catching up. The median time of market exclusivity for a breakthrough drug has fallen by nine full years, from 10.2 years in the 1970s to 1.2 years in the late 1990s already.[163] As a practical example: While Inderal (propanolol / AZN) had a monopoly in the beta blocker market for 10 years until its competitor Lopressor / Troprol XL (metopropol / Novartis) entered the market, Viagra (sildenafil / PFE) had nearly six years of market exclusivity until the entrance of Levitra (vardenafil / Bayer) and Cialis (tadalafil / LLY), who entered the market within less than three months of each other.[164]

[162] Cf. Datamonitor (2004b), p. 9; Fischer, Breitenbach (2010a), pp. 11-12; Kuhn (2007), p. 137
[163] Cf. DiMasi, Parquette (2004), pp. 1-14
[164] Cf. Cohen (2006), p. 288; Fischer, Breitenbach (2010a), p. 12

Some experts deem that the importance of blockbuster drugs is decreasing over time, as many current blockbusters become generic and the trend for new drugs goes towards medications that target specific patient (group) needs, as the market access hurdles are getting higher.[165] On the other hand, other experts believe that blockbusters are far from dead, predicting 8 biologics to be in the top ten of best-selling drugs by 2016, led by Humira (adalimumab / Abbott, Eisai) with over 10 billion in sales.[166] Either way it is important to be aware with which kind of product is to be launched and to address the specific market requirements (e.g. required indication, spending levels) accordingly and in a timely fashion.

4.1.2 Niche Markets and Products

In general, a niche product is defined as a product that is made and marketed for use in a small and specialized but profitable market. A general industrial innovation study reviewing 221 product launches suggest that niche strategies are generally more successful than mass market strategies, and within the niche realm, innovators are usually more successful than followers.[167] In the bio / pharmaceutical world, a niche market generally addresses a small patient population with comparatively small returns.[168] Niche products - also called 'niche busters' when successful - focus on a single, distinct market segment[169] as more specific disease mechanisms will be identified[170], and hold a large clinical and commercial promise, if the necessary focused launch efforts are carried out successfully.[171] On specific use are biotechnology drugs that provide targeted therapy, addressing a specific genetic makeup of the patient[172]. The drawback of their development and marketing is that the development costs have to be spread amongst and recovered

[165] Cf. Seiter, Holz (2009), p. 924; Fischer, Breitenbach (2010c), pp. 299-304; Teichmann, Twelsiek, (2008); Vanderveer (2003), p. 2
[166] Cf. EvaluatePharma (2011), p. 19; Law (2010), p. 4
[167] Hultink, Griffin, Hart, Robben (1997), pp. 243-257
[168] Cf. Datamonitor (2004), p. 9; Jørgensen (2008), p. 55
[169] Cf. Bruhn (1995), p. 63
[170] Cf. Vanderveer, Pines (2003a), p. 2
[171] Cf. Kuhn (2007), p. 138; Robinson (2010)
[172] Cf. Terblanche (2008), p. 205

from a significantly smaller patient population than blockbusters, leading to higher prices. If the bio / pharmaceutical market was to grow at the current rate, it would be at $1.4 trillion by 2020, a number so high that it is only logical that payers are trying to slow down their use.[173]

Figure 4-1 visualizes the launch implications of the decision to develop products for the blockbuster market vs. the niche market. Oftentimes, a potential molecule or antibody is discovered or developed without a specific target in mind, or it does not work does not work as well as predicted on the envisioned target (see the Viagra example in the following). Another strategy can be to start off with one niche indication and then build the market from there, covering more and more indications over time (see the Gleevec / Glivac example in the following).

Figure 4- 1: Product launches in blockbuster and niche markets

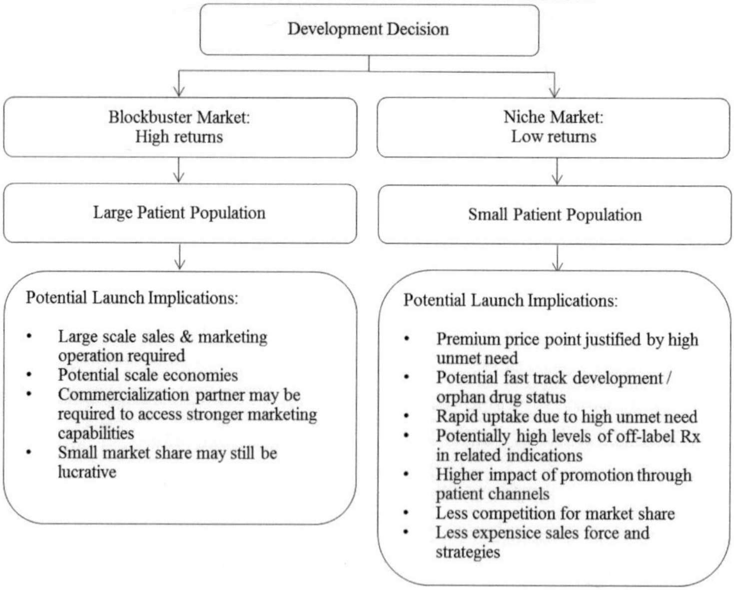

Source: Based on Datamonitor (2004), p. 9

[173] Cf. PriceWaterhouseCoopers (2009), pp. 13-14

4.2 Implications of Market Entry Order and Treatment Lines

Product launch decisions are taken on a strategic level and compare risks, trade-offs and potential returns.[174] While the market entry position as well as the potential market size cannot necessarily be influenced by the company about to launch as product, it is important to know the implications of the market entry position and product potential. These factors may play a role in deciding when and if to launch a product, or even continue with its development in earlier phases. According to a McKinsey study analyzing all specialty launches from 1994 to 2003, market size at launch accounts for 25% of the outcome prediction of the launch product's success, with another 19% determined by the 5-year market growth rate post-launch. The only more important factor was the average differentiation of the product relative to the standard-of-care (51%).[175] Based on market experience, a marketable innovation is usually only successful if it is able to reach minimum sales of 200 million Euros.[176] It needs to enter all large markets within the first 1-2 years after its first launch to maximize its patent protection and its market success also depends on marketing, pricing, and life cycle management.[177] Thus, the market entry position influences the overall strategy for the product and warrants a closer look.

4.2.1 First-to-market Products

Being an innovator, and thus first in a marketplace has a variety of potential advantages. If executed correctly, it can lead to increased margins (since there are no reference prices available yet and the product is addressing an unmet medical need), and allows to create product loyalty and a subsequently sustained leader-

[174] Cf. Spanjol, Tam, Qualls, Bohlmann (2011), p. 623-640
[175] Cf. Gudiksen, et al. (2008), pp. 563-564
[176] An exception to this rule are orphan drugs, which receive special treatment by authorities and companies alike (see chapter 4.2.3.1).
[177] Cf. Fischer, Breitenbach (2010a), p. 24

ship position.[178] For these products that will face competition in the foreseeable future, a tailored market protection strategy is particularly important.[179]

As a pioneer, the goal is to make up for the cost disadvantage by being first-to-market by a long-term profit advantage.[180] Research done in different industries showed that there are substantially different outcomes when estimating the cost / profit ratio of a first-in-class product, depending on the overall industry setting.[181] In the pharmaceutical market, entry order is positively correlated with approval time, as established in a study reviewing 1,629 New Medical Entities (NMEs) between 1950 and 2000.[182] Entering a market first may even be less costly than entering as a follower, despite the resources it takes to establish the marketplace.[183]

Also, first-to-market products (just like all market leaders), have an interest in growing the, oftentimes still immature, marketplace as they benefit from it solely (or disproportionally),[184] e.g. through awareness campaigns or free testing for a disease (a prevalent approach for infectious diseases, such as HIV or Hepatitis B). Market expansion can take place by increasing the number of patients (earlier or increased rate of diagnosis, change of treatment standards) or by increasing the value of a patient (more frequent treatments, increased adherence).[185] In the IMS Health Excellence Study, almost half (46%) of the successful launches also did so by expanding the market.[186] This is a point to be considered when preparing for a first-to-market product launch.

Being first to market, it is also possible to position an entire condition, which will be illustrated with the following four examples:

---

[178] Cf. IBM (2006), p. 2
[179] Cf. Boulding, Christen (2009), p. 966; Kucher, Janssen (2004), p. 1
[180] Cf. Cohen (2006), pp. 285-286
[181] Cf. Boulding, Christen (2009), p. 958
[182] Cf. Carpenter, Rynbrandt (2003)
[183] Cf. Bolesh (2006), pp. 20-22; Buzzell (2004), p. 481
[184] Cf. Bruhn (1995), p. 80; Datamonitor (2008a); Zeiner, Schiel (2007), p. 1399
[185] Cf. Seiter, Holz (2009), p. 927
[186] Cf. McGuire (2007), p. 26

A market creator example is Rituxan (rituximab / Genentech / Roche), for the treatment of non-Hodgkin's lymphoma, that was able to grow the market by 7500% (from ~$20 million to $1.5 billion) in 5 years.[187]

In the case of Lyrica (pragabalin / PFE), the treatment of fibromyalgia was identified as a patient-driven and thus Pfizer closely collaborated with patient organizations and focused on DTC advertising in the US, while educating physicians on diagnosis and treatment. This way, Lyrica firmly established itself as the agent for the treatment of this underdiagnosed and previously untreatable disease.[188]

Detrol (tolterodine tartrate / PFE) was defined as a treatable condition for something that was previously just known as 'incontinence'. Research showed that patients practiced 'bathroom mapping', meaning that they build their daily activities around easy and frequent access to bathrooms. Treating this condition gave them a whole new freedom in the way they lived their lives.[189]

Another well-known example is the definition of 'treatable erectile dysfunction' at the launch of Viagra (sildenafil / PFE), where beforehand there has only been 'impotence'.[190]

On the other hand, being first-to-market bears the disadvantage that the marketplace is not well-established and might need considerate work to explain mechanisms of action and other clinical or disease state details. Also, it is possible to grossly misestimate the market's potential for a certain compound, leading to suboptimal decisions in areas such as pricing, production, and sales staffing. Nevertheless, being first to market allows the company to clearly and widely position the product without regard to competitive claims. In this case, the company has to actively take advantage of this lead-time in the market, though.[191]

---

[187] Cf. Gudiksen, et al. (2008), p. 564
[188] Cf. Datamonitor (2008a)
[189] Cf. Vanderveer (2005a), p. 4
[190] Cf. Cohen (2006), p. 288; Simon, Kotler (2003), pp. 102-103; Vanderveer (2005a), p. 4
[191] Cf. Rodriguez-Pinto, Rodriguez-Escudero, Gutierrez-Cillan (2008), p. 164

In summary, being first to market may contribute to the product's success, but not necessarily so. A marketing study of leading industrial companies found that generally speaking the better product wins, not necessarily the first to market[192], and another international quantitative study shows that, ceteris paribus, it is better to enter a market six months later and well-prepared than to rush to market without being commercially quite ready.[193] Decisive factors are a refined safety profile and a more desirable indication.[194]

4.2.2 Follow-on Products

It is necessary to spend a significant amount of resources on promotional activities to build the necessary share-of-voice in a saturated market, not to mention the work and time it takes to generate the data needed to convince payer organizations and formulary committees of the medical need of the follow-on product based on clinical and financial rationale. Due to these factors, the budget to launch a follow-on product is up to four times larger than its first-in-class counterparts according to a study by Cutting Edge Information, as depicted in figure 4-2.[195]

[192] Cf. Cooper, Kleinschmidt (1995), p. 320
[193] Cf. Corstjens, et al. (2005), p. 327
[194] Cf. Gudiksen, et al. (2008), pp. 565-566
[195] Cf. Bolesh (2006), pp. 20-22

Figure 4- 2: First-in-class and follow-on product launch budgets

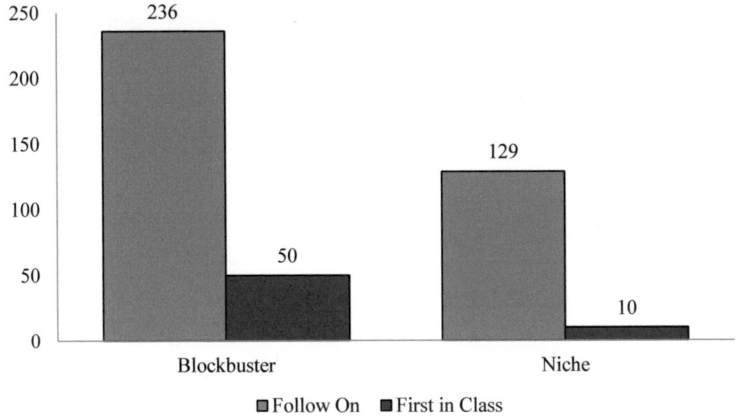

Source: Bolesh (2006), p. 22

Nevertheless, due to the saturation of the blockbuster markets, follow-on products are becoming more prominent and important in companies' portfolios: While one of the top therapeutic areas for NCEs is the cardiovascular field[196], only 5% of these NCEs are first-in-class.[197] Based on studies done assessing market strategies, it has been concluded that the incremental improvements achieved by follow-on drugs through thoroughly planned and executed R&D programs can overcome the perceived pioneer advantage.[198]

Since profits decline as the number of competitors increases in a marketplace, usually only the first three products in a class recover their R&D investment post launch.[199] Thus, time is of the essence. Studies show that while the first-in-class drug does not have a direct price advantage as there is no comparator yet, number two and three to enter the market receive higher prices compared to later market entrants.[200] Also, with additional products on the market, pricing becomes more

---

[196] Note: Regarding the number of new product introductions, it is a close tie between cardiovascular, systemic anti-infectives and central nervous system drugs (Grabowski, Wang (2006), p. 456)

[197] Cf. Grabowski, Wang (2006), p. 456

[198] Cf. Cohen (2006), p. 287; DiMasi, Parquette (2004), pp. 1-14

[199] Cf. Kyle (2006), pp. 612-614; Ortwein (2001), p. 57

[200] Cf. Danzon, Epstein (2009), pp. 32-33

important. The new product's price has to be in line with the in-market competitors and it is possible that the prices of incumbent products are dropped, or contracted at a lower rate, to keep out the new competitor.[201] These general market data, as well as the specific current market situation, need to be factored into the market entry strategy and financial planning of the company prior to launch.

4.2.3 First-line Treatments

First-line treatments are the first treatments used for a certain disease (see figure 4-3). Oftentimes, in more mature markets, these first-line positions are taken by generic drugs. In these markets, second-line treatments are becoming more important to the manufacturer. In the markets that are not genecrically dominated yet, launch products target both naïve and switch patients, i.e. patients that have previously been on another therapy. IMS Health stipulates that successful launches are particularly more successful in winning over switch patients than average launches; making switches is an interesting early launch success indicator.[202] Options such as market expansion, treatment guidelines to allow for earlier treatment (e.g. statins[203]), and better and earlier diagnosis are key factors to consider in preparation for and during the launch. In case a first-line indication is required or desired in an established market, even if it is still a patent-protected disease state without generics, major up-front work regarding health-economic data, guideline discussions and updates with payers and Key Opinion Leaders (KOLs) are necessary to secure this first-line position.[204]

---

[201] Cf. Karakaya, Yannopoulos (2011), p. 171-185
[202] Cf. Bernhard (2010a), p. 2
[203] In a concerted effort, the threshold for cholesterol levels was lowered in the guidelines, making a significantly larger part of the population (18% in the US) eligible for statin treatment, tripling the number of scripts (Burton, Adams (2001)).
[204] Cf. Seiter, Holz (2009), pp. 923-930

Figure 4- 3: **First- and second-line treatments**

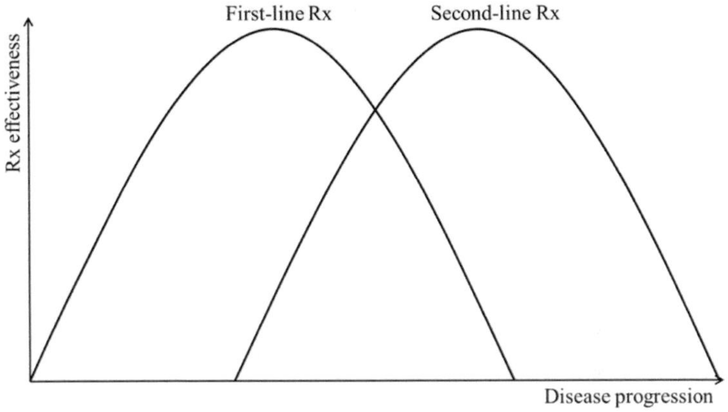

Source: Own depiction

4.2.4 Second-line Treatments

As most major markets already have (generic, and thus cheaper) players in it[205], new (original, and thus expensive) launches often times receive a second-line or add-on status instead of becoming first-line or gold standard treatments.[206] This is a change upcoming product launches have to take into account and manage going forward.

It is important to have the necessary data to support the line of treatment the drug is trying to achieve. Especially in disease states that are managed by drug resistance, such as HIV / AIDS, the respective cross-resistance information in the label at launch is crucial for the product's success.

To incorporate all these considerations in a product launch preparation, it is advisable to create a product and corporate SWOT (Strengths, Weaknesses, Oppor-

---

[205] Note: In Germany, the markets for the top 8 indications already are more than 90% generic (Seiter, Holz (2009), p. 926)
[206] Cf. Seiter, Holz (2009), p. 926

tunities, Threats) analysis highlighting all key factors of the impending product launch, such as the market conditions mentioned above.[207] Based on this, key activities as well as the necessary funds to carry these out need to be identified and quantified. This has to happen in a timely manner, as some activities (such as KOL development, patient organization work, or mechanism of action establishment in the marketplace) need a sizeable amount of lead time prior to the launch.

One example for a comprehensive pre-launch market strategy is the introduction of Gleevec / Glivec (imatinib mesylate) into the market for Chronic Myelogenous Leukemia (CML). At launch in May 2001, Gleevec / Glivec was only indicated for the treatment of CML in blast crisis, accelerated or chronic phase after interferon-alfa therapy had failed.[208] While this was a niche indication with a small patient base (and receiving orphan status), Gleevec / Glivec is believed to have been used off-label in first-line settings already before its first-line use approval in 2002, 18 months after its initial approval for second-line use.[209] This proves that even a small, second-line indication in a niche market might prove profitable, as it generates interest in the drug and increases its off-label use, even though this may not be supported promotionally.[210] Novartis' challenge was to communicate the product's superior efficacy to physicians, payers and patients alike. Patients became so excited about the drug, that they sent a letter with 3,000 signatures from patients and caregivers to the Chief Executive Officer (CEO) of Novartis to accelerate trials so that more patients could access the drug more quickly.[211] Novartis filed the NDA within 32 months of Gleevec / Glivec first having been tested in humans and the FDA gave it priority review, approving it within 10 weeks of submission, a new record in the history of cancer drug approvals.[212]

The patient loyalty paid dividends for Novartis, as NICE initially refused approval of Gleevec / Glivec in October of 2002 due to insufficient evidence (high price

[207] Cf. Knoke (2008), pp. 10-11
[208] Cf. National Cancer Institute (2011)
[209] Cf. Cameron (2007); Datamonitor (2004), p. 7; Pray (2008)
[210] Cf. Datamonitor (2004), pp. 6-7; Ng (2004),p. 214
[211] Cf. Vanderveer, Pines (2003), p. 4
[212] Cf. Dagher, Johnson, Williams, Keegan, Pazdur (2004), p. 1503; Datamonitor (2004), pp. 8-11; Schilsky (2004), p. 1495

and lack of long-term survival data), but due to patient pressure allowed second-line use of Gleevec / Glivec within 3 months of its initial, negative decision and allowed first-line treatment by October of 2003.[213]

Also, since Gleevec / Glivec as an oral agent was not covered under Medicare, one of the key medical providers in the US, Novartis implemented a Patient Access Program (PAP), helping potential patients figure out eligibility for and access to treatment.[214]

By now, Gleevec / Glivec has also been approved for five indications outside of oncology, and while all of these are niche indications, their sequential build up into one large program made Gleevec / Glivec on of the biggest success stories for the new niche buster market model.[215]

4.3 Market Selection and Competitive Assessment

When assessing the overall marketplace to ensure a successful launch, it is also necessary to strategically review all current and future players, including the competitive landscape. Market intelligence has to be shared within the company and concerns both the internal operations as well as competitors'. A successful competitive strategy coordinates current and future measures to be able to defend a competitive advantage.[216]

A time-tested way of doing this is using the five competitive forces by Michael Porter. Here Porter identifies the vertical competitive forces, specifically the bargaining power of suppliers and buyers within the supply chain, as well as the horizontal competition, consisting of new market entrants, established rivals, and substitute products and services. This framework for business strategy has been

---

[213] Cf. Datamonitor (2004), pp. 8-11;National Institute of Clinical Excellence (NICE) (2003)
[214] Cf. Datamonitor (2004), p. 11
[215] Cf. Robinson (2010), p. 2
[216] Cf. Cohen (2006), pp. 291-292; Golder (2000), p. 335; Henderson (1994), p. 122

adapted and expanded with specific forces in the pharmaceutical realm by Simon, as shown in figure 4-4:[217]

Figure 4- 4: The Five Forces by Porter, adapted for the bio / pharmaceutical world

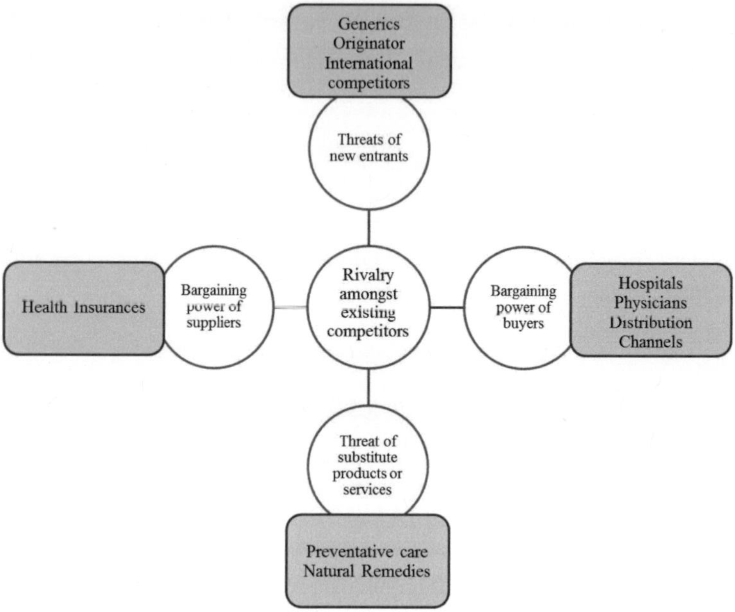

Source: Based on Porter (2008), p. 4; Simon (1989), p. 4

The competitive analysis is essential in determining the launch product's role in the marketplace at launch as well as through its life cycle. Unfortunately, the pharmaceutical industry has done a less thorough job in this area than other industries in the past.[218] As part of this analysis, not only already approved products need to be taken into consideration, but also pipeline products that are expected to enter the marketplace during the product's lifespan.[219] Competitive products have to be defined as products that are used to treat the same condition, whether they are officially indicated for it, available over-the-counter or as a prescription drug.

---

[217] Cf. Porter (2008), pp. 1-17; Simon (1989), p. 4
[218] Cf. Simon (1989), pp. 8-9
[219] Cf. Falk (2005), p. 248

In some cases, even herbs (e.g. Traditional Chinese Medicine used for the treatment of Hepatitis) and vitamins (e.g. Calcium and Vitamin D for the treatment of osteoporosis) have to be taken into consideration. In general, alternative and herbal treatments are more commonly used in Europe than in the US, but their popularity is also increasing in the latter.[220]

4.3.1 Intellectual Property (IP) Strategy

In general, patents increase the return on R&D spending by providing a time-limited exclusivity to the inventor. In the bio / pharmaceutical industry, the patent life determines and limits the marketability and life cycle length of an originator drug, as generics are likely to enter the market and undermine the originator drug's position as soon as the patent expires. Thus, patents play a central role in the management of drugs and need to be factored into the overall life cycle plan.[221] In context with the competition, it is also important to ensure exclusive rights to the product, the processes involved, as well as the product name. While an in-depth analysis of patent requirements and laws is beyond the scope of this dissertation, it is important to note and remember throughout the pre-launch phase that a variety of aspects of the product need to be patented in time to ensure protection from the competition.[222] The strategic use of patents also includes safeguarding future technologies and can constitute a bargaining chip for potential alliances and business deals.[223]

Usually, patents have to be applied for individually in every country, or – in case of Europe – for a specific region. Based on the Patent Cooperation Treaty (PCT), established in 1970, it is possible to file for an international patent for all participating countries.[224] Unfortunately, the EU still has not created a Community pa-

[220] Cf. Kyle (2007), p. 90
[221] Cf. Bureth, Penin, Wolff (2010), p. 259
[222] Cf. Riedl (2010), pp. 217-241
[223] Cf. Thumm (2004), p. 532
[224] Cf. Riedl (2010), pp. 223-226; World Intellectual Property Organization (2011a)

tent that would give inventors to obtain one legally valid patent for all EU countries, a simplified protection of inventions that would reduce patenting cost for filing and translation.[225] In the absence of this, it is important to diligently file patents for the product and/or its production process in all relevant countries.

Brands can be internationally registered for the participating countries based on the Madrid System Concerning the International Application of Marks, also simply known as the 'Madrid System', established in 1891.[226]

In WHO (World Health Organization) countries, pharmaceutical patents have a duration of 20 years[227] and a 5 year extension option (details, likelihood, sources). Since product development takes about 10-12 years and patents need to be filed at the onset of research, to ensure legal protection, this means that products have an on-the-market protection of no more than 8-10 years.[228]

The ability or inability to protect patents in a country also influences the likelihood of a launch in this country. This has been a problem for the growing markets in low- to middle income countries, such as the BRIC countries.[229]

The patent status changes the market landscape significantly: While Lipitor (atorvastatin/ PFE) was already the leading statin in the market when Crestor (rosuvastatin / AZN) entered the marketplace, the company decided to invest strongly into Crestor. Crestor remains in an inferior position versus Lipitor until now, but since Lipitor's patent expires in 2011, Crestor is estimated to be the leading statin, one of the top ten products worldwide, by 2016. While generic atorvastatin sales are expected to remain strong after Lipitor's patent expiration, Crestor (rosuvastatin) is estimated to be the leading patented statin.
Knowing this, Astra Zeneca's Crestor (rosuvastatin) entered the statin market for the treatment of cholesterol, going up against the market leader Lipitor (atorvas-

---

[225] Cf. Ernst & Young (2005), p. 64-65
[226] Cf. Riedl (2010), p. 237; World Intellectual Property Organization (2011)
[227] Cf. Terblanche (2008), p. 207
[228] Cf. Ortwein (2001), p. 38
[229] Cf. Lanjouw (2005), p. 25

tatin / PFE). In the US alone, the company spent $1 billion to commercialize Crestor within the first year. The product launched in August 2003 and had a market share of 4.6% of new prescriptions by the end of the year, 5 months post launch.[230] With sales of 4.8 billion worldwide in 2009, Crestor is expected to be one of only two small molecules in the top 10 drugs in 2016 with estimated sales of 6.3 billion.[231] This shows that the IP status of a competitive drug needs to be scrutinized as it strongly influences the life cycle of the launch product, thus influencing the launch plan decision, such as level of marketing spend and investments at the beginning.

4.3.2 Market Selection

Selecting the right markets to enter into is one of the key decisions that have to be made and taken into consideration regarding study design and product features prior to a product launch.[232] According to recent studies by IMS Health, the fastest growing healthcare market will be China in a class of its own, followed by the other three BRIC countries.[233]

More than a third of all high net worth individuals (defined as owning financial assets over $1 million) already live in Asia Pacific, Latin America, and the Middle East. With increasing wealth and a population growth rate the multiple of the growth rates in Western countries, these countries – headed by the BRIC countries - are becoming more and more important for bio / pharmaceutical companies.[234] While the established markets in North America, Europe and Japan experienced only modest growth between 2009 and 2010, the markets in Asia / Africa / Australia and Latin America experienced double-digit growth, as depicted in figure 4-5.[235]

---

[230] Cf. Kucher, Janssen (2004), p. 1
[231] Cf. EvaluatePharma (2011), p. 19; Law (2010), p. 4
[232] Cf. Gaston-Breton, Martin (2011), p. 268
[233] For more details please see: Campbell, Chui (2010), pp. 1-8; Eleveld, Chui (2010)
[234] Cf. PriceWaterhouseCoopers (2009), pp. 18-19
[235] Cf. Cacciotti, Clinton (2011), p. 6

Figure 4- 5: Bio / Pharmaceutical market growth 2009–2010 by region

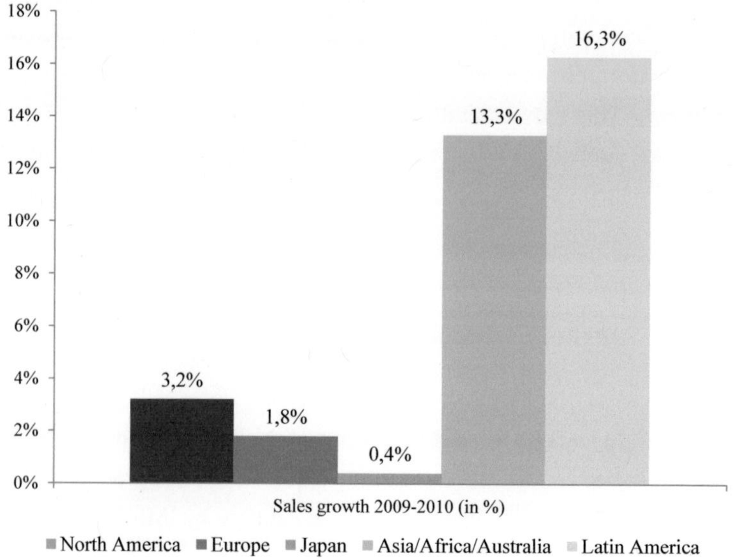

Source: Cacciotti, Clinton (2011), p. 6

The CAGR for these regions is estimated to be around 11-14% over the next years, accounting for up to 40% of the total market by 2020.[236] Unfortunately, many bio / pharmaceutical companies do not have any experience in these countries and need to acquire talent or build competencies in these areas to be successful over the long term. For the individual product launch, this might mean an overall shift in the company's fabric (if it is a small company and/or the product of crucial importance for the company) or will necessitate a decision whether to partner with another company to also launch the product in a country currently not in the corporation's purview. (also see Strategic Partnership, chapter 5.1.6). Once it is decided which markets to enter into, it is also crucial to consider the order. This can be determined by the location of the company, the market size and opportunities, strategic alliance partners and other factors.

[236] Cf. PriceWaterhouseCoopers (2010), pp. 10-11

4.3.3 Current Market Selection Criteria

The size of a market is also important as one develops a launch plan. While the UK and Germany only rank 10th and 13th in product price, they rank 2nd and 4th in number of product launches due to the importance of their markets and their size.[237]

Since the US and Europe are not only the largest markets[238], but also apply the toughest regulatory standards (see regulatory chapters 2.5.2 and 5.3.1), failure to seek approval in these countries suggests that the compound would not pass the standard hurdles for the US and the EU.[239]

Local market structures are also to be taken into consideration. As an example, new products generally enter the UK market quite slowly. In 2002, only 15% of products prescribed had entered the market in the previous 5 years, which is one of the lowest percentages in the EU and only half compared to the US, where 30% of all prescribed drugs had been launched within the past 5 years. This is due to the fact that British system is complex, often requiring a NICE recommendation before making the product available in the marketplace. An additional factor might be that British physicians are conservative and that office software (with the latest products) is only updated every few months.[240] Also, the comfort level with technology varies from country to country (highest in the US, medium in Germany and the UK, rather low in France) and is based on varying legislation (e.g. phone detailing is banned in France), potentially requiring different channels to reach the key stakeholders.[241]

---

[237] Cf. Danzon, et al. (2005), p. 282
[238] Cf. Campbell, Chui (2010), p. 5
[239] Cf. Danzon, et al. (2005), p. 271
[240] Cf. Hermansson (2005), pp. 142-143
[241] Cf. Knoke (2008), pp. 41-42; Simon, Kotler (2003), pp. 285-286

A longitudinal study done from 1982 to 2003 showed that both foreign and domestic firms favored the US market for the first launch of their important products.[242]

Overall, product launches are becoming increasingly more global: While only 24% of drugs launched in all G7 countries (Canada, France, Germany, Italy, Japan, United Kingdom, and United States) between 1970 and 1981, this number increased to 37% from 1982-1992, and went up to nearly half (47%) in the time period from 1993-2003, as shown in figure 4-6.[243]

Figure 4- 6: Increase of product launched in all G7 countries

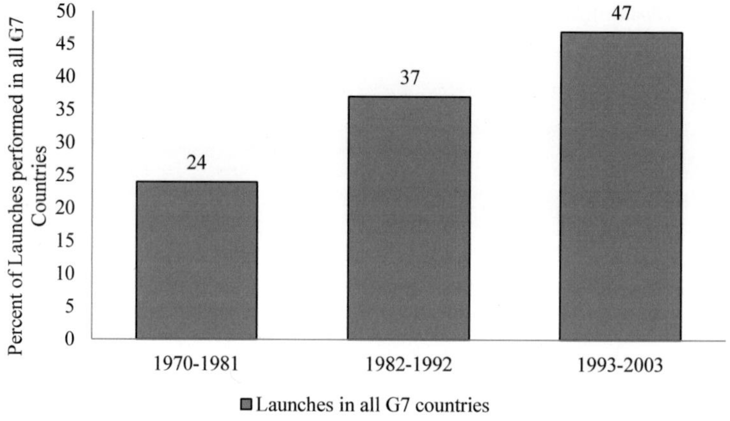

Source: Based on Kyle (2006), pp. 602-603; Kyle (2007), p. 88

Nonetheless, only on third of all products that launched in one of the G7 countries also launched in all others, despite obvious advantage to amortize large and sunk development costs across as many markets as possible. This is due to the heterogeneity of a company's cost of entry in various countries, the market size, the level of competition and the fixed costs associated with a product launch.[244] Accord-

[242] Cf. Grabowski, Wang (2006), p. 457; Note: The US also accounted for 68% of all first-in-class launches, 45% of biotech launches, and 69% of orphan drug launches since 1993. Only regarding global NCEs the EU still holds the leadership position (Grabowski, Wang (2006), p. 457).

[243] Cf. DiMasi, Grabowski (2007), p. 213

[244] Cf. Kyle (2006), pp. 602-603; Kyle (2007), p. 88

ing to the aforementioned IMS Excellence Study, only 38% of products were successful in the majority of the countries they were launched in.[245]

4.3.4 Influence of Regulations on Launch Timing and Price

In an international launch setting, pricing for bio / pharmaceutical products is influenced by many factors. Not only internal considerations, such as production costs, play a role, but also the price of comparative drugs and substitution products or procedures[246], as well as – increasingly - the regulatory environment.[247]

Internationally, the comparative pricing issue continues to be discussed and even tried in courts[248] and must be taken into consideration when establishing launch patterns[249], setting prices and calculating profits for a new product launch.

In Europe, drug prices are still state-regulated, which leads to price discrepancies between EU countries and subsequent 'parallel' trade from low-price countries to high-price countries, which is legal since May 2004 under the Treaty of Rome.[250] In this context, it needs to be mentioned that prices in Germany usually remain above the prices in the rest of Europe, which leads to political controversies in Germany and the EU, the impact thereof is going to be discussed in the following.

Since it is hard to adjust prices post launch, an ongoing look at the international pricing structure, including regulatory and government requirements and updates, is mandatory to establish an overall sustainable pricing structure.[251]

---

245 Cf. McGuire (2007), p. 26
246 Cf. Müller (2005a), p. 152; Ortwein (2001), p. 99
247 Cf. Rao (2008), pp. 95-98
248 Cf. Ernst & Young (2005), p. 64
249 Cf. Kyle (2007), p. 98
250 Cf. Danzon, Epstein (2009), pp. 12-13; Köstlin (2005), p. 233
251 Cf. Köstlin (2005), p. 237

4.3.5 Reference Pricing

Various studies have looked at the impact of regulations on drug launch and pricing: Since some countries function as reference countries for others, especially within the EU, most companies strategically launch in high-price countries first (Germany, Netherlands, Sweden, UK) to avoid undermining these prices before launching in low-price countries (France, Greece, Italy, Portugal, Spain). This is also one of the reasons companies insist on high list prices in reference countries, even though they might be giving major rebates within the country, as to not dilute the reference price, which is deferred from the list price.[252]

It is important to note that only drugs within the same subclass influence each other pricewise. Drugs for treating the same condition, but with different mechanisms of action (MOAs) – such as proton-pump inhibitors and H2-antagonists in the class of anti-ulcerants - barely influence each other pricewise.[253] Generics do not influence originator drugs either.[254]

4.3.6 Parallel Trade and Reimports

To discourage parallel trading, a narrow price band in the various launch countries is desirable.[255] Yet even if the price is set at parity at launch, it might fluctuate due to variations in exchange rates, and it cannot be freely adjusted anymore due to various country-specific price controls.[256] Thus, parallel trading needs to be factored into the post-launch projections and is a key factor particularly in the EU countries.[257]

---

[252] Cf. Danzon, Epstein (2009), pp. 1-13
[253] Cf. Danzon, Epstein (2009), pp. 3-4
[254] Cf. Danzon, Epstein (2009), p. 32
[255] Cf. Falk (2005), p. 248; Köstlin (2005), p. 233
[256] Cf. Darba, Rovira (1998), p. 132
[257] Cf. Kotzian (2004), p. 191

In the UK, parallel imports play an important role for products that are priced at least 10% lower in other EU countries than in the UK and make up about 18% of a product's sales.[258] In 2003, 5 million Euros worth of sales were done as parallel trade, about 5% of the European drug market.[259] In addition to the companies' financial loss due to parallel trading, some countries end up being medically underserved. In Greece, for example, about 16% of drugs sold are re-imported into higher price countries, such as Germany and the UK.[260]

4.3.7 Impact of Launch Sequence on Pricing

For drugs in new drug classes, a comprehensive study in 15 countries for 12 drug classes between 1993-2002 concludes that the median launch lag is less than one year in high-price EU countries and the US, and between one and two years for all other countries that are involved in the launch, except for France, Portugal, and Japan, which usually launch later.[261] This shows that companies take into account the effects of reference pricing, as well as respective market sizes as they prepare their international launch plan (also see chapters 6.3.1 and 6.3.2, launch plan and country plan, respectively). Launch delays in low-price markets might in the end lead to higher prices in these markets due to spillover effects from the high-price markets and avoids early contamination of prices in high-end markets (through reference pricing and parallel trades).[262]

For everyday business this means that companies usually launch in their own country first, as the barriers to entry are the lowest. Firms headquartered in free-pricing countries tend to launch in price-controlled countries as late as possible in their launch order, and choose the higher priced countries for their launch. Firms

[258] Cf. Hermannson (2005), pp. 134, 141
[259] Cf. Weißbäcker, Müller (2005), p. 206
[260] Cf. Weißbäcker, Müller (2005), p. 207
[261] Cf. Danzon, Epstein (2009), pp. 25-28
[262] Cf. Danzon, Epstein (2009), pp. 33-34

headquartered in price-controlled markets generally tend to introduce their products in fewer foreign countries.[263]

Studies have shown that countries with price controls tend to have fewer new product launches (about a 75% reduction in the probability of entry relative to a country without price controls).[264] Oftentimes, these affect the launch of high-quality drugs that are usually able to charge a premium price. If this is impossible in the respective country, also taking into account reference pricing and parallel trading concerns, the innovative drug might not launch in this price-controlled country.[265]

In general, it can be said that within the EU, launching in the UK and Germany first, followed by France, Spain and Italy last is the optimal launch order. An integrated launch strategy, however, also has to take into account other considerations, such as the fact that launch sequencing delays can lead to sales volume losses that outweigh the price advantage gained from this strategy. Also, at times the market does not allow for an optimal launch sequence, due to competitive products or smaller markets or slower market growth.[266] Thus the established rules need to be assessed on a case-by-case basis and to be optimized according to the market's, the product's and the company's strategic specifications.

[263] Cf. Kyle (2007), pp. 91-92
[264] Cf. Kyle (2007), pp. 97-98
[265] Cf. Lanjouw (2005), p. 3; Kyle (2006), p. 615
[266] Cf. Simon, Kotler (2003), pp. 241-242

5. Product-based Considerations

The product is at the core of the product launch. A launch's success (and the subsequent sales) depends on the properties of the product itself that need to be tailored to market demands. Contrary to the common belief that 'a good product sells itself', studies have shown that only 50% of a product's success depend on the product itself, the other 50% depend on other factors, such as the market conditions and the skill set of the launch team. Interestingly, a quantitative study shows that nurture is worth a lot in this industry meaning that having the best product alone is not enough to win. Also, a survey amongst executives on their product performance revealed that nearly two thirds of them (63%) were disappointed in their new product efforts.[267] This warrants a detailed discussion of the necessary product properties as well as the methods applied to develop it in order to achieve a successful product launch in the bio / pharm marketplace. These factors include both clinical as well as commercial aspects.

5.1 Research & Development Considerations

In a longitudinal study, based on data from 1990 until 2005, the clinical phase lasts about 6-8 years, while the approval phase takes 1-2 years. The authors looked for and found differences between the length of these phases between oncology drugs and all other drugs: While oncology drugs were favored by the FDA in the approval process, they did take longer in the clinical phase and had a higher rate of failure in the last phase (Phase III) of the clinical process.[268]

The focus of current research oftentimes is still on the discovery of an individual molecule without the necessary context. This context has to be provided both

[267] Cf. Bonney (2008), p. 34; Copper, Kleinschmidt (1993), p. 74 ; Corstjens, et al. (2005), p. 327
[268] Cf. DiMasi, Grabowski (2007), p. 212

- on the scientific side: The disease's pathway and the molecule's interaction with it, as well as
- on the commercial side: the viability of this molecule in the marketplace, including factors such as biomarkers that allow for targeted therapies to cut overall cost.[269]

As previously mentioned, the successful, market-oriented bio / pharmaceutical launch process necessitates commercial as well as clinical aspects as early as during the pre-clinical phase. For this purpose, major corporations have instituted cross-functional teams, such as Novartis' "Innovation Management Board" that discussed the pipeline and reviews the portfolio on a quarterly basis. To ensure an appropriate value proposition for patients and payers alike, it is advisable to start thinking about and working on these commercial aspect of the product in question by the end of Phase II of clinical development.[270]

The following table 5-1 provides an exemplary overview of necessary actions both in the clinical and commercial realm from the get-go.

[269] Cf. PriceWaterhouseCoopers (2008), p. 29; Sakamoto, van de Ven, Godin et al. (2010), p. 57
[270] Cf. Barnett (2009), pp. 55-56

Table 5- 1: Clinical and commercial activities throughout the launch preparation process

PHASE	Pre-Clinical	Phase I	Phase II	Phase III	Launch
Clinical Actions	• Assess unmet medical needs • Thought-leader identification and input • Targets (indications, dosages) • Investigaor recruitment (Phase I)	• Dosage and safety • Global advisory board • Leader development • Trial investigator recruitment (Phase II)	• Safety and efficacy data • Opinion leader recruitment • Phase II conference presentations • Plan articles • Shape labeling	• Efficacy and safety data • Early access programs • Phase IV planning • Publications • Global Continued Medical Education (CME) program	• Physician monitoring (attitude/ acceptance) • Phase IV clinical start (new indications) • Continue publication efforts
Commercial Actions	• Competitive comparators • Preliminary pricing study • Pre-clinical positioning • Initial attribute mapping	• Global brand teams • Early advocacy collaborations • Global payer assessment • Pharmacoeconomic studies • Early segmentation • Product profile development	• Market needs: validate early insights • Refine physician and patient segmentation • Quantitative product profile • Competitive analysis • ROI modeling • Build communi-cations	• Forecast and financials • Patient/physician pretests • Advocacy program expansion • Final pricing/reimbursement • Labeling/monograph • Sales training • Communication plan	• Marketing ROI analysis • Positioning assessment • Monitor promotional effectiveness • Monitor competitive response • Link with advocacy groups for Phase IV trials

Source: Simon, Kotler (2003), p. 117

Unlike other industries, such as high tech and other manufacturing, the scientific risk of commercial R&D projects cannot be staked out clearly from the onset. The viability of a potential drug, i.e. its safety and efficacy – and lately also its cost-effectiveness – can only be tested in a lengthy clinical trials (and error) process.[271]

In the 1990s, Pharmaceutical companies spent an average of 15% of their revenue on R&D[272], with an increasing tendency as the pipelines are drying up. In this century, bio/ pharmaceutical R&D spending is estimated at between 19-20%, with $124.5 billion (19.3% of sales) in 2009.[273]

The so-called four hurdles to be overcome for the launch of a bio / pharmaceutical product, which are making it such a pricey process, are efficacy, safety, product quality, and – as of lately and with the introduction of cost efficiency agencies – the proof of an adequate cost-benefit ratio.[274] In recent years, a decrease in regulatory predictability along with increased regulatory requirements has complicated the approval and launch process.[275]

As previously mentioned, patents are a high barrier to entry in the bio / pharmaceutical market, making it a lucrative business to be in once established.[276] On the other hand, once a patent expires after its 20-year patent protection[277] granted to WTO (World Trade Organization) member countries in the Uruguay GATT (General Agreement on Tariffs and Trade) round[278], it immediately makes room for new competition. For example, as soon as the Merck's patent for Zocor (simvastatin), a statin for the treatment of elevated cholesterol, expired, three generic competitors entered the market.[279] As another example: when Zantac (cimet-

---

[271] Cf. Pisano (2006), p. 119
[272] Cf. Ortwein (2001), p. 37
[273] Cf. EvaluatePharma (2011), p. 10
[274] Cf. Dietrich (2003); Glaeske, Klauber, Lankers, Selke (2003), p. 8
[275] Cf. Honig (2011), p. 151
[276] Cf. Porter (2008), p. 10
[277] Cf. Ng (2004), p. 10
[278] Cf. Danzon, et al. (2005), p. 291
[279] Cf. Porter (2008), p. 11

idine / GSK) lost its US patent, it lost nearly 90% of its sales within four years, from $2.1 billion in 1995 to $277 in 1999.[280]

While the first generic entrant prices a product only slightly below the originator drug, as soon as the second generic enters the prices fall by about 50%. Since it is not uncommon for an average pharmaceutical product to face 8 competitors within 9 months of patent expiration, it loses about 55 to 75% of its business within the first year, as depicted in figure 5-1 below.[281]

Figure 5- 1: Remaining market share after patent expiration

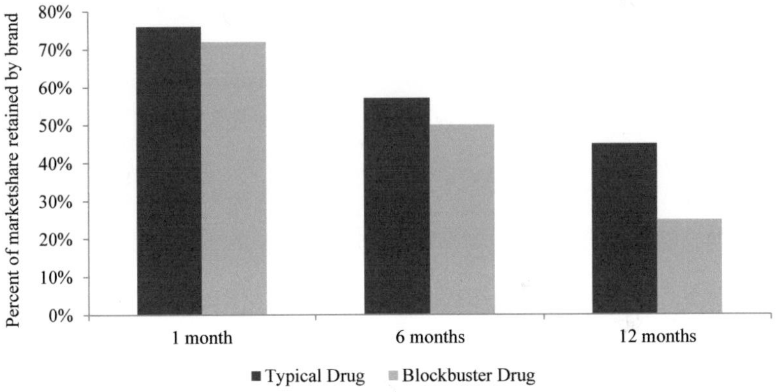

Source: Bolesh (2008), p. 23

5.1.1 Trial Design

An innovative product and well-documented clinical trials are necessary to allow for market approval by the regulatory authorities.[282]

[280] Cf. Ng (2004), p. 10
[281] Cf. Bolesh (2008), pp. 23-24
[282] Cf. Falk (2005), p. 244

Over time, a variety of steps have to be taken and carefully decided upon, as summarized in table 5-2:

Table 5- 2: Key considerations for clinical trials

Trial Design	**Site Selection**	**Patient Recruitment**	**Data Capture / Scrubbing**	**Analysis, Reporting, Submissions**	**Data Mining, Warehousing**
Design questions, endpoints, databases Define patient eligibility criteria Determine treatment protocol	Select investigators based on research, patient base, performance (enrollment/retention success)	Recruit via investigators Recruit through targeted media Screen for demographic and medical eligibility	Complete data entry Correct errors	Report final data (endpoints and descriptive statistics) Submit NDA to regulators	Compile data from multiple sources into single format Mine data to set up physician and patient databases, use in forcasting and for market intelligence

Source: Based on Simon, Kotler (2003), p. 273

To ensure a successful product launch addressing the four hurdles mentioned above, companies have to work more closely with payers and providers to determine what kind of medications are needed[283] and plan ahead on what kind of questions the clinical trial design must be able to answer to clearly position itself in the marketplace while differentiating the product from the standard of care.[284]

Trial designs, and their easy accessibility online these days[285], do impact the marketplace and the product perception. Here it is important to involve experts, such as clinical pharmacologists, who do not only understand the drug development process, but also ways that trial design can help position and differentiate a prod-

[283] Cf. PriceWaterhouseCoopers (2009), p. 10
[284] Cf. Ernst (2002), p. 9; Gudiksen, et al. (2008), p. 567; Zeiner, Schiel (2007), pp. 1399-1400
[285] Cf. Trial information is available on clinicaltrials.gov and similar websites

uct in the marketplace. It is necessary to be aware of all strengths and limitations of the methodologies used to design studies and to quantify their results.[286]

As patient and payer requirements change, this will also impact the necessary endpoints in clinical trials, necessitating qualitative data in addition to efficacy and safety to make a drug attractive and successful in the marketplace.[287]

A comprehensive overview on the kind of health-economic evaluation options is provided in table 5-3:

Table 5- 3: Health economic evaluations

Non-comparative		**Comparative**			
Cost analysis	Healthcare cost analysis	Cost-cost-analysis	Cost-benefit analysis	Cost-effectiveness analysis	Cost-user benefit analysis
Only takes into account the cost of a certain treatment or procedure (e.g. cost of a kidney transplant)	A special kind of cost analysis, evaluating the cost of a disease as a whole (e.g. cost of psoriasis in a country)	Compares the cost of two alternate treatments to minimize cost (e.g. cost of kidney transplant vs dialysis)	Monetarizes the economic aspect as well as intangible components (e.g. QOL, effects on morbidity and mortality)	Expresses effects that cannot be monetarized in natural units (e.g. % reduction of tumor size, number of successfully treated cases)	Takes the results of the cost-effectiveness analysis and translates them into patient-centric results (QALY)

Source: Schöffski (2007), p. 66; Schöffski, Fricke (2008), pp. 76-78

Out of the abovementioned health economic evaluations, the cost-benefit analysis is most commonly taken into account by payers. Additional considerations, such as cost-user benefit analyses, are becoming more and more important as the patient benefit, and his or her improvement of quality of life (QOL) and life span, jointly measured as quality-adjusted life years (QALY), becomes the focus of

[286] Cf. Honig (2011), p. 155
[287] Cf. PriceWaterhouseCoopers (2009), p. 8

treatments and study designs. As an example, the NICE in the UK, which will be discussed further in the subsequent chapter, requires QALY studies for its cost effectiveness evaluations.[288]

One example for successful trial design strategy is Tykerb (lapatinib / GSK). After receiving approval in late-stage cancer for Tykerb (lapatinib) in combination with the oncology market leader Herceptin (trastumzumab / Genentech/Roche), GSK decided to do Phase III head-to-head trials of Tykerb against Herceptin, both in combination with chemotherapy, in the first-line treatment of metastatic breast cancer. This study (EGF108919 or 'COMPLETE') is still enrolling, but already sending a strong signal to the market and its stakeholders about GSK's confidence about their product in this attractive first-line setting. At this point, Tykerb is approved in 92 countries and showing positive sales results.[289]

5.1.2 Patient Selection Criteria for Clinical Trials

Inclusion and exclusion criteria for clinical trials are crucial beyond the regulatory authorities' requirements that are discussed and agreed upon in the phasing meetings. It is advisable to have a large enough quantity of relevant target groups (e.g. women of child-bearing years, older patients, various races) in the clinical trials to ensure a relevant and credible data set, which aids the marketability of the drug post launch. As an example, Novartis was the first company to conduct their pivotal clinical trials for their chronic Hepatitis B (CHB) drug Tyzeka (US) / Sebivo (ROW) (telbivudine) in a predominantly Asian population. As the majority of CHB patients are of Asian descent, this lent additional credibility to their product data.[290] At the same time it is prudent not to overpower clinical trials, i.e. recruiting too many patients, since this might slow down the development process and drive up cost without a benefit at the time of approval.[291] The pivotal GLOBE trial

[288] Cf. Schöffski, Fricke (2008), pp. 83-87
[289] Cf. Clinical Trials.gov (2011); Global Insight (2008); National Cancer Institute (2011)
[290] Cf. Sebivo Package Insert (2010), p. 5
[291] Cf. David, et al. (2009), p. 609

for Tyzeka / Sebivo was powered with 1367 patients in four treatment arms[292], which might be considered overpowered.

On the other hand, it is important to have a clear set of exclusion criteria as well, as to not muddy the waters unexpectedly. A good example for this is the clinical data for Xolair (omalizumab / Genentech, Novartis, Roche). Since this asthma-treatment drug is a protein-based biologic with a clean side effect profile, a history of cancer was not an exclusion criterion for the pivotal trial participants. Phase III trial results showed a numerical, statistically non-significant difference between patients treated with Xolair vs. patients treated with standard treatment. An FDA oncologist expert panel reviewed these data as part of the approval process and deemed these irrelevant, the FDA nonetheless decided to add the 'risk of malignancies and cancer' to the product's label, creating an issue in the mind of (non-)prescribing physicians and thus leading to endless discussions on the matter of cancer for the sales team, research physicians and the companies in general. An exclusion of cancer patients, or patients with a family history of cancer, might have solved this issue before it occurred.[293]

Some market research (discussed further in chapter 5.2.1) can be beneficial early on in the development process: Optimizing both the patient profile as well as the target product profile early in the development process helps qualify and quantify the target group depending on the profile the product under development can offer at the time of launch. This is oftentimes done in a custom choice modeling process, matching product characteristics with patient needs and by involving practicing clinicians early on in the process.[294]

Once the clinical trial design and patient selection criteria are set, timely patient recruitment to secure an early launch date is of the essence. Oftentimes patients are unaware of trials or unsure of their impact on their health (fear of getting the placebo / standard treatment as much as fear of being a 'guinea pig'). Once re-

---

[292] Cf. Lai, Gane, Liaw, et al. (2007), p. 2580
[293] Cf. FDA (2003); Xolair Package Insert (2010), pp. 5-6
[294] Cf. Gudiksen, et al. (2008), p. 567; more details at: Hull, Ramakrishan (2006)

cruited, patients need to be retained as well, as usually nearly 25% of volunteers drop out before completing their study courses. Thus, some marketing activity, such as defining the target audience's needs and motivations, addressing them in all communications, advertising clinical trials as far as legally possible (which varies with each country, the US being one of the more lenient ones), and branding the clinical trial (e.g. by using a recognizable acronym and visuals) is essential for a quick and successful development process.[295]

5.1.3 Go / No-Go Decisions

During the clinical development phase, it is crucial to assess the product profile with regards to the market potential[296], including the price the market could bear for the product. As the development of the product becomes more and more costly as time goes by, the earlier the correct no-go decision is taken, the more money the company can save.[297] This screening process in critical, but difficult to execute due to the uncertainty and complexity, as well as limited information, associated with it.[298] The real challenge lies in collecting the right kind of necessary information prior to a go / no-go decision to make the right choice, which is one of the reasons these difficult decisions often get pushed out.[299] Phase III trials constitute the most costly and time-consuming aspect of the drug development process. By validating targeting and activity in the preclinical stages, carefully constructing the Phase I and II trials to provide information on pharmacokinetic properties, activity, and toxicity of the agent, sensible go / no-go decisions can be made earlier in the process and overall development cost can be reduced. The necessary changes in the R&D project attrition are schematically visualized in figure 5-2. It shows that through slightly higher investments, including early evaluations of the

---

[295] Cf. Avitabile (2006)
[296] Cf. Trilling (2008a), pp. 220-221
[297] Cf. Christopher, McDonald (1995), p. 135 ; Hart, et al. (2003), pp. 22-36
[298] Cf. Johne, Snelson (1988), p. 119; Lin, Chen (2004), p. 197
[299] Cf. Khurana, Rosenthal (1998), p. 57

R&D project in early research phases, decisions can be taken earlier, leading to significant savings in later phases of development.[300]

Figure 5- 2: Shifting the R&D attrition curve

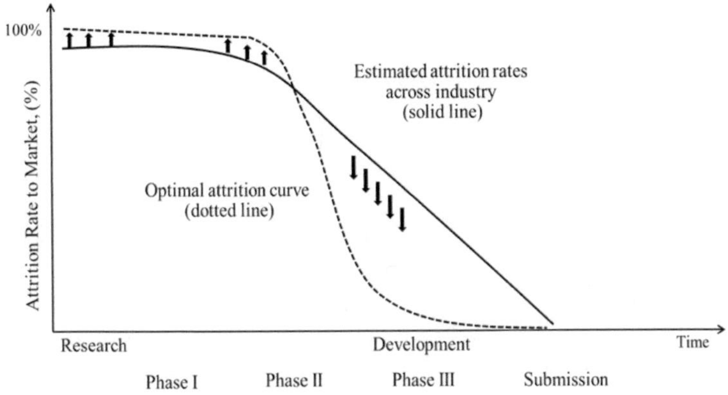

Source: Based on Accenture (2007), p. 12

It is also prudent to do costly safety studies, such as carcinogenicity studies, after proof of concept has been reached, and not – as it is often done – before Phase II is reached.[301] On the other hand, a promising drug should not be overlooked or 'accidentally' killed on its way to the market. Factors to be considered are the agent's potential role in the treatment of a disease (whether as a single treatment or an add-on agent) and the potential for a product market niche or the strategic value of a product for the corporation (e.g. breaking into a new disease state, or fortifying its position therein).[302] Here early stage pricing and forecasting studies can help make informed decisions.[303] In practice, the reasons for discontinuation are initially based on the clinical data received during clinical trials (see figure 5-3 below).

[300] Cf. Accenture (2007), p. 12
[301] Cf. David, et al. (2009), p. 609
[302] Cf. Roberts, Lynch, Chabner (2003), pp. 3688-3693
[303] Cf. Robinson (2010), p. 4

Figure 5- 3: Top reasons for stopping clinical development

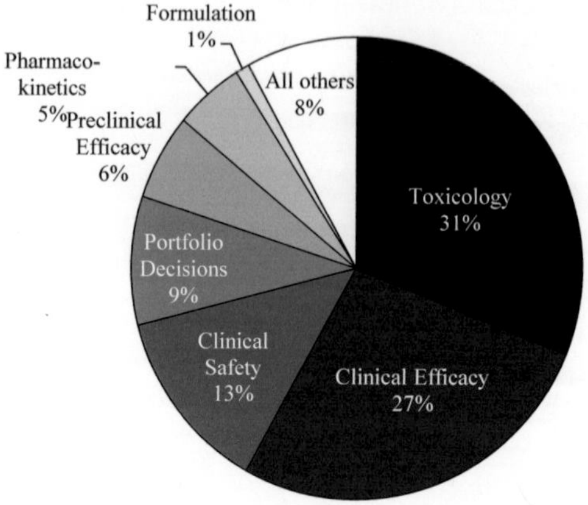

Source: Becker (2010), p. 112

In the final market-based evaluation though, it is estimated that about a third of all clinical trial developments are abandoned due to economic reasons.[304] This can be avoided (or preponed to an earlier point in the development process) by asking difficult commercial questions, and doing the respective market research, in early phases of development (also see chapter 5.2.1).[305]

A more economically-oriented decision making process throughout the development process is crucial in discussions with investors, regulators, and payers, as well as providers, patients, the public and other stakeholders through the entire product life cycle (see figure 5-4).[306]

---

[304] Cf. DiMasi (2001), pp. 297-307
[305] Cf. Bonney (2008), pp. 34-35
[306] Cf. Köstlin (2005), pp. 236-237; PriceWaterhouseCooper (2009), p. 11

Figure 5- 4: Stakeholders involved in new product decisions over time

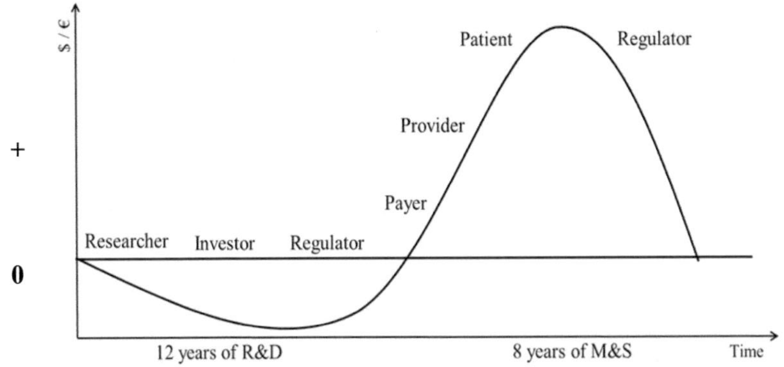

Source: PriceWaterhouseCooper (2009), p. 11

In general, developing contingency plans that are triggered by certain, defined events is helpful to not be blind-sighted in the process.[307]

In this context, milestones and check in points are defined before the clinical trial process and redefined during. At the point of these milestones, decisions are made. This also means oftentimes that spending budgets are gated, meaning that depending on the outcome of a certain milestone additional funds are released or withheld for the specific project. This ensures that an individual product does not squander funds, but continues to compete with other products in the pipeline through the course of the development process. Since the outcome of these milestones is not foreseeable and might harbor surprises, this process ensures that all successful projects still have a fair chance at funding over the course of their development and that funds are divided based on research results and market promise.

[307] Cf. Aaker (1995), p. 348

5.1.4 Special Attention to Side Effects

In the process of product development, in addition to the usual look at serious adverse events (SAE) and other adverse events (AE) that might limit the product's indication and launch potential, it is also important to keep a keen eye on potential positive side effects:

Viagra (sildenafil / PFE) was initially tested as a hypertensive drug, failing to reach the hoped-for effectiveness in this indication, it was subsequently tested for the treatment of angina. While it was not very effective in this disease state either, trial participants reported increased erectile function (which turned out was due to the increase of nitric oxide levels with the intake of sildenafil, which is necessary for erections). So the hypertensive invention, tested for angina, turned out to be the first oral medication for the treatment of erectile dysfunction and became a household name worldwide.[308] Additionally, but with a lot smaller commercial success, sildenafil is also marketed a subset of its initial indication, the treatment of pulmonary artery hypertension (PAH) under the brand name Revatio.

Also, taking another look at previously unsuccessful entities within another disease state might be worthwhile:

Retrovir® (zidovudine / GSK, still known as Burroughs Wellcome at the time of its discovery) had failed as an anti-cancer drug in 1964 but was revived and retested at the onset of the AIDS epidemic in this disease state in the 1980's and subsequently approved as the first treatment against HIV in 1987.[309]

---

[308] Cf. Gilbert, et al. (2003), p. 6; Ng (2004), p. 72
[309] Cf. Grabowski (2005), p. 465; Ng (2004), p. 72

5.1.5 Market Positioning Based on Clinical Profile

An example for a successful launch based on clinical differentiation poses the launch of Singulair (montelukast / Merck). Not being able to provide strong clinical data against the competition due to limited efficacy compared with products already on the market, Merck opted for clinical trials that presented Singulair as an add-on therapy, leading to a lower use of rescue medication (bronchodilators) and a tapering off of inhaled steroids. As both physicians and patients are historically steroid-phobic, due to potential side effects, the promise of fewer steroids by adding a convenient oral agent with a clean side effect profile proved successful.[310]

Additionally, Merck opted to focus on a pediatric indication from the get-go (first for patients under the age of 6, then down to the age of two years), thus capturing an important part of the asthmatic population (25% of sufferers are under the age of 14). This also signaled to physicians that this product is extraordinarily safe, dispelling all safety concerns oftentimes connected to asthma treatment (such as steroid-induced side effects).[311]

In the US, the launch was accompanied by a strong DTC campaign, aimed at the parents of asthma sufferers. The campaign pointed out that Singulair is not a steroid (thus not having the usually feared side effects) and is a once-daily tablet (providing stronger convenience than the inhalers commonly used in the everyday treatment of asthma, oftentimes more than once a day, which are commonly presenting a challenge for young users, leading to suboptimal use and lack of adherence). So while the focus for physicians lay on safety, for patients (and their parents) convenience was an additional factor.[312]

---

[310] Cf. Datamonitor (2004a), pp. 7-9
[311] Cf. Datamonitor (2004a), p. 9
[312] Cf. Datamonitor (2004a), p. 9-10

5.1.6 Strategic Partnerships

In general, it has been acknowledged in the literature that strategic alliances and partnerships, oftentimes in form of horizontal alliances, can be beneficial in the successful introduction of a new product or service package.[313] In the bio / pharmaceutical field, the trend goes towards the integrated offer of disease management package, including all necessary drugs as well as patient education, monitoring and counseling to improve relationship and adherence, nutritional and physical therapy advice etc.[314] Providing an entire package to patients is financially interesting for both payers (whose patients get more comprehensive care) as well as the drug manufacturer (whose patients are more compliant and have a stronger connection to the company and its services than in the past).

Oftentimes, the value of a product is not only based on the product itself, but the whole 'package' it is offered in, to solve the problem around an entire disease state. This also includes soft factors such as information provided, trust in the company, quality of sales representatives and company services rendered, relationships with Key Opinion Leaders etc. These soft factors have to be taken into consideration as part of the differentiation strategy, which is key to set the launch product apart from the competition.[315] Offering a full service and product spectrum using all available distribution channels, is a key focus area for the bio / pharmaceutical venture of the future.[316] It is also becoming increasingly important to offer a full solution to a healthcare problem, for example a full array of products to treat a certain disease state, which may consist of a mix of branded and generic prescription drugs and OTC medications.[317] An example for this is a 'five in one' poly pill developed by the Wolfson Institute of Preventative Medicine in

[313] Cf. Golder (2000), pp. 335-336; Sullivan, Coughlan (2007), p. 203
[314] Cf. Cooper, Kleinschmidt (1995), p. 315; PriceWaterhouseCoopers (2008), p. 37
[315] Cf. Gudiksen, et al. (2008), p. 564
[316] Cf. Fischer, Breitenbach (2010b), pp. 270-272; PriceWaterhouseCoopers (2008), p. 16; Riemenschneider, Sprandel (2007), pp. 159-160
[317] Cf. Gilbert, et al. (2003); PriceWaterhouseCoopers (2009), p. 20

London that contains one statin, three hypertension-treating drugs and a folic acid.[318]

Alternatively, therapeutic drugs might be marketed with the appropriate diagnostic[319], testing for the validity of the product use. On the one hand, it boosts the value proposition of a product, as only people likely to benefit due to their specific diagnostic results are getting the drug. On the other hand, safety concerns are diminished by the fact the likely responders are the only ones receiving the drug and potentially experiencing side effects along with its efficacy.[320] One of the key developments in biotechnology is the addition of targeted screening, which means the patient's Deoxyribonucleic Acid (DNA) is tested for certain gene expressions to ensure that it will respond to a specific therapeutic.[321]

One prominent example of this is Genentech / Roche's cooperation with Dako to devise a test for identifying the right patients for its expensive biologic breast cancer treatment Herceptin (trastuzumab / Genentech / Roche):[322] Only about 25% of all breast cancer patients respond to the treatment with Herceptin. Bayer and Onkogene jointly developed an assay that tests for the epidermal growth factor (EGF), coded by the Her2-gene. This enables the treating physician to determine the stage of the tumor and thus the potential usefulness of the patient's treatment with Herceptin, reducing time in the selection of appropriate treatment and avoiding any unnecessary resistance of the tumor to the drugs provided.[323] Successful and cost-effective disease management is the ultimate goal, an objective beyond the classic pharmaceutical product development and marketing.[324]

To get a good grasp on the clinical profile of the launch product and its potential market implications, it is worthwhile to build a checklist that spells out the market implications as soon as relevant clinical data are available and revisit it on a regu-

---

[318] Cf. PriceWaterhouseCoopers (2009), p. 20
[319] Cf. Müller (2005a), p. 157
[320] Cf. Honig (2011), p. 155
[321] Cf. BCG (2006), p. 16
[322] Cf. Herceptin Development Timeline(2011); PriceWaterhouseCoopers (2009), p. 12
[323] Cf. Fischer, Breitenbach (2010c), pp. 299-301
[324] Cf. Ortwein (2001), p. 23

lar basis, to appropriately pre-plan, pre-position, and prepare the marketplace for the new product, as depicted in table 5-4.

Table 5- 4: Exemplary market implications of clinical product features

Clinical Product Feature	Market Opportunity	Market Challenge
Side Effect A		
Side Effect B		
…		
Mechanism of Action		
…		
Administration		
Dosing Schedule		
…		

Source: Own depiction

5.2 Marketing Considerations

In addition to good science, a product launch also requires top notch marketing. Good marketing needs to be based on solid data, acquired through thorough market research.[325] The drug needs to be differentiated based on its, often small, differences which have to be clearly and consistently communicated across the board with all customers.[326] Here it becomes relevant not to decide if to include customers in shaping the product and its positioning and messaging in its development process, but how to best do this.[327] After all, it is crucial to differentiate one's product, especially in a highly competitive market.[328] To help effectively differen-

[325] Cf. Bolesh (2006), p. 18
[326] Cf. Kucher, Janssen (2004), p. 1-2
[327] Cf. De Luca, Verona, Vicari (2010), p. 315
[328] Cf. Kucher, Janssen (2004), p. 1

tiate the launch product and find a space in the marketplace, solid market research is necessary.

5.2.1 Market Research Process and Steps

Third party data received through market research are crucial for a successful launch process. In its absence, companies run the risk to market to themselves and their perceived needs versus to the customer and their needs.

Usually, market research is conducted during the entire launch process and beyond. All aspects of the product launch decision can and probably should be subject to market research to ensure that they are being properly addressed. Here we need to distinguish between primary (hands-on) market research and secondary market research (using already available data).[329] While primary market research is advantageous as can be tailored to the specific product requirements and company questions, secondary market research is usually readily available and cheaper. It also provides a good basis for primary market research as a second step after all relevant available (or affordable) secondary market research has been reviewed and evaluated.[330] Qualitative market research has long been the basis of bio / pharmaceutical marketing, as the nature of the product (health, prevention or cure of a disease, or even death) is an emotional driver. In this context, product selection is not a purely rational process and the wealth of detailed information available needs to be presented and condensed into decision-driving factors.[331]

To make product development decisions during the early pre-launch phase, market research focuses on market analysis, such as: competitive analysis (currently available products), new product ideas, market size and attractiveness, and com-

---

[329] Cf. Bruhn (1995), pp. 88-91
[330] Cf. Troll (1989), p. 100
[331] Cf. Schweitzer, Siewert (2007), pp. 625-627

petitive pipeline actitivies.[332] To successfully launch a product, it is essential to continuously assess it with the commercial aspect in mind.[333]

As an example for lack of market orientation cited by Kevin Sherer, the CEO of Amgen, he and his team did not listen to the marketplace and objective opinions of outsiders during the launch of Kineret (anakinra), a treatment for rheumatoid arthritis. While the product was effective for a subset of patients, it did not have the market potential Amgen attributed to it. Having spent their funds on the product launch based on its (over)estimated revenue potential, the company lost money, thus wasting shareholder money.[334]

Specific launch-related market research is usually started as the product is nearing the end of Phase III trials and enough relevant data is available, taking between 9 to 12 months. It can be summarized and will be described as follows (figure 5-5)[335]:

[332] Cf. Ortwein (2001), p. 101
[333] Cf. Ernst (2002), p. 9
[334] Cf. Hemp (2004), p. 73
[335] Cf. Kelly, Liftin, Vaughn (2009); Vanderveer, Pines (2003)

Figure 5- 5: Market research process for launch products

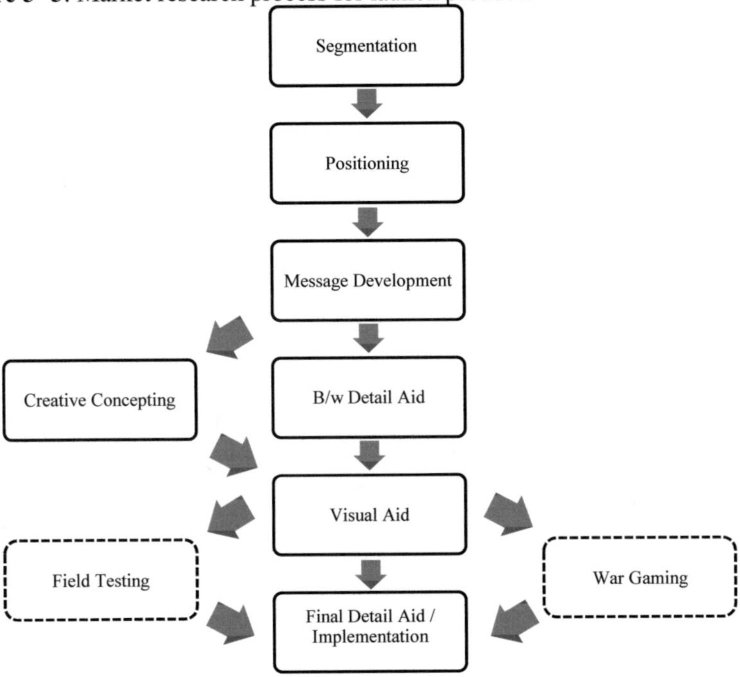

Source: Kelly, Liftin, Vaughn (2009), p. 2; Vanderveer, Pines (2003)

5.2.1.1 Market Segmentation

Market segmentation is the sectioning of the relevant market into homogenous sub-markets that is the basis for differentiated marketing.[336] To ensure the viability of a market segment, it needs to be identifiable and measurable, relevant to the product, contain enough market potential to provide a sufficient return on investment, and to be accessible, meaning that it is also commercially viable.[337] A market segment thus consists of consumers (or decision makers) that respond similar

[336] Cf. Bruhn (1995), pp. 60-64
[337] Cf. Christopher, McDonald (1995), pp. 74-75

to a given set of marketing stimuli.[338] Market segments strive to be internally homogenous while being externally heterogeneous, thus clearly distinguishing themselves from other segments. Comprehensive market segmentation examines the target audience in three ways:

- Demographically (who they are)
- Behaviorally (what they do)
- And attitudinally (why they do what they do).[339]

To ensure a product's success in the pharmaceutical marketplace, it is necessary to segment the market appropriately and thus realize a favorable position within a viable market segment.[340] Segmentation helps target the right customers, i.e. the ones that hold the largest ROI, delivering tailored messages that address the customers' needs, and to tactically inform the optimal media mix to reach these customers.[341]

A good example of a targeted segmentation is the promotionally based attitudinal segmentation, which posed an extensive battery of attitudinal and experiential questions at 800 US physicians and derived with the following 6 physician segments in table 5-5 (in order of diminishing pharmaceutical sales influence upon the respective segment)[342]:

---

[338] Cf. Kotler, Armstrong (1989), pp. 42-43
[339] Cf. Green, Krieger (1991), p. 21; Kelly, Liftin, Vaughn (2009), p. 1
[340] Cf. Green, Krieger (1991), pp. 25-26; Simon (1989), p. 7
[341] Cf. Johne, Snelson (1988), p. 121; Kelly, Liftin, Vaughn (2009), p. 1
[342] Cf. Vaughn, Gruber (2009)

Table 5- 5: Attitudinal prescriber segmentation

Segment	Characteristics
Industry Enthusiasts (27%)	• Reps valued, interactions welcomed • Low concern for applying business principles to practice • Patient-specific treatment decisions • Aggressive seekers of latest clinical info • Highly data driven • Active attendees of pharma-sponsored events • Brand loyalists
Patient-Overloaded Independents (5%)	• Small staff • Average nearly 600 patients per month • Reps valued • Generalized treatment decisions • Low concern for applying business principles to practice • Early brand adopters • Brand loyalists
Hometown Altruists (40%)	• Small staff • Reps regarded as valued colleagues • Patient-specific treatment decisions • Enjoy managing practice • Professionally active • Adaptive prescribers
Academic High Achievers (10%)	• Moderate-size staff • Reps appreciated, but with skepticism • Generalized treatment decisions • Passion for academics • Interested in latest research studies • Appreciate alternative detailing methods • Strong preference for specific brands

Occupational Traditional-ists (7%)	• Large staff • Average 450+ patients per month • Reps not valued • Patient-specific treatment decisions • Conservative prescribers • Late brand adopters but willing to switch
Corporate Professionals (11%)	• Large staff • Reps not valued nor depended upon • Practice treated as a business • Generalized treatment decisions • Highest proportion of patients with no prescription plans • Adaptable prescribers

Source: Based on Vaughn, Gruber (2009), p. 2

In case of lower budget launches, using these kinds of established, actionable segments[343] to think about and categorize target physicians and provide a tool to the sales force might be helpful. The drawback is that these categories were not specifically crafted for one therapeutic area and thus might overlook market-specific idiosyncrasies. Nonetheless, this kind of available secondary research is helpful in a pinch and up to the launch team to decide which tools to include in their tool kit. Here both the decision makers and channels (step 1) and the ultimate users (step 2) have to be reviewed and potentially segmented appropriately. In a first step, to ensure that a market-specific segmentation is done within the relevant physician / channel customer base, one helpful suggestion is to follow this three-part approach:

First, the company focuses on the relevant customer base. Historically, there has been a bias towards physicians, but other healthcare staff (such as nurses, nurse practitioners, medical assistants etc.) and other players in the healthcare system

[343] Note: While the segments and their characteristics are listed above, additional information about how to address these segments can be found in the respective article by Vaughn, Gruber (2009)

(such as payers) also need to be taken into account.[344] Once the target base has been established, they get further analyzed based on their customer value. E.g. a single pharmacy has a significantly higher economic value to the company than an individual patient; a health insurance's value is higher than that of a physician etc. Thus, resources need to be allocated accordingly. Last but not least, individual approaches and offers have to be formulated for these customers that made it through the first two cuts. While companies do appreciate the targeted approach in theory, letting go of historically important customers and beliefs in practice proves to be hard and is oftentimes insufficiently executed.[345]

In a second step, on the patient level, segmentation is also valuable, as it allows the company to focus on a specific patient type, and maybe even take a leadership position in this subset. While it is tempting to keep the patient segment as broad as possible, to not limit the available patient base and thus limit profits, this is the most viable option to secure a relevant position in the busy bio / pharmaceutical marketplace.[346]

The dynamic part of the market - meaning the new, switch and add-on patients - are essential to the product's growth. Studies show that in the decisive first 6 months post-launch, excellent launches seem to have a higher number of switch patients than less successful launches. It is important to note, that in more established markets, only about 10% of the market is dynamic.[347]
Mapping the patient experience throughout the launch process helps gain a deep understanding of the patient's experience and can guide the marketing and development process.[348]

In practice, it makes sense to use the same vendor for international segmentation analyses. This ensures consistency of the methodologies and comparability of the data provided.[349]

---

[344] Cf. Vanderveer (2009), pp. 27-28
[345] Cf. Albiez, Danielsohn-Weil, Scholl (2007), pp. 1133-1137
[346] Cf. Seiter, Holz (2009), p. 927
[347] Cf. Pfister (2010), p. 3; Wartenberg, Ziedman, Rickwood (2010), p. 7
[348] More details and maps can be found in Taenzler (2006)

5.2.1.2 Product Positioning

The unified and coordinated branding and positioning of the launch product is also crucial for its success.[350] Strategic positioning aims to address a specific unmet medical need that is supported by relevant clinical data. Note that a specific unmet need does not necessarily mean that the drug is overall more effective than the competition (see Singulair case), but specifically that it addresses an unmet need (safe, easy-to-use and steroid-sparing in the case of Singulair).[351] Positioning determines the overall impression the customer is supposed to take away from the product, the place the product occupies in his mind, supported by key messages that are derived from key data points.[352] As customers transcend borders or simply go online, it is crucial for the positioning to be internationally unified and not watered down by being adjusted to local differences.[353] This brings with it the difficult task of having a focused position that is relevant and applicable in all launch countries. Here it is essential to ensure a unique positioning for the product, meaning distinguishing it from competing products in the customers mind, as well as a relevant positioning of the product. The competitive advantage has to be crystallized to effectively position a product.[354]

The positioning is usually done about 12-18 months pre-launch, when the product's profile is already well-known, but also allowing for enough time to test all materials that need to be developed and tested prior to launch.[355] Overall preparation for a product launch, nonetheless, should be started on the commercial side about three to four years prior to the anticipated launch date to effectively coordinate with and participate in the development decisions.[356]

---

[349] Cf. Müller (2005a), p. 159
[350] Cf. Falk (2005), p. 245; Ortwein (2001), p. 100
[351] Cf. Datamonitor (2004a), pp. 10-11
[352] Cf. Kotler, Armstrong (1989), pp. 43-44; Falk (2005), p. 247
[353] Cf. Müller (2005a), pp. 151-152
[354] Cf. Simon (1989), p. 7
[355] Cf. Vanderveer, Pines (2007), pp. 71-76
[356] Cf. Robinson (2010), p. 4

Bringing a distinct and perceived advantage to the market is crucial for a successful market entry.[357] This is also and particularly the case for combination products where a clear decision has to be made, if the product is to be positioned as the combination of the heritage drugs to enhance the existing brand or as a new entity in itself to expand the franchise. Of course, these decisions also impact the branding of the drug, which will be discussed in a subsequent chapter.[358]

In practice, the urge to include as many key benefits as possible into the positioning statement of a product oftentimes leads to a diluted positioning, as it is not focused enough for the customer to keep in mind and distinguish it from the competition. While the positioning of a product usually is nothing more than a short sentence, it is the essence of the brand and thus needs appropriate amounts of time and attention to be created successfully. To avoid corporate or top management bias or to avoid 'consensus-driven' cluster positioning statements that end up diluting the brand and not being unique versus the competition, it often is advisable to let this positioning workshop be run by outside experts specializing in positioning. As a second step, the positioning might be tested with key customers, such as key opinion leaders and top prescribers[359], to test their relevance. One of the key points for a product's success is defined by how well it meets customer wants and needs.[360] Thus it is imperative to develop a thorough understanding of the customers' mindset, desires and needs early in the development process.
As explained above, the core of pre-launch market research is made up by a product's positioning. Positioning can be defined as the advantageous location that a product owns in the minds of physicians, or: 'where the company wants its product to be placed in the customer's mind so that it will achieve optimal utilization.[361]

The positioning is an internal statement that informs and drives all other marketing activities, communications and materials. A successful positioning statement

---

[357] Cf. Simon (1989), p. 14
[358] Cf. Datamonitor (2008b), pp. 1-9
[359] Cf. Falk (2005), p. 247
[360] Cf. IBM (2006), p. 5
[361] Cf. Ries, Trout (2001); Vanderveer, Pines (2007), pp. 71-72

has to be credible regarding the clinical performance of the product, unique and thus differentiating it from the competition, clinically relevant, sustainable across the product's life cycle - and ultimately drive prescribing behavior.[362]

Ideally, the product's positioning stays the same, while the messages and materials derived from it can be adjusted for the respective audiences and, as additional data becomes available or competitors enter the marketplace, also over time (see figure 5-6). Messaging can be seen as the product's story, where a new chapter begins at the point the old one left off, consistent in its approach and anchored by the same positioning platform. Once a product has been introduced to and positioned in the market, it never can 'start over' with a clean slate. Thus it is crucial to get the positioning right the first time around.[363]

Figure 5- 6: Consistent positioning for all stakeholders over time

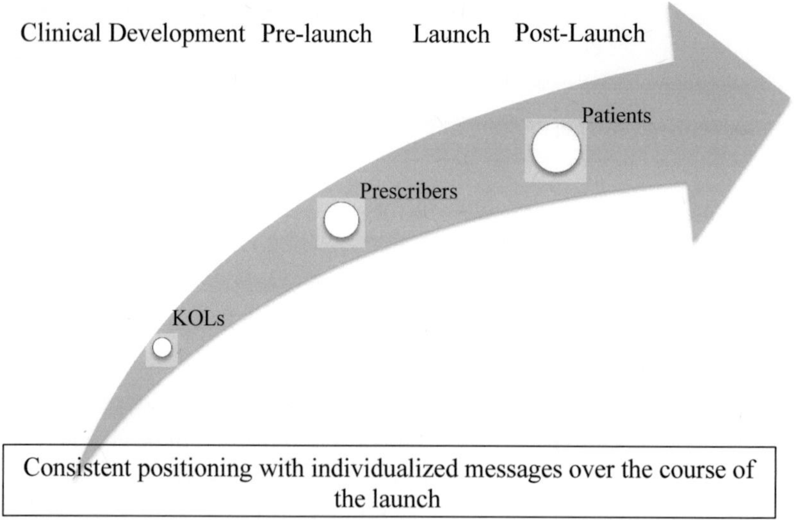

Source: Based on Vanderveer (2005a), p. 3

In summary, the positioning statement is traditionally developed by the cross-functional brand team in-house 12 to 18 months prior to launch and then tested

[362] Cf. Kelly, Liftin, Vaughn (2009), p. 1; Vanderveer, Pines (2007), p. 72
[363] Cf. Stephen (2009); Vanderveer (2005a), p. 3

qualitatively in individual in-depth interviews with physicians, and subsequently validated quantitatively.[364] Novel approaches, such as the customer-driven positioning suggested by leading market research organizations, postulate that instead it should be developed by physicians. This successful approach allows physicians to develop their own preferred positioning of the new product in question based on clinical data and positioning building blocks provided by the brand team.[365]

Table 5-6 provides a detailed example of an imaginary drug's ('Cizplam') positioning statement, including all its elements, which eventually lead up to a single focused positioning, the 'elevator pitch' statement.[366]

Table 5- 6: Exemplary positioning statement highlighting key elements

Positioning Statement Element	Definition	Example ('Cizplam')
Problem Statement	Optional components to the positioning statement include the problem statement, which articulates a specific unmet need in the marketplace that is being met by the brand in questions	For the treatment of pain, prescribers currently have to make compromises between safety and efficacy (the safer, the less effective)
Functional benefit	The essential clinical properties of a medication that intrinsically differentiate it from other medications	Cizplam acts quickly, easy on the stomach, enhances physical functioning, without increased cardiovascular or cancer risk

[364] Cf. Prounis (2007), pp. 57-61; Vanderveer (2005a), p. 2
[365] Cf. Kelly, Liftin, Vaughn (2009), p. 2
[366] Cf. Vanderveer, Pines (2003), p. 3; Vanderveer, Pines (2007), pp. 74-75

Reason to believe	A reference to some scientific or mechanistic aspect of the brand that substantiates its main clinical benefits (optional)	Cizplam is unmatched in its class because of its unique mechanism of action
Emotional benefits	Emotions that customers may derive from using the brand in question	Physicians can trust (feel reassured, confident) to be making the right choice by prescribing Cizplam)
Main theme	The truly unique and aspirational advantage offered by the product in question	Full efficacy without compromising safety

Positioning Statement ('elevator pitch'):

"Effective on pain and fast-acting, Cizplam, because of its unique mechanism of action, can also treat headaches, is easy on the stomach, beneficial to physical functioning, and does not result in any increase in cancer or cardiovascular risk."

Source: Based on Vanderveer, Pines (2003), p. 3; Vanderveer, Pines (2007), pp. 74-75

In some instances, it is also advisable to include a comparator in the positioning architecture, meaning that is also addresses the key competitor's features and the own product's advantages over it.[367]

Instead of being exposed to the more emotional or aspirational elements of a positioning that might go against the scientifically oriented physician, the physician is first exposed to the clinical and functional benefits of the drug, followed by rea-

[367] Cf. Demeire (2011)

son to believe and only then the emotional benefits. This allows physicians to first buy into the clinical aspects of the drug and be more (for)giving when getting to the emotional and aspirational ones, instead of shooting them down right away, as the 'weakest link' in the overall statement. While physicians tend to be focused on the clinical aspects and need to believe these before moving forward, a product's positioning needs to also include the emotional side and even aspirational elements (e.g. trying to change the way the disease is treated) to fulfill its full potential post launch. At the end of the interview, the physician is asked to develop his own positioning based on the chosen elements and then compare it to and to defend it against the statements developed by the brand team. This allows for a detailed analysis and an in-depth understanding of the physician's take on the suggested positioning statements, leading to potential adjustments and sharpening of focus and language.[368]

This novel approach allows for testing a solid positioning statement with all necessary elements with the target physicians while optimizing the aspirational and emotional aspects of the positioning.[369]

Taking the time and effort to get the positioning right is crucial as it forms the basis for all subsequent marketing communications, including materials, messages, advertising etc. In addition to being clinically correct and compelling, the positioning statement also needs to be 'ownable', which means that the claims made, and thus the space owned in the customers' minds, cannot be taken by a competitor.[370]

One good example of successful positioning and subsequent messaging is Eli Lilly's launch of Cialis (tadalafil) for erectile dysfunction in a market dominated by Viagra. Cialis was positioned as the 'weekender' drug (which in more clinical terms refers to its longer 'duration of action') and subsequently successfully positioned itself against Viagra. Levitra (vardenafil) failed to clearly position itself

---

[368] Cf. Schulz (2001), p. 13; Vanderveer, Pines (2007), pp. 71-76
[369] Cf. Vanderveer, Pines (2007), pp. 71-76
[370] Cf. Demeire (2011); Prounis (2007), p. 55

versus the competition and subsequently suffered in the marketplace. Successful positioning creatively combines the hard facts that create the backbone of every bio / pharmaceutical positioning (in Cialis' case: 'up to 36 hours of action') with emotional benefits (in Cialis' case: 'separating the pill from the pillow', meaning that the patient with erectile dysfunction (ED) feels less rushed and medical when using Cialis in comparison with Viagra).[371]

Studies done in the innovative and growing Rheumatoid Arthritis market in the UK have shown that well-positioned products such as Enbrel (etanercept / Amgen) and Humira (adalimumab / Abbott) have a significantly higher market share, driven by both new patients and switch patients, than its less well-positioned competitors Remicade (infliximab / Centocor / Merck) and MabThera (rituximab / Genentech / Roche), while having comparable recall data.[372]
To validate the success of segmentation and product positioning, or to adjust it, conjoint analyses have been a tool used since the early 1990s to truly understand the trade-offs certain customer groups are making in their product decisions.[373]

While this dissertation focuses on the launch of new products, the implications and opportunities of a relaunch of an existing one should not be forgotten in this context, as it can apply the same tools as a new product. In a more mature phase of the product's life cycle and particularly under changed market conditions, a re-launch and repositioning poses an option to extend the product's life.[374] The main goal is to enhance the overall life cycle of the product, oftentimes based on a change in the competitive environment.[375]

An example for this is the repositioning and relaunch of the Hepatitis B drug Hepsera (adefovir / Gilead) as a new, potent competitor Baraclude (entecavir / BMS) entered the marketplace and started to chip away at the market share of Hepsera. This way, Gilead was able to hold on to a significant amount of market

---

[371] Cf. Vanderveer (2005a), pp. 3-4
[372] Cf. Zeiner, Schiel (2007), p. 1399; Zeiner (2008), pp. 435-436
[373] More details can be found here: Green, Krieger (1992), pp. 117-132
[374] Cf. Bruhn (1995), p. 67
[375] Cf. Knoke (2008), pp. 13-14

share until the launch of a new drug, Viread (tenofovir), for the treatment of CHB.[376]

Another good example for successful (re)positioning is Raptiva (efalizumab / Genentech/ Roche), which was launched for all kinds of moderate to severe psoriasis only to realize that it was unable to gain a leading position versus the competition, such as Amgen's Enbrel and Abbott's Humira (adalimumab). Only by segmenting the market and repositioning the product to specifically treat hands and feet, where Raptiva had an effectiveness advantage, was the brand successfully positioned in the physician's minds.[377]

---

[376] Baraclude (2011), Hepsera (2011), Viread (2011)
[377] Embrel (2011), Humira (2011), Raptiva (2011)

5.2.1.3 Messaging and Final Material Development

Following the successful product positioning, key messages (that are to be communicated to the stakeholders) are developed and tested with the help of potential customers, followed by sales materials that integrate these key messages into full stories – first based on simple black-and-white outlines to get the story right, then more and more detailed, integrating key visuals and logos (which are also tested in parallel).[378] Here it is important to note that cultural differences may lead to varying perceptions and might necessitate different messages, which needs to be considered in the brand book and addressed in individual country plans (see chapter 6.3.2).

5.2.1.3.1 Key Messages

The brand team and the advertising agency, sometimes with the help of the market research company of choice, if they are well-versed in the marketplace, are developing key selling messages based on all claims that are likely to be approved by the regulatory authorities.[379] After these have been pared down to a manageable amount of messages (20-30), a compelling 'story' has to be built, based on the key points of the positioning statement:

- Attention getters – to gain the stakeholder's attention and want them to listen to what the representative has to say
- Benefits – key advantages the product holds for the stakeholder and patient
- Reasons to believe – substantiating the benefits with clinical data
- Obstacle handlers – (proactively) addressing the stakeholder's concerns
- Close / call to action – providing direction or impetus towards the goal, such as prescribing the drug in question[380]

---

[378] Cf. Adams (2009), p. 16; Vanderveer, Pines (2007), p. 73
[379] Cf. Vanderveer, Pines (2003), p. 3
[380] Cf. Dobni, Zinkhan (1990), pp. 110-119; Vanderveer, Pines (2003), p. 3

5.2.1.3.2 Black and White Detail Aid

The mock-up of the detail aid is kept simple in black and white, focusing on the words, graphs and charts that tell the story of the product. This technique avoids any distraction by imagery and colors at this point in time to fine-tune the story, providing final input for content flow and wording. In individual in-depth interviews (IDI), the detail aid is presented with a sales representative's voice over (to simulate a real situation without variances, such as varying performances of a real person).[381]

5.2.1.3.3 Creative Concept Development

While the story line is tested in form of a black and white detail aid, the creative elements undergo a test as well. Here we are mainly concerned with the imagery, logos, and potentially headlines and taglines, which also have to support and substantiate the product's positioning statement. The research is focused on understanding which imagery best reflects the positioning, gets the stakeholder's attention and helps them remember the product, and how motivating the imagery is to use the product (as well as potential issues with the imagery, such as it being offensive or otherwise problematic).[382]

5.2.1.3.4 Final Detail Aid

Once the black and white detail aid has been fine-tuned and the creative elements vetted, these are brought together in the final detail aid. This, in turn, is tested similar fashion as the black and white detail aid, ensuring it includes all necessary information and flows well. It is important to select both stakeholders that are likely to use the product as well as the ones that are hesitant to do so. The detail

---

[381] Cf. Vanderveer, Pines (2003), p. 4
[382] Cf. Vanderveer, Pines (2003), pp. 3-4

aid has to stand up to all audiences, and varying responses best test the validity of the material.[383]

Optional, yet time tested additions to the market research process are war games and field testing.

5.2.1.4 War Games

One proven way to ensure fresh thinking and illuminate the launch from the competitors' point-of-view is doing so-called 'war games'.[384]

As a first step, internal role playing sets the stage to understand the competition and the market. It also serves to inoculate non-core team members with the realities of the marketplace. Specifically speaking, usually about 40 members of the launch team, top management, key vendors (such as advertising executives or business consultants) split into two teams. The competing teams consist of the launch product team as well as a team representing the largest (future) competitor (usually the current market leader). While the launch team develops a selling story and positioning for the launch brand, the competing team uses the current market leader's or key competitors' data and profile to bolster its position in light of the new market entrant. In mock sales pitches in front of a neutral jury, both teams are trying to poke holes into the competing team's product profile, its positioning, key messages, and materials. Subsequently, the teams are using the information gathered in the first round to develop counter-strategies and tactics. Following this structured, moderated interaction, the entire team gets together and evaluates the overall outcome, resulting into an action plan for improvement[385] that, if done right, anticipates competitive steps and thus is able to deal with these issues and questions as they arise during the launch process.[386]

---

[383] Cf. Schweitzer, Siewert (2007), p. 627; Vanderveer, Pines (2003), p. 4
[384] Cf. Falk (2005), p. 249
[385] Cf. Falk (2005), p. 249
[386] Cf. Vanderveer, Heasley (2005)

War gaming can also be tested in market research. In its most basic form, the launch product's key selling messages are tested against the key competitor's. Here the goal is to create a compelling story that holds up against the competition and 'wins' in the market research setting. Under certain circumstances, various story lines can be tested and established for different customer segments, addressing their specific needs and concerns. The value of war gaming in market research consists in gaining real-life feedback on the launch product's potential versus the competition, crafting the most compelling story under optimal testing conditions, and – last but not least – to provide confidence to the sales team that their materials and messages stand the test of real life physicians, the people they have to go sell to in face of the competition.[387] Ideally, war-gaming starts off with a round of focus groups to identify the best strategies, which is then followed by IDI to further hone and refine specific messages and counter-arguments.[388] War-gaming cannot only be used to inoculate one's own product against the competition, but also to preemptively position a competitive product. One example for this is Eli Lilly's successful positioning of the incumbent Pfizer drug Geodon (ziprasidone) as a drug with a higher cardiovascular risk. The lesson learned for the launch product is that if one does not address (and lay to rest) concerns about the product, the competition will do this for you and use it to their advantage.[389]

Even with an objectively superior product, it is not always easy to take away market share from the competition due to brand loyalties, the comfort of the known product and aversion to change.[390] This is particularly true for customers who are conservative in their choices (see Rogers' diffusion of innovation). Especially when new in a marketplace without existing ties and connections, the manufacturer has to take this fact into consideration.

---

[387] Cf. Kelly, Garcia (2009), pp. 83-88; Vanderveer, Heasley (2005)
[388] Cf. Kelly, Liftin, Vaughn (2009), p. 2
[389] Cf. Vanderveer (2005a), p. 4
[390] Cf. Simon (1989), p. 13

5.2.1.5 Field Testing

Another optional part of the development process is the so-called field testing. Companies provide mock ups of the detail aid to sales representatives and let them test them with their prescribers in real life situations.[391] This not only provides a good test under full market conditions, but also generates buy-in from the sales force as they are included in the decision making process.[392] One drawback is that, to remain credible, problems arising at this (late) stage need to be addressed and time and funds need to be allotted for this. Secondly, in case of a launch situation, respective legal paperwork has to be drawn up and the material handled appropriately confidentially, to avoid any charges or issues regarding off-label promotion of a not-yet approved drug.

On the other hand, this pressure test ensures that the detail aid is really ready to go into the marketplace, providing helpful a priori information about the launch situation.

5.2.2 The 7Ps of Bio / Pharmaceutical Marketing

Since the 1960's, the marketing mix of the so-called '4Ps' has been applied to successfully market products:

- Product – This first P relates to all decisions made to market a specific goods-and-service range.[393] Here it is important to provide a better product, or problem solution, for the customer than the competition.[394]
- Price - This second P regards the price setting for each product, service range, or offer.[395]

[391] Cf. Vanderveer, Pines (2003), p. 4
[392] Cf. Kavanaugh, S. (2008), p. 8; Schweitzer, Siewert (2007), p. 625
[393] Cf. Christopher, McDonald (1995), p. 24; Kotler, Armstrong (1989), p. 46
[394] Cf. Zollondz (2008), pp. 28-31
[395] Cf. Christopher, McDonald (1995), p. 24; Kotler, Armstrong (1989), p. 46

- Place - This third P regards the company activities to make the product in question available, i.e. the decisions on the appropriate channels of distribution.[396]
- Promotion[397] - The forth classic P addresses the activities to communicate the merits of the product to the target audience, with the intent to ultimately persuade them to buy the offered product and/or service.[398] Here we can also distinguish between personal promotion, such as the sales force, and impersonal promotion, such as advertising.[399]

Figure 5- 7: The 4Ps of marketing

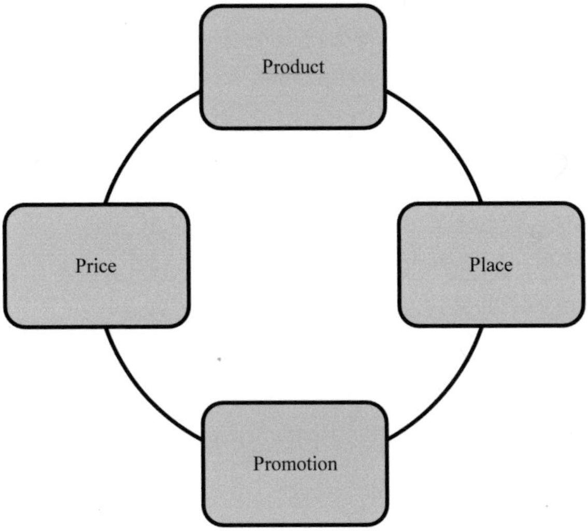

Source: Own depiction

Based on corporate and market objectives, the decisions made to meet the 4Ps objectives make up the traditional marketing plan.

[396] Cf. Christopher, McDonald (1995), p. 24; Kotler, Armstrong (1989), p. 46
[397] Cf. McCarthy (1964), pp. 38-40
[398] Cf. Kotler, Armstrong (1989), p. 46
[399] Cf. Christopher, McDonald (1995), p. 24, pp. 26-27

Unlike other common markets, the pharmaceutical market is also influenced by three additional forces - players, processes, and positioning –which as a total are known as the '7P'. This is depicted in figure 5-8, with the three additional Ps having a darker gray background.

- Players (including politics and patients) – which means specifically the needs and expectations of all stakeholders in the healthcare market (discussed in detail in chapter 5.3)
- Processes – the understanding of the processes within this highly regulated marketplace, including informal processes and communication processes.[400] Accordingly, bio / pharmaceutical companies are more and more focused on the processes they use to do their business. In this context, processes refer to the production of a service, such as the integration of patients and other stakeholders into the treatment with a drug.[401]

Last but not least, the final of the 7Ps of pharmaceutical marketing, as depicted in figure 5-8, refer to

- Positioning – the positioning of the service and product provided based on the insights gained from the observations and interactions with stakeholders / players and their processes.[402]

As discussed in the previous chapter, the goal of positioning a product is to ensure that the properties of the product and services offered by the company are noted by the potential customers and ultimately meet their needs.[403] Studies, such as the one done by IMS Health, have shown that the product's positioning and content

[400] Cf. Harms, Drüner (2003), pp. 191-193; Wolf Sussman (2008), p. 234
[401] Cf. Ernst (2002), p. 9; Zollondz (2008), p. 107
[402] Cf. Harms, Drüner (2003), pp. 191-193; Wolf Sussman (2008), p. 234
[403] Cf. Bruhn (1995), pp. 64-65

of its message are more important than the sheer intensity of the promotional push.[404] This means that all the promotional funds in the world will not make up for a botched positioning, and subsequent messaging of a product. So while this can be a tedious, sometimes esoteric-sounding, part of the process, it is important to get it right and to get the right minds involved.[405]

Figure 5- 8: The 7Ps of bio / pharmaceutical marketing

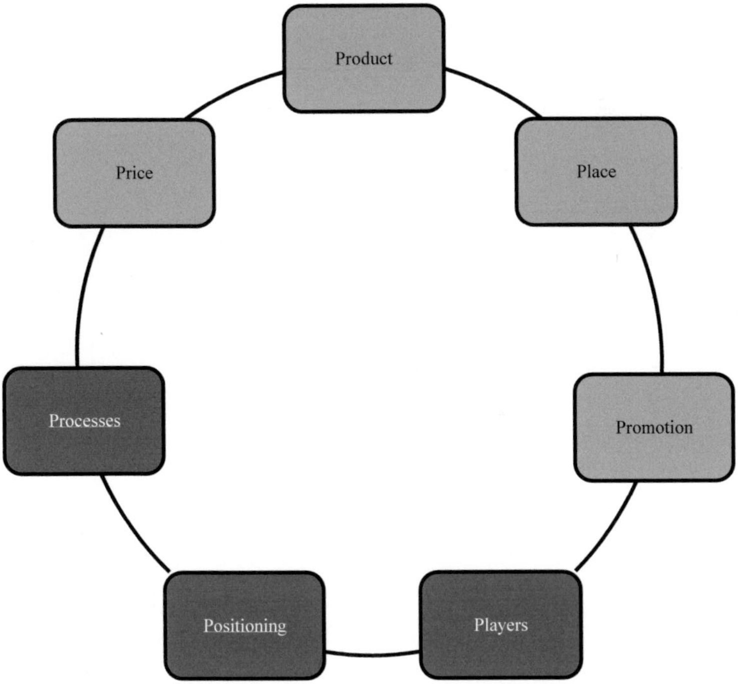

Figure: Own depiction

Both business and socio-political considerations have to be taken into account in the marketing of pharmaceuticals, complicating the process and – at times – leading to lower results than the product itself suggests.[406]

---

404 Cf. Zeiner, Schiel (2007), p. 1399
405 Cf. Fischer, Breitenbach (2010a), p. 2; Harms, Drüner (2003), pp. 191-193
406 Cf. Ortwein (2001), p. 100

5.2.3 Branding

It is crucial not to confuse the 'brand' with the 'product' itself, or to even use them synonymously. A brand is 'the set of associations a product or service engenders in the mind of its users'[407]. While products become generic or are superseded by rival products, a brand can live forever and can be linked to newly introduced products and services as well. Thus brand creation, while in its intricate details beyond the scope of this dissertation, is a key factor to consider.[408]

A brand is a product's, a product ranges, or a corporation's intangible surround, such as quality perceptions, reputation, and image. It differentiates a product, and its services (or the company itself) from the competition and creates loyalty, thus preventing substitution.[409] Branding is part of a coherent strategy and has to be carefully considered and prior to launch a decision has to be made, if the new product is to be positioned by itself, as part of a product line or extension, for example in form of a combination product, or even under the corporate umbrella.[410] To ensure a unified brand, details of the product's branding are summarized and visualized in the launch-relevant brand book (see chapter 6.3.3).

5.2.3.1 Brand Name

The new product also needs a brand name in addition to its international nonproprietary name (INN), which is designated by the WHO.[411] Usually, this name is to be memorable for all parties involved (pharmacists, physicians, and consumers) and not easily confused with another medication. Oftentimes, it makes sense to have a reference to the disease state in the brand's name. Others are pure fantasy names. One example of this is the fibromyalgia drug Lyrica (pregabalin),

---

[407] Cf. Aaker (2007), p. 9; PriceWaterhouseCoopers (2009), p. 20
[408] Cf. Fischer, Breitenbach (2010b), pp. 265-266; PriceWaterhouseCoopers (2009), p. 20
[409] Cf. Aaker (1995), pp. 206-213; Christopher, McDonald (1995), pp. 167-173
[410] Cf. Aaker (2007), p. 9; Comiteau, Fahey (1996), p. 2; Datamonitor (2008b), pp. 1-9
[411] More details regarding this process can be found at WHO (2011); WHO (2011a)

which is to be associated with music and harmony rather than with a specific ingredient or benefit.[412] Brand names can be individual brand names (one for each drug, such as 'Lyrica', 'Prilosec', 'Nexium' etc.), or a company trade name combined with an individual product name (such as 'Claritin 12-hour RediTabs' or 'Aspirin plus C' etc.).[413]

In the US, the FDA updated its industry guidance for the submission for the evaluation of proprietary names in February 2010. It uses a special algorithm to ensure the product does not get confused with another, called POCA (Phonetic Orthographic Computer Analysis), to which it has given access to specialized companies, such as Thomson Compumark and CT Corsearch. Only if the guidelines are met and these tests are passed, bio / pharmaceutical companies pass a set of name suggestions to the FDA entity in charge of the name approval.[414]

In the EU, the EMA has developed similar guidelines for the 'acceptability of names for human medicinal products'.[415]

This does not necessarily mean that these agencies come to the same conclusions, as they have slightly different guidelines. As an example, the HIV drug is called Epzicom (GSK) is a combination of Epivir (lamivudine) and Ziagen (abacavir), thus the name 'Epzicom' is associated to be the abbreviation for <u>Ep</u>ivir <u>Zi</u>agen <u>Com</u>bination. While this name was approved in the US, in the EU and Australia the same product is called Kivexa.
Eli Lilly named its human Growth hormone (hGh) drug <u>Gen</u>otropin, positively associating it with the leading biotechnology company and first inventor of the synthesized growth hormone, <u>Gen</u>entech. (Genentech's own hGh drug is called Neutropin, which continues to lead to confusions and wrong associations much to Genentech's dismay in this highly competitive market).

---

[412] Cf. Birkner (2011), p. 6; Ortwein (2001), p. 53
[413] Cf. Kotler (1972), p. 449
[414] Cf. FDA (2010); Heavner, Harlan (2010); Thompson Compumark (2011)
[415] Cf. EMA (2007)

For international product launches, it is important to consider the sound and meaning of a name in another language. Gilead Sciences' and BMS's joint HIV combination drug of Viread (tenofovir), Emtriva (emtricitabine) and Sustiva (efavirenz) ended up being called 'Atripla'. In launch case studies conducted with German university students, this name was repeatedly pointed out as sounding inappropriate to the German ear. 'Atripla' sounded too much like 'Tripper', the German slang term for the venereal disease 'gonnorhea'.

5.2.3.2 Product Packaging

Packaging is another factor to be considered during the launch process. One the one hand, it poses a manufacturing issue, ensuring that the drug is appropriately and safely stored. But it also has commercial implications, as package size also influences the price: units in packages with over 100 units are significantly cheaper, but strength does not influence the price much.[416] (Also see price setting example for Lipitor in chapter 5.3.3.3). Overall, injectables and non-oral drug forms bear a significantly higher price in the marketplace. This needs to be evaluated and benchmarked in the marketplace when deciding on the product's price.[417]

Another reason packaging might be valuable is to avoid illegal parallel trading. The option is to brand and package products differently for various markets:[418] To avoid re-imports of at-cost donations of its HIV drug Truvada (a tenofovir and emtricitabine combination Nucleoside / tide Reverse Transcriptase Inhibitor (NRTI)) to third world countries, Gilead Sciences gave the pill a different color in third world countries (dark blue) from its color in first-world countries (light blue) where the drug is available on the open market. Country officials in these third world countries had used the opportunity of cheap high-value drugs to make some money by selling them back into first world countries instead of giving them to their population in need.

---

[416] Cf. Danzon, Epstein (2009), p. 35
[417] Cf. Danzon, Epstein (2009), pp. 32-33
[418] Cf. PriceWaterhouseCoopers (2009), p. 19

5.3 Stakeholder Considerations

To secure market access and acceptance at launch, it is crucial to be in touch with the respective players prior to that point in time.[419] As previously mentioned and depicted in figure 5-4, a number of stakeholders are involved in new product decisions throughout the launch process and beyond, as it is not sufficient to solely address the direct customers' needs, but to also lower adoption barriers for further influential stakeholders.[420]

On a tactical level, it is important to address all stakeholders in accordance with the launch strategy established in the previous chapter. Here it is important to note that different countries require different approaches as the influence of the stakeholders varies from country to country.[421]

This chapter focuses on specific tactics in regards to the stakeholder are being discussed. These have to be assessed, coordinated and carried out in each country the company decides to launch, as depicted in table 5-7.

---

[419] Cf. Bernhard (2010), p. 3
[420] Cf. Talke, Hultink (2010), p. 548
[421] Cf. Bernhard (2010a), pp. 1-2

Table 5- 7: Exemplary stakeholder grid

Stakeholder Group	Key Players	Action Items
Regulators		
Payers		
Investors		
Prescribers		
Patients		
Patient Groups		
Media		
...		

Source: Own depiction

5.3.1 Regulatory Stakeholder Considerations

For all businesses, legislative and regulatory rules, and their changes, pose major threats or opportunities.[422] This is particularly true for the highly regulated bio / pharmaceutical industry, as will be discussed in the upcoming chapter.

To successfully launch a product, it is imperative to have a thorough understanding of the regulatory environment in the respective countries and to formulate the launch strategy accordingly. Some of the key factors to consider are as follows.

Launch delays are pricey.[423] Based on an estimate done by Datamonitor in 2008, each day a product launch is delayed can cost the manufacturer up to $23 million in sales in the US alone as well as an additional $37,000 in development costs.[424]

---

[422] Cf. Aaker (1995), p. 112
[423] Cf. Danzon, et al. (2005), p. 269
[424] Cf. Datamonitor (2008), p. 24

Another study, done by McKinsey in 2009, estimates that a 6-month launch delay leads to a loss of $100 million in Net Present Value (NPV) and a reduction of the IRR (internal rate of return) of .5%. Nonetheless, launching a product is not just a matter of speed, but also depends on carefully choosing what processes to accelerate and how, such as the novel parallel development techniques, e.g. various forms of drug components, in granulated and in fully blended form. The parallel development technique employed for Januvia (sitagliptin / Merck) for the treatment of diabetes, which accelerated the launch by an estimated 3-4 years.[425] Increasingly, companies are looking into ways to streamline their operations, enabling them to take early decisions and to move from one clinical trials phase to another without delay by having preplanned and predefined the next steps. Merck, for example, was able to speed up the development and testing of a promising diabetes drug MK-0431 from the usual 4.12 years needed for Phase III trials to 2.25 years by improving their information technology and decision making processes.[426] Applying new procedures should be preceded by a clear understanding of the socio-political background, such as the perception of the public of national laws that might impact them.[427]

On the other hand, a regulatory submission should not be rushed, as the labeling of the product is the basis for nearly all commercial (marketing and sales) activities and needs to be thoroughly reviewed by all parties involved. It is thus advisable to establish a labeling committee with experts from regulatory, clinical and commercial departments. Each of them brings a unique view on the product that is necessary to develop a well-balanced submission and product label.
In France, Italy, Spain, Switzerland, and Japan, being a local player (a company with headquarters in this country) had a significant positive effect on launch timing, getting approved more readily.[428] This is to be taken into account as well, as it might (positively) influence the overall launch plan. Business drivers in the UK are to get a relevant indication that is prioritized by the government, that the

---

[425] Cf. David, et al. (2009), p. 609
[426] Cf. Carr, D., Cone, E. (2004), p. 52
[427] Cf. Günzel, Bass (1991), p. 300
[428] Cf. Danzon, Epstein (2009), pp. 28-30

product is in line with national guidelines, and local hospital guidelines and drug lists.[429]

Studies also show that success rates do vary between therapeutic classes: Endocrine and central nervous system (CNS) success rates were consistently below average, while success rates for anti-neoplastic and anti-infective categories were well above average.[430] These clinical success rates are a good indicator on how well bio / pharmaceutical companies are able to translate new drugs available for clinical testing into drugs approved for marketing.[431] In a study reviewing 85 NCEs in 14 EU countries, it was noted that HIV / AIDS products had chosen to take the faster, centralized process, as pressures for market approval and market needs were high.[432] Products most likely to choose the mutual agreement track were those most likely to be exposed to parallel trade. Interestingly enough, these also included first-in-class drugs, which can be rationalized by the fact that these drugs usually retain their first mover advantage for a long period of time, thus being exposing to parallel trade when launched simultaneously in all EU countries, as well as spillover effects by being used for reference pricing.[433] Since the sample size is relatively small and this study was done early on in the EMA's existence, new strategies might evolve and are to be observed with interest.

Due to the still large unmet medical need and the lethal nature of the disease, cancer drugs account for the largest share of biotechnology products in phase III trials, showing the focus of the future of biotechnology.[434] In 2004 alone, Avastin (bevacizumab / Genentech, Roche), Erbitux (cetuximab / mClone and Merck KGaA), Tarceva (erlotinib / Genentech, Roche, OSI Pharmaceuticals), Clonar (clofarabine / Genzyme) were approved for the treatment of cancer.[435] As of 2010, the top three cancer products in terms of sale are all monoclonal antibodies (Avas-

[429] Cf. Hermansson (2005), pp. 142-143
[430] Cf. DiMasi (1995), p. 9
[431] Cf. DiMasi (1995), p. 13
[432] Cf. Danzon, et al. (2005), p. 286, 289
[433] Cf. Danzon, et al. (2005), p. 289
[434] Cf. Ernst & Young (2005), p. 57; BCG (2006), p. 4, 22
[435] Cf. Ernst & Young (2005), p. 57

tin (bevacizumab), Rituxan (rituximab), and Herceptin (trastuzumab) / all Genentech/Roche).[436]

As could be seen throughout the review of the regulatory requirements, oncology drugs seem to hold a special status from a regulatory point-of-view. As has been shown in a longitudinal US study from 1990-2005[437] and also been observed in various European reviews, special provisions were made more frequently in this disease state than in any other. This is due to the lethal nature of the disease, a strong advocacy and patient community[438] and the still large unmet medical need in the treatment of cancer, which makes it an attractive area to venture into for pharmaceutical and biotech companies alike, despite the fact that the late-stage failure risk is comparatively higher.[439]

For general comparison, in 2001 the median approval time for pharmaceuticals at CDER was 14 months; the median approval time for biologics at CBER was a little over 20 months.[440] Thus, due to the more complex nature of biologics, a company has to factor in longer review periods until the approval and launch of biologics.

Regulatory reviews can have a clear outcome, such as yes (approved letter) or no (non-approvable letter), but also outcomes that are in the gray zone (approvable letter). In this case, minor deficiencies need to be corrected before the drug can finally be approved.[441] To save time and money, companies naturally aim to avoid all flaws and provide clear information to the FDA to immediately receive an approval letter, which enables them to launch the new product without delay.

Also formalities need to be considered: E.g. if the company chooses a Centralized Procedure in the EU, it has to notify the EMA 6 months prior to MAA submis-

[436] Cf. EvaluatePharma (2011), p. 14
[437] Cf. DiMasi, Grabowski (2007), pp. 209-216
[438] Cf. Vanderveer; Pines (2003), p. 4
[439] Cf. DiMasi, Grabowski (2007), p. 212
[440] Cf. Ng (2004), p. 164
[441] Cf. Ng (2004), pp. 190-191

sion.[442] As bio / pharmaceutical companies are dealing with government authorities (and timelines) in all countries, integrating these deadlines and review timelines into the overall launch plan is crucial for a successful launch.

It is also possible to include the authorities in the development process. In 2007, Novartis was the first company to take a new approach to its Phase III design of an experimental new drug when it involved NICE as a consultant to provide advice on its design.[443] In 2008, GSK let various government healthcare officials in Europe decide which compounds should progress in clinical trials.[444]

Another way to optimally take advantage of the regulatory process is by using the special provisions for certain drugs. These are:

- Orphan Drugs
- Conditional Market Authorization (EU) and Accelerated Approval (US)
- Fast Track (US), Priority Review (US), Accelerated Assessment (EU) and Compassionate Use (US and EU)[445]

5.3.1.1 Orphan Drug Track

Both the FDA and the EMA provide special rules for orphan drugs, established in 1983 and 2000 respectively.[446] The term 'orphan drug' refers to drugs that treat diseases that only afflict a small number of patients, and thus might not be lucrative for an individual corporation, despite their high value of a small set of patients in the overall population. Here the governments are providing special push

---

[442] Cf. Ng (2004), p. 198-200
[443] Cf. PriceWaterhouseCoopers (2009), p. 12, Jack (2008)
[444] Cf. PriceWaterhouseCoopers (2009), p. 12; Whalen (2008), p. B1
[445] Cf. EMA (2007a); FDA (2010a); Official Journal of the European Union (2006)
[446] Cf. Ernst & Young (2005), p. 58; DiMasi, Grabowski (2007), p. 214; Fischer, Breitenbach (2010a), p. 20; Grabowski (2005), p. 458

and pull incentives to stimulate the discovery and development of drugs for these disease states.[447]

In the US, the Orphan Drug Act applies to conditions with a prevalence of less than 200,000 people. For treatments addressing these conditions, the FDA is required to facilitate the approval, which is the same process as for regular drugs, and provide counseling to ensure a more effective R&D process. The company receives a 50% tax credit for its orphan drug clinical trial expenditures. And, apart from any patent protection of the drug, a 7 year marketing exclusivity is granted.[448] The FDA also combined this with a Phase I and II clinical research grant program, providing between $150,000 and $300,000 in research grants.[449] In the US, more than 1,400 drugs have been qualified as orphan drugs and the number of approved orphan drugs since 1983 has increased tenfold, and more than doubled in the last decade. By the end of 2010, 367 orphan drugs have been approved by the FDA.[450]

About 5,000 of the 30,000 known diseases are considered orphan diseases whose treatment options would qualify as orphan drugs.[451] Practice shows that more nearly half of all orphan drugs are concentrated in the three areas of oncology, AIDS and genetic diseases.[452]

Within the EU, orphan drug status can be given based on prevalence or lack of profitability (expected revenues from this disease state).[453] A prevalence of .05% (or less) or 230,000 people of the general population qualifies a drug as an orphan drug in the EU.[454] Due to market exclusivity, reduced filing fees and protocol assistance, many European companies decided to pursue niche treatments. These

---

447 Cf. VFA (2011)
448 Cf. DiMasi, Grabowski (2007), p. 214; Haffner (2006), pp. 445-447; Ng (2004), p. 191; Schlemminger (2010), p. 139
449 Cf. Grabowski (2005), p. 464
450 Cf. Grabowski (2005), p. 465; Karst (2011); Schlemminger (2010), p. 139; Tufts Center for the Study of Drug Development (2010)
451 Cf. Ortwein (2001), p. 22
452 Cf. Grabowski (2005), pp. 467-468
453 Cf. Ernst & Young (2005), p. 63
454 Cf. Aigner, et al. (2010), p. 100; BCG (2006), p. 23

filings are reviewed by the Committee for Orphan Medicinal Products (COMP), established in 2000, which issues an opinion regarding the potential orphan drug status within 90 days, which in turn is then decided upon by the Commission within 30 days.[455] These timelines have to be factored in for drugs that are to be developed and launched under the preferential orphan drug status. By the end of 2004, 237 drugs had received orphan drugs and 20 were already approved.[456] By 2011, the number of approved drugs with European orphan drug designation has increased to 63, with another 770 potential orphan drugs in the clinical development.[457]

To provide an overview, table 5-8 depicts the orphan drug criteria and provisions by the EMA and FDA.

Table 5- 8: Comparison of EMA and FDA orphan drug regulations

Orphan Drug	**EMA (EU)**	**FDA (USA)**
Criteria	< 230,000 patients/year (<5 per 10,000 inhabitants)	< 200,000 patients/year (<7.5 per 10,000 inhabitants)
Provi-sions	• Reduced filing fees (100% for SMEs, 50% for non-SMEs) • Priority Review (6 months) • Protocol assistance • Market exclusivity for up to 10 years	• No regulatory fees • Federal tax credit (up to 50% of research cost) • Orphan Products Grants Program • 7 year market exclusivity

Source: Own depiction based on EMA and FDA websites

Some well-known examples for orphan drugs are Caradase (Alglucerase / Genzyme) for Morbus Gaucher patients, Leustatin / Litak (cladribine / Janssen-Cilag)

[455] Cf. Official Journal of the European Communities (2000); VFA (2011)
[456] Cf. Ernst & Young (2005), p. 58, 63
[457] Cf. EMA (2011); Orphanet Report Series (2011); VFA (2011)

for hairy cell leukemia, and Xagrid (anagrelid / Shire) for the treatment of essential thrombocytemia.[458]

The term, 'orphan drug', has to be further clarified and leads to uncertainty of the financial incentive to develop orphan drug in Europe.[459] As for their profitability, orphan drugs range widely: A 10-year sales study done for orphan drugs launched between 1990 and 1994 showed that the top quintile earned over $500 million in its tenth year on the marked, the median quintile had sales of $29.5 million at that time, while the lower quintiles earned less than $10 million in their tenth year.[460] Thus, due to their government support and financial potential, these 'wealthy' orphans are worth pursuing as a company strategy.

Yet, the subsequent success of Novartis' Gleevec / Glivec (imantinib mesylate, a treatment for chronic myeloid leukemia) led the European authorities to reconsider orphan drug designations and decide that the exclusivity should be removed if the orphan drug is 'earning unreasonable profits'.[461] Specifically, according to article 8(2) of the European Orphan Medicines Regulation 141/2000, the market exclusivity of ten years can be reduced to six years at the end of the fifth year in case the product is sufficiently profitable not to justify maintenance of market exclusivity'.[462] This is a factor to keep in mind when planning an orphan product launch, as it impacts the overall financials and life cycle of the product. Smaller companies, such as Santhera[463], have used this development in the orphan drug segment to find a niche to establish themselves in the fiercely competitive pharmaceutical market.[464]

---

[458] Cf. Schlemminger (2010), p. 139
[459] Cf. Ernst & Young (2005), p. 58
[460] Cf. Grabowski (2005), p. 469
[461] Cf. Ernst & Young (2005), p. 58
[462] Cf. Commission of the European Communities (2008); Ernst & Young (2005), p. 63
[463] For more information, please go to Santhera (2011)
[464] Cf. Schlemminger (2010), p. 139

Industry leaders have suggested that this rule should only apply for orphan drugs that received its status based on financial considerations, but not for products that received orphan status based on prevalence data.[465]

A longitudinal study done by DiMasi and Grabowski showed that out of the 27 orphan drugs introduced in the US between 1990 and 1994, their median global peak sales were $29.5 million, compared with the median global peak sales of the non-orphan drugs during this period of time of $236 million.[466] Thus the prevalence model used by the FDA seems to be effective in designating the orphan drug status to the appropriate drug. Yet it is noteworthy that the orphan drug status was given to 48.5% of oncology drugs from 1990-2005, while only 18.5% of drugs received orphan status in all other disease states in the same time period.[467]

A problem for orphan drug development is the lack of knowledge of potential side effects prior to launch, as it is hard to collect sufficient data in these disease states.[468] In the EU, this oftentimes leads to a long-term conditional market authorization.

5.3.1.2 Regulatory: Conditional Marketing Authorization (in the EU)

In Europe, this so-called 'conditional marketing authorization' allows a company to market new products to get innovative medicines to patients faster. Thus, these products must yield an important health benefit and the company agrees to conduct further trials and monitoring. After the year, this conditional approval could expire, be extended or proceed for regular approval.[469]

Some experts estimate that 'live licenses' will become a reality, which means that new products can be launched conditional on further clinical studies to substanti-

---

465 Cf. Ernst & Young (2005), p. 63
466 Cf. DiMasi, Grabowski (2007), p. 214
467 Cf. DiMasi, Grabowski (2007), p. 212
468 Cf. Ortwein (2001), p. 22
469 Cf. Ernst & Young (2005), p. 63; Official Journal of the European Union (2006)

ate the data set. This would simplify the initial approval process, but necessitate additional regulatory and clinical work during and after the launch process.[470] If this was to come to pass, the current 'big bang' approach of a product launch would be replaced by a more subtle launch, followed by additional waves as new information, in form of extended labels (new indications or dosing schedules etc.), becomes available.[471]

For now, a one-time launch still is the practitioner's reality and needs to be planned and prepared for accordingly.

5.3.1.3 Accelerated Development and Approval Processes (in the US)

In the US, it is possible to receive a variety of accelerated development and review timelines from the authorities. This is based on the anticipated advantage of the new product over the currently available ones, and can be especially impactful in case of severe and deadly diseases.[472]

Time-to-market, and thus accelerated approval times, is a crucial success factor[473], especially since patent lives are limited and when the competition is following closely behind. To demonstrate the intricacies of clinical trial work with the involvement of regulatory stakeholders in the bio / pharmaceutical industry, the various options available in the US are shown in figure 5-9 below and then briefly discussed in increasing order of impact in the following.

---

[470] Cf. PriceWaterhouseCoopers (2009), p. 18

[471] Cf. PriceWaterhouseCoopers (2009), p. 20

[472] Cf. Aigner, et al. (2010), pp. 99-101; Dagher, et al. (2004), p. 1500-1501; Ng (2004), p. 182; Schilsky (2004), pp. 1495-1496

[473] Cf. Carbonell, Rodriguez-Escudero (2010), p. 501; Carbonell, Rodriguez (2006), p. 1; IBM (2006), pp. 8-9

Figure 5- 9: Impact of accelerated FDA programs on development timeline

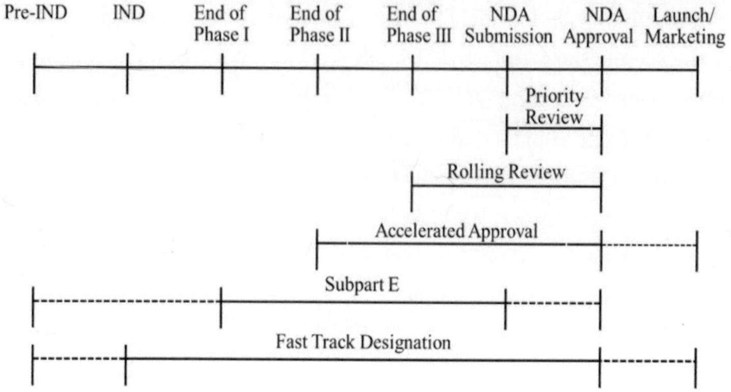

Source: Milne, Bergman (2001), p. 74

Priority Review means that the FDA aims to complete the NDA review (for products that fill an unmet medical need in a serious disease) within 6 months instead of the usual 10-month timeframe. The request for priority review can be initiated at any time during the drug development process and will be accepted or denied by the FDA within a 60-day-timeframe.[474] For best chances to receive priority review, it is prudent to be able to provide substantial scientific proof necessitating a priority review at the time of the request.

Rolling Review is the only part of the Fast Track Designation instituted in 1997 that was not previously available in other accelerated processes with the FDA. It means that the company may submit chapters of its documentation for review as they are finalized one after the other, instead of waiting for the entire submission documentation to be final. In theory, this might save the company and the review process a lot of time. Nonetheless, getting Fast Track Designation is not a guarantee for a rolling review, though – and even a rolling review does not guarantee that documents are actually reviewed before everything is received as it normally would in a standard submission. So in effect, a rolling review might be nothing more than a rolling submission process.[475]

---

[474] Cf. FDA (2010a)
[475] Cf. Milne, Bergman (2001), pp. 72-74

Accelerated Approval means that drugs are approved based on surrogate endpoints instead of the usual primary endpoints (e.g. tumor shrinkage rather than survival data). They then are required to conduct confirmatory Phase IV trials post-launch to confirm the validity of the primary endpoint (e.g. survival data).[476]

Established in 1988 and last revised in 2010, Subpart E specifically serves the expedited development, evaluation and marketing of therapies - both biologic and pharmaceutical drugs - that are intended to treat life-threatening and severely-debilitating illnesses. Qualifying treatments may, but do not necessarily, receive accelerated approval.[477] Companies also receive additional attention and support from the FDA committees, such as early consultations, pre-IND meetings and end-of-phase 1 meetings. As a drawback, promotional launch materials that are to be used within the first 120 days after launch have to be submitted to the FDA for prior review.[478] In reality, this usually leads to a launch without sales aids, advertising, or any other promotional materials other than the package insert and maybe simple reminder items, such as pens, with the brand name printed on them.

For a Fast Track Designation, the US government provides various programs under the FDA Modernization Act (FDAMA) of 1997[479], which help speed the development process along:

Other than individual expedited development and review programs, such as Subpart E, the fast track designation instituted under the FDAMA in 1997 has the potential to facilitate the entire development and approval process for drugs that fill an unmet medical need for the treatment of a serious illness.[480] Four basic programs are provided: Meetings, written correspondence, review programs and dispute resolution. The only part of the Fast Track Designation that is not covered in

---

[476] Cf. DiMasi, Grabowski (2007), p. 210; FDA (2010a)
[477] Cf. DiMasi, Grabowski (2007), p. 210; FDA (2010a)
[478] Cf. Code of Federal Regulations Title 21 – Part 312 (2010); Code of Federal Regulations Title 21 – Part 601 (2010)
[479] Cf. 105th Congress of the United States of America (1997)
[480] Cf. Milne, Bergman (2001), p. 71

other programs is the Rolling Review.[481] Most drugs that are eligible for a Fast Track also receive priority review, which means that the FDA aims to complete the NDA review within 6 months instead of the usual 10-month timeframe.[482]

As an example for particularly short FDA review times, the previously cited Gleevec / Glivec (imantinib mesylate / Novartis) was approved for the treatment of life-threatening chronic myeloid leukemia (CML) within four months.[483] Crixivan (indinavir / Merck), another orphan drug, was approved for the treatment of HIV within 42 days.[484] Just like these two drugs, more than half of all fast-track drugs have orphan designations.[485]

So far Switzerland is the only European country that allows for a 'fast track' approval for certain indications. This usually means that products are approved in an accelerated manner, usually saving multiple months. This also enables physicians and patients worldwide to acquire the product from Switzerland through an international pharmacy.[486]

5.3.1.4 Further Considerations

Besides these clearly distinguished development and approval tracks, there are a couple of additional factors that might play a significant during the development of the product and should be taken into consideration within the launch planning stage. These are the compassionate use of a drug and parallel track development.

---

[481] Cf. Milne, Bergman (2001), p. 72
[482] Cf. FDA (2010a)
[483] Cf. FDA (2010a)
[484] Cf. Ng (2004), pp. 164-165
[485] Cf. FDA (2010b), Grabowski (2005), p. 467
[486] Cf. Falk (2005), pp. 244-245

5.3.1.4.1 Compassionate Use

In case of life-threatening diseases that lead to death without treatment, such as cancer, it is possible to provide not-yet-approved drugs to patients in need against the current medical and legal standards.[487]

In Europe, compassionate use implementation remains in the competence of the member states. The member states, not the company providing the compassionate use drug[488], has to notify the EMA of their intention to make a product available for compassionate use. It is possible, though, to receive a Committee for Medicinal Products for Human Use (CHMP) opinion to facilitate access to these programs within the EU, to favor a common approach regarding the conditions of use, and to increase transparency between member states. It falls on the company providing the drug to ensure that patients receiving the product as part of a compassionate use product still receive it uninterruptedly during the period between marketing authorization and the product being available in the marketplace.[489] Compassionate use products do not only create goodwill for the company and their product range by providing life-saving medication prior to approval, but also provide the opportunity for a head-start during launch: Prescribers already have experience with the launch product prior to launch, and compassionate use patients can be turned into regular patients of the marketed product, also providing a good rationale for payers, as the aim is to keep these patients on drug versus starting a new treatment.

One example for compassionate use is Alimta (pemetrexed / LLY), a chemotherapy drug for the treatment of pleural mesothelioma and non-small cell lung cancer, which proved an average lifespan extension of 13 months (vs. 7 months with

[487] Cf. Aigner, et al. (2010), p. 100; Ng (2004), p. 182
[488] Note: Companies are allowed to notify the EMA of compassionate use applications or ongoing procedures taking place in a member state
[489] Cf. EMA (2007b)

conventional treatment) in Phase III and was thus allowed to be legally used for compassionate reasons prior to NDA submission.[490]

The EMA instituted a compassionate use program for not-yet-authorized new medicinal products in 2007.[491]

It is essential for the manufacturer to ensure that compassionate use patients continue to receive the drug through the usual channels once it is commercially available on the market. This leads to a faster product adoption in the marketplace and a steeper launch curve, and thus a shorter time to peak sales.[492]

5.3.1.4.2 Parallel Track for HIV (US)

Another way to provide treatment to patients prior to approval is the parallel track. If patients do not qualify for the strict enrollment criteria of a clinical trial, but are in need of treatment to save their lives in the case of HIV positive / AIDS patients they can be enrolled in a parallel track in the US.[493]

The previous review of regulatory intricacies drives home the point that depending on the disease state and local legislation, specific rules and requirements do apply that need to be investigated and optimized as part of the launch preparation process.

5.3.2 Payer Considerations

Another key stakeholder is the payer, be it a public or private entity, depending on the local health care system. It is important to establish the true value of a product

[490] Cf. Ng (2004), p. 182; Eli Lilly (2002)
[491] Cf. EMA (2007b); Ernst & Young (2005), p. 63
[492] Cf. Zeiner, Schiel (2007), pp. 1400-1401
[493] Cf. FDA (2009a); Ng (2004), pp. 182; Schilsky (2004), p. 1495

(and potentially its overall benefit including delivery systems and services) to find the right price for it.[494] This is one of the most important, and difficult, issues for the marketing executive.[495]

Strategically speaking, products are usually priced at a premium based on the superiority of the product in the marketplace, or – lacking such a competitive advantage – they are priced at a discount, the so-called cost- and price leadership. Any other approach usually leads to a 'stuck in the middle' position for the product.[496] Yet pricing is not an independent, free market exercise in the pharmaceutical marketplace: Pricing restrictions due to government constraints, parallel trade and reference pricing make pricing one of the most difficult parts in the launch process, which is why this section is relatively longer and more in-depth than some of the other 7Ps of bio / pharmaceutical marketing. Patent exclusivity for ethical drugs leads to a time-limited monopoly and thus usually a high, skimming pricing scheme within the constraints of the marketplace mentioned above and depicted in figure 5-10 below.[497]

---

[494] Cf. Riemenschneider, Sprandel (2007), pp. 165-166
[495] Cf. Christopher, McDonald (1995), p. 209
[496] Cf. Bruhn (1995), pp. 78-80
[497] Cf. Kucher (1989), pp. 121-123; Suh, Manning, Schondelmeyer, Hadsall (2000), p. 531

Figure 5- 10: Interrelated pricing considerations

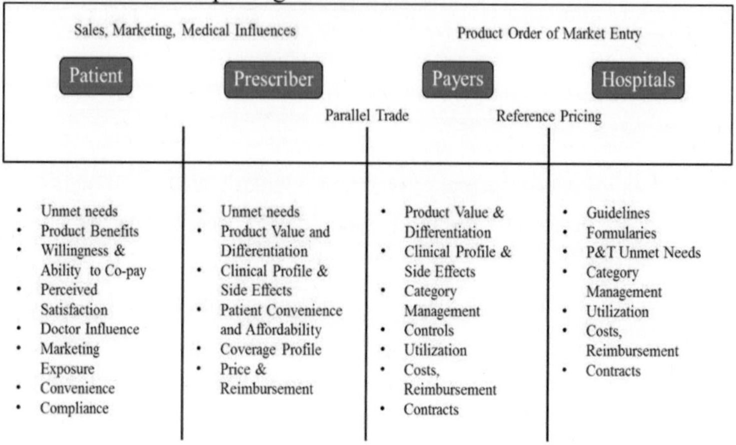

Source: Rao (2008), p. 96

5.3.2.1 Specific Pricing Considerations

Pricing studies, such as conjoint analyses[498], are important for the entire set of launch decisions. Not only do price scenarios deliver financial information, but also influence marketing and sales strategies, not to mention potential Public Relations (PR) communication strategies. After all, every price impacts players such as payers and patients, and it is crucial to be prepared for their response.[499]
IMS Health proposes the following seven steps to effectively address payers:

1. Ensure that these seven steps are addressed in a timely, complete and effective fashion
2. Identify and understand the funding flows for the disease area
3. Identify decision makers controlling these funds – or potential future funds
4. Understand what motivates decision makers, and their decision criteria

---

[498] For more information regarding the usage of conjoint analyses as a basis for pricing decisions, please see Kucher, Hilleke (1993) on value pricing

[499] Cf. Köstlin (2005), p. 240-241

5. Adapt product development based on insights into decision making criteria
6. Develop value dossiers tailored to each type of payer, segmented both by group and motivation type
7. Before, and during launch, target the segmented payers with appropriate messages
8. Monitoring the impact of this activity[500]

5.3.2.2 Reimbursement

The approval of a product is only part of the post-launch process of getting a product to patient, as it does not necessarily mean that the product is also reimbursed.[501]

While physicians usually focus on the safety and efficacy of a product in their decision making process, payers put cost effectiveness and risk first.[502] Thus health-economic studies are becoming more valuable to deliver the necessary economic arguments to these gatekeepers.[503]
Government authorities, pharmacy chains, are suppliers are becoming more influential and relationship management with all players is paramount, in Europe it might make sense to have a centralized approach to ensure consistency.[504]

5.3.2.3 New Payer Trends

Health outcomes and comparative effectiveness are playing a larger role and are even considered to be a paradigm shift in the bio / pharmaceutical market. This

---

500 Cf. Wartenberg, Ziedman, Rickwood (2010), pp. 5-6
501 Cf. Falk (2005), pp. 244-245
502 Cf. PriceWaterhouseCoopers (2008), p. 16
503 Cf. Seiter, Holz (2009), p. 926
504 Cf. Anashkina (2005), p. 132; Müller (2005a), p. 157

means that for a successful launch, companies need to build these new capacities in time and be able to negotiate the reimbursement landscape.[505]

Over time, the global access to information and medications (e.g. through the internet) might lead to a single global price.[506] This is something that the companies have to take into consideration as they are planning their future launches.

In general, bio / pharmaceutical companies have been cautious to use differential pricing to address all consumer groups. Nevertheless, GSK (as well as other companies) has started offering medicines at variable prices within as well as between countries in 2008, tailored to the customers' needs and abilities. Some experts predict that variable pricing, on a sliding scale for countries and customers, will become the norm over the next decade.[507]

5.3.2.3.1 Risk Sharing

Risk sharing is a new trend in pharmaceutical reimbursement. It is a viable option for bio / pharmaceutical companies to prove their belief in the effectiveness of their product by sharing the financial risk with the payers.[508]

Going forward, as government institutions are gathering longitudinal data, bio / pharmaceutical companies will have to face a value-based product pricing that is based on the product's performance: it works, it provides value for money, and it is better than alternative treatment options.[509]

Performance-based pricing, also known as 'pay-for-performance' (P4P), of new medical products is under discussion and some market experts estimate that it

[505] Cf. Robinson (2010), pp. 2-3
[506] Cf. PriceWaterhouseCoopers (2008), p. 14
[507] Cf. PriceWaterhouseCoopers (2009), p. 19
[508] Cf. Cook, Vermon, Manning (2008), pp. 551-555
[509] Cf. PriceWaterhouseCoopers (2008), p. 16-18

might be a reality for all launch products within the next 10 years.[510] Critics, on the other hand, believe that due to the inherent difficulty in assessing and policing risk sharing agreements and because of lack of empirical evidence of their success at this point, P4P might not be a lasting trend.[511]

Current risk sharing agreements between manufacturers and payers can be categorized into four types:

1. Budget caps
   (such as is customary in agreements in France, Australia and New Zealand)
2. Effective discount price from list price
   (e.g. Lucentis in the UK: the National Health System (NHS) only pays for the first 14 injections, then Novartis picks up the tab in full)
3. Outcomes uncertainty
   (e.g. a money back guarantees in case simvastatin in combination with dietary changes does not lower low-density lipoprotein (LDL) in the US)
4. Subgroup uncertainty
   (e.g. in the UK non-responders to Velcade (bortezomib) receive additional doses of the product at Johnson & Johnson's cost).[512]

This new trend has to be taken into consideration when entering reimbursement discussions, as payers might require a performance-based payment scheme for the new drug to be launched. As the power shifts to payers and patients, qualitative data (QOL) in addition to the traditional efficacy and safety information, will become increasingly important.[513]

---

[510] Cf. PriceWaterhouseCoopers (2008), pp. 38-39; PriceWaterhouseCoopers (2009), p. 8
[511] Cf. Towse, Garrison (2010), pp. 100-101
[512] Cf. Global Insight (2008); Pollack (2007); Towse, Garrison (2010), pp. 96-101; PriceWaterhouseCoopers (2009), pp. 7-8
[513] Cf. PriceWaterhouseCoopers (2009), p. 8

The trend towards increased P4P necessitates the discussion how (e.g. according to which markers and standards) the launch product is to be established with payers. Early discussions are recommended to avoid unpleasant surprises at launch.

In summary, it is essential to have a thorough understanding of the political and reimbursement landscape to determine the optimal price for the various countries.[514] Even in the US, the least price-conscious country at this time, cost determines whether drugs are added to managed care healthcare plans, and if so, at which tier.[515] Again, this is oftentimes done by outside consultants in the area of PharmacoEconomics pricing, managed by the in-house PharmacoEconomics manager who reports to and is part of the launch team. PharmacoEconomics data, and cost-benefit-analyses, are key to gain market access when the markets are controlled by payers and subject to financial restrictions.[516]

5.3.2.3.2 Country-specific Pricing Examples

Every country, even every individual state within the EU, has its own price setting structure.[517] Most price regulatory regimes disallow price increases post-launch, or even demand price cuts, thus the launch price decision is significant for the drug's entire life cycle.[518] This dissertation focuses on the key aspects of product pricing, including specific considerations within three key countries: Germany, the UK, and the US.

Pricing mistakes cannot be made undone. Is the price set too low, the company leaves money on the table and does not realize the product's potential. Is the price too high, the government's cost effectiveness agencies, such as NICE and IQWiG, and payers might not give their green light or reimburse the drug, which can lead

[514] Cf. Falk (2005), p. 248
[515] Cf. Vanderveer (2005a), p. 3
[516] Cf. Zeiner, Schiel (2007), pp. 1399-1400
[517] Cf. Köstlin (2005), p. 226
[518] Cf. Danzon, Epstein (2009), p. 10

to a complete failure and virtually no sales for a potent, otherwise promising drug.[519]

As an example for a poor pricing position on the low end, Eli Lilly priced the first insulin analog too low when it was originally launched. When the company realized their pricing mistake, they were able to increase the prices quickly in the US. Due to the price control in European countries, this was not possible and profit was left on the table. Obviously, the product's potential had not been recognized and communicated prior to launch.[520]

5.3.3 Cost Effectiveness Agencies

Competitive performance in a dynamic industry like the bio / pharmaceutical one is strongly affected by national policies.[521]

Additionally, European Countries have instituted authorities that add cost effectiveness to the usual approval criteria of efficacy and safety. The UK-based NICE was installed in 1999.[522] The Commission for Health Improvement (CHIMP) monitors the observance of the NICE guidelines.[523] In Germany, IQWiG was established in 2004.[524]

This means that after approval of a product by the EMA based on efficacy and safety data, additional hurdles of cost effectiveness, usually measured in QALYs (quality-adjusted life years)[525], have to be overcome to be able to launch the product in the individual European markets.[526] This might lead to a delayed and suc-

---

[519] Cf. Köstlin (2005), p. 241
[520] Cf. Kucher, Janssen (2004), p. 1
[521] Cf. Grabowski (1989), p. 32
[522] Cf. Hermansson (2005), pp. 135-139
[523] Cf. Köstlin (2005), p. 232
[524] Cf. Ernst & Young (2005), p. 64
[525] Cf. Hermansson (2005), p. 140; Schöffski, Fricke (2008), pp. 83-87
[526] Cf. PriceWaterhouseCoopers (2008), p. 16; Terblanche (2008), p. 207

cessive launch process across the EU that necessitates additional planning and consideration.

5.3.3.1 Germany: IQWiG

In Germany, bio / pharmaceutical companies were able to set their own prices until the initiation of IQWiG. Also, due to budget pressures, the government has requested across-the-board rebates of 6% in 2003 and 16% in 2004.[527]
An example for how price-focused the evaluations of cost effectiveness agencies can be found in the German IQWiG's evaluation of Lantus (insulin glargine / SNY). While the company provided extensive QOL data and overall disease management data and cost estimates, this product was rejected based solely on price, which led to subsequent complaints from both industry and academic sides.[528]

In 2011, the AMNOG law (Gesetz zur Neuordnung des Arzneimittelmarktes – Law for the Restructuring of the Pharmaceutical Market) came into effect. Since then, all new bio / pharmaceutical products are evaluated based on their additional patient benefit at launch, as compared to other available therapies and treatments. A federal joint committee then decides how to monetize the additional value by setting a fixed price for the new product and decide which patients are eligible for the new product: This means that free pricing is officially a thing of the past in Germany, and the federal government is hoping to save a total of 2.2 billion Euros in 2011.[529] The effect this has on the overall German market, based on the decisions taken on upcoming launches, remains to be seen.

[527] Cf. Köstlin (2005), p. 230
[528] Cf. Schöffski (2010), pp. 1033-1035
[529] Cf. Bundesgesetzblatt (2010), pp. 2262-2277; Bundesministerium für Gesundheit (2011)

5.3.3.2 United Kingdom: NICE

Drugs make up about 13% of the NHS expenses.[530] The Association of British Pharmaceutical Industry (ABPI) has self-imposed an agreement with the health ministry that regulates prices, called pharmaceutical price regulation scheme (PPRS). The PPRS does not only set prices, but also sets a maximum profit under consideration of maximum expenses for production, research, promotion and administration.[531] This allows for a still-free price regulation in the UK, but once a price is set, it cannot be increased for the duration of the drug's patent life. An exception to this is the line-extension, where a price cannot be set freely, but requires an additional approval of the Medicines and Healthcare Products Regulatory Agency (MHRA), an executive arm of the health ministry. The PPRS plan is renegotiated every 5 years, at which point prices are usually reduced (between 2.5 to 4.5% between 1993 and 1999, 7% for all drugs in 2005, indicating an increasing price control).[532] Nevertheless, some recent pharmaco-economic studies suggest that NICE underestimates the cost-effectiveness of some evaluated drugs, especially in the chronic disease realm, by assuming price increases with inflation instead of factoring in the real future drug prices. In sum, the calculations of NICE and other similar agencies are not considered flawless and might lead to some unexpected hurdles in the launch and acceptance process.[533]

A positive NICE ruling strongly influences the product's sales in the UK. A positive NICE review of nicotine patches led to sales of 121 million Euro in the UK, while sales only reached 20 million Euro in Germany. On the other hand, a negative review of Remicade (infliximab / Centocor / Merck) led to sales of merely .2 million Euro in the UK, while sales totaled 43 million Euro in Germany.[534]

---

[530] Cf. Hermansson (2005), p. 135
[531] Cf. Köstlin (2005), p. 231-232
[532] Cf. Hermansson (2005), pp. 138-139; Köstlin (2005), p. 232
[533] Cf. Hoyle (2008), p. 589
[534] Cf. Hermansson (2005), p. 140

The UK's NICE is also seen as a role model for medical reviews and its rulings might have an impact beyond UK borders (also see reference pricing chapter 4.3.5).[535]

5.3.3.3 United States

In the US, private health plans negotiate their prices (and discounts) in return for preferred formulary status individually without governmental influence; the government payer Medicaid demands discounts on these individually established private payer prices.[536] As a result, an analysis of ex-manufacturer product prices of blockbuster pharmaceuticals stated the price was about 40% of the US prices in France, Italy and Spain.[537]

With an aging population and growing medical expenditure as a consequence, the price pressure on all healthcare services, including bio / pharmaceutical products, will only increase over the next years. While only 12% of US-Americans are over the age of 65, they incur more than 33% of all drug costs, with 71% of this population taking one or more prescription drugs for chronic illnesses.[538]
One example for the result of free price setting in the US is Lipitor (atorvastatin / PFE), which at in 2006 was priced at $92, around 61 times the manufacturing cost, for its 10mg dose. The 20mg dose costs an additional 30 cents to manufacture per month, but is priced at a markup of $39 at $131. Since all other costs (packaging, distribution, and marketing) are the same, this leads to a pure profit of $38.70, a 13,000% markup over the gross and net profits for the 10mg pill. This example shows the unusual price structure of pharmaceutical drugs in the US that is void of competition in a patent-protected market.[539]

---

[535] Cf. Hermansson (2005), p. 140
[536] Cf. Danzon, Epstein (2009), p. 11
[537] Cf. PriceWaterhouseCoopers (2010), p. 12
[538] Cf. Fischer, Breitenbach (2010c), pp. 301-302
[539] Cf. Light (2007), p. 909

Interestingly enough, a generic alternative, simvastatin (marketed under Zocor, Simvacor et al.) is more expensive than the non-generic Lipitor ($104 instead of $92 for the 10mg dose), making it not financially lucrative to switch a patient from an originator's to a generic product.[540]

An example for market-based pricing is Atripla, which was priced at parity to the two individual components, despite the fact that it provided more convenience and thus, logically, could have demanded a higher price. Due to the highly sensitive nature of the HIV market, and the large influence of patient groups, the company decided to price it at parity with the individual components. Thus Gilead received goodwill from payers, patient groups, lobbyists and advocates and was able to make this drug the number one seller within months of launch.

These examples show that an in-depth market analysis is necessary to arrive at the right price. Not only driven by manufacturing or marketing costs and profit margins but also based on competitive and generic pricing, as well as public opinion.

In the US, already spending 17% of the GDP (Gross Domestic Product) on healthcare while 16% of the population is indigent, similar trends like the ones that already took place in Europe might be observed over the next years. Specifically, a governmental cost savings program is under discussion.[541] Already, the negotiations of the six government agencies with their pharmaceutical providers led to an average discount of these drugs by 51-59%.[542]

Nonetheless, the US market is the most liberal market when it comes to pricing, with the fewest government restrictions on company decisions.[543] Consequently, prices in the US are nearly twice as high as in the leading European countries.[544]

---

[540] Cf. Light (2007), p. 910
[541] Cf. PriceWaterhouseCoopers (2008), pp. 11-13
[542] Cf. Congress of the Congressional Budget Office (2005)
[543] Cf. Light (2007), p. 908
[544] Cf. UK Department of Health (2006), p. 14

In general, it is advisable to de-risk the pricing strategy of a product early in its development. Traditionally, companies develop product pricing towards the end of Phase III clinical trials. Ideally, pricing should be already considered and discussed with potential stakeholders as early as Phase II.[545] New trends suggest flexible pricing, allowing the companies to adjust prices based on their effectiveness and overall success in the marketplace.[546]

5.3.4 Prescriber Considerations

Another key stakeholder group are the prescribers. The main access to a prescriber is the sales representative, which will be covered in the organizational section later on. Additional areas of contact are symposia, congresses and scientific consulting situations, such as advisory boards. All these play a role in the increased diffusion of the new product innovation.[547]

It is important to know ahead of time, how physicians would respond to the certain kind of new drug, who is open to prescribing new, less tried and tested products.

To ensure market access, it is important to know who the relevant key opinion leaders (KOLs) are, who sits on the relevant guideline committees to learn their perspective on the disease state and the new product's potential space in their decision making, recommendations and guidelines.[548]

[545] Cf. PriceWaterhouseCoopers (2009), p. 12
[546] Cf. BBC News (2008)
[547] Cf. Troll (1989), pp. 99-101
[548] Cf. Zeiner, Schiel (2007), pp. 1399-1400

5.3.4.1 Guidelines

Guidelines, such as generally available disease state guidelines issued by medical authorities, as well as specific guidelines issued by individual entities, such as hospitals or payer groups, influence the usage of a launch drug and should be reviewed with ample time to address, and even change, these guidelines, if necessary and possible.

A good example is the launch of the statin Lipitor (atorvastatin / PFE). Using health-economically relevant data, Pfizer was able to show the effect of Lipitor in regulating lipids and its cost effectiveness as it prevented more serious, costly hospital and outpatient treatments. The entire statin class, despite its higher cost, became the gold standard for the treatment of dyslipidemia.[549]

Historically, bio / pharmaceutical companies used to focus most efforts (up to 90% of their resources) on physicians, neglecting other key players such as regulatory authorities and payers. Also, within the physician segment, most physicians were treated equally, receiving similar amounts of attention and resources.[550] As mentioned in the market research chapter (5.2.1), it is important to revisit these assumptions and to carefully review the nature and importance each player type prior to making further allocation decisions for the launch process.

5.3.4.2 Promotional Activities Toward Prescribers

Promotion has been already defined as one of the 7Ps in bio / pharmaceutical marketing. In most cases, these are directed towards prescribers and, increasingly, towards other key stakeholders.

---

[549] Cf. Zeiner, Schiel (2007), p. 1400
[550] Cf. Albiez, et al. (2007), p. 1135

Not all products are susceptible to the same kind of promotional activity, and not all countries have the same opportunities and restrictions.[551] Thus, the promotional mix needs to be reviewed, discussed and adjusted well prior to launch to ensure optimal utilization of the local market conditions to favorably position the product in the players' minds.

Based on a product's positioning and life cycle stage, the communication towards the players needs to be adjusted over time.[552] Classical promotional activity in a bio / pharmaceutical company can be distinguished between direct promotional activity (materials provided to and used by the sales force) and indirect promotional activity, such as advertising and journal ads.[553]

Not technically considered a promotional tool, and oftentimes funded through the medical budget of a company, Medical Education needs to be mentioned as a key communication vehicle to the key customer group of physicians and other healthcare providers.[554] All medications, but especially first-in-class and specialist medicines, require additional knowledge about the disease state, the mechanisms of actions and latest medical advances. Thus bio / pharmaceutical companies need to focus and increase their efforts in the realm of medical educational programs, usually run by academic institutions, to help their prospective prescribers understand the disease and the potential new product's impact in this new marketplace.[555]

In practice, with diminishing promotional possibilities due to stricter regulations (especially in the US and increasingly in Europe), companies are shifting previous marketing and promotional funds to the more 'neutral', but potentially just as effective realm of medical education. While medical education has long been a part of the company's marketing efforts, some corporations are moving this function to the development part of the business to ensure a clear division, that is visible to

[551] Cf. Müller (2005a), p. 153; Terblanche (2008), p. 206
[552] Cf. Müller (2005a), pp. 153-154
[553] Cf. Wolf Sussman (2008), p. 245
[554] Cf. Wolf Sussman (2008), pp. 242-243
[555] Cf. Datamonitor (2004a), p. 10; PriceWaterhouseCoopers (2009), p. 19

the regulating authorities, between promotional activities and medical education efforts.[556]

5.3.4.3 Niche Marketing to Physician Stakeholders

The special nature of niche drugs also has an impact on the marketing and sales activities. Since they are prescribed by specialist physicians with a deep knowledge in this medical area, they require a more in-depth scientific base of their marketing and sales people and materials.[557] This will be important for the launch plan, such as in selecting the launch team, developing materials and sales training.[558]

A company's focus on specialist products only, such as is the case for Genentech (now part of Roche), requires different organizational and cultural characteristics.[559]

5.3.4.4 E-prescriptions

E-prescriptions are another way payers are trying to influence physician's prescription behavior. They clearly show which medications are reimbursed or preferred by the healthcare provider and thus sway the physicians in their decision making process.[560] Working with payers becomes more important under these circumstances, as the payers' choice, i.e. the tiering of the launch product and its integration into their (e-prescription) databases, also impacts the physicians prescribing behavior. Some generic companies, like 1A Pharma for example (the low-end generic arm of Hexal, which in turn in part of Novartis), actively selected

---

556 Cf. Wolf Sussman (2008), pp. 242-243
557 Cf. PriceWaterhouseCoopers (2009), p. 14-22
558 Cf. PriceWaterhouseCoopers (2009), p. 14
559 Cf. PriceWaterhouseCoopers (2009), p. 16; For the interested party, an overview can be found in the appendix (PriceWaterhouseCoopers (2009), p. 17, table 4)
560 Cf. PriceWaterhouseCoopers (2009), pp. 5-6

their product name based on where it shows up on the pharmacist's computer screen (all products starting with '1A' receiving the top spot here).[561] In an increasingly automated world with limited time for extensive decision making processes for healthcare providers and decision makers, the output and ranking of electronic databases need to be taken into consideration in the overall marketing plan.

5.3.4.5 KOL Management and Mapping

In addition to the promotional side of product management, there is a more scientific side, focusing on purely medical information, such as Phase III and IV study analyses, scientific publications etc.).[562]

While the efficacy of promotional activities is generally declining, both due to stronger restrictions imposed by regulatory agencies or preventative cautionary measures by the bio / pharmaceutical companies, the value of marketing to informal networks is increasing.[563] This is due to improved communication technologies and overall globalization of the marketplace, both formally in form of conference as well as informally, in form of one-off conversations, websites and blogs.[564] In the context of the bio / pharmaceutical marketplace, the network hubs that influence the behavior of other and thus need to be effectively integrated into the launch process are KOLs. KOLs do not only get information but also 'vet' information for their colleagues.[565] They are the 'go to' people for medical information, especially on new drugs, and thus need to be involved in the launch process early on. One way of doing this is establishing regular advisory boards[566], wherein the KOLs give input on the current status and open questions on a product's development. This integrated KOLs into the launch process and provides

---

561 For more information on this company, please see 1A Pharma (2011)
562 Cf. Ortwein (2001), pp. 106-107
563 Cf. Robinson (2010), p. 3
564 Cf. Chakravorti (2004), pp. 59-60
565 Cf. Vanderveer (2006), p. 3
566 Cf. Seiter, Holz (2009), p. 929; Wolf Sussman (2008), pp. 242-243

helpful information pre-launch. Also, by reaching these KOLs, the company can reach his or her entire network in a short series of steps.[567] KOLs are traditionally known to be physicians, but with the increasing importance of the regulatory environment, regulatory KOLs also need to be considered.[568]

KOL management can be seen as a special pharma-specific aspect of the generally-known customer relationship management, the company's focus on the specific needs of the customers, as KOLs are the company's key customers.[569] Details of this well-documented approach are beyond the scope of this dissertation, but it can be likened to parts of Customer Relationship Management (CRM) in the non-pharmaceutical world.[570]

KOLs oftentimes act internationally, thus they have to be managed and accounted for on an international level, requiring further coordination between the teams in various countries in case of an upcoming launch.[571]

When forecasting or modeling the product uptake, lag times have to be factored in as appropriate. Product loyalties need to be taken into consideration in all disease states, but especially in chronic diseases (Diabetes, HIV, Hepatitis) physicians are hesitant to switch treatments.[572] Oftentimes, competition from older drugs is stronger than from newly introduced ones, as building a brand takes time and doctors tend to have 'sticky', meaning: hard to change, prescribing habits.[573] On the other hand, studies show that anticipated drug need for first-in-class products leads to an initially strong sales uptake, which tends to taper off, if the expectations are not met or the early followers ride the pioneer's wave and fill an unmet need not met by the first.[574]

[567] Cf. Chakravorti (2004), p. 63
[568] Cf. Zeiner, Schiel (2007), p. 1399
[569] Cf. Müller (2005a), p. 156
[570] Cf. Riemenschneider, Sprandel (2007), pp. 162-165
[571] Cf. Müller (2005a), p. 151
[572] Cf. Kucher, Janssen (2004), p. 3
[573] Cf. Kyle (2006), p. 612
[574] Cf. Cohen (2006), p. 288

For a launch, it is thus important to identify and target those potential prescribers that are most likely to change their prescribing patterns. These innovator doctors do not only prescriber earlier than their more conservative colleagues, but also prescribe more than the others for about 20 months post-launch.[575]

These findings are based on the diffusion of innovations model by Everett Rogers in the 60s. He scientifically established that new ideas and products are spread by certain people, namely innovators and early adopters that are most likely to try new technologies, such as a newly launched product. Without going into further theoretical detail[576] in this dissertation, it is crucial to keep this concept in mind, and to focus on innovators and early adopters, as one is preparing for a launch (see figure 5-11). The idea of KOLs as initiators of new trends, who help the diffusion of innovation gain speed, is also rooted in this model.[577]

Figure 5- 11: Diffusion of innovations

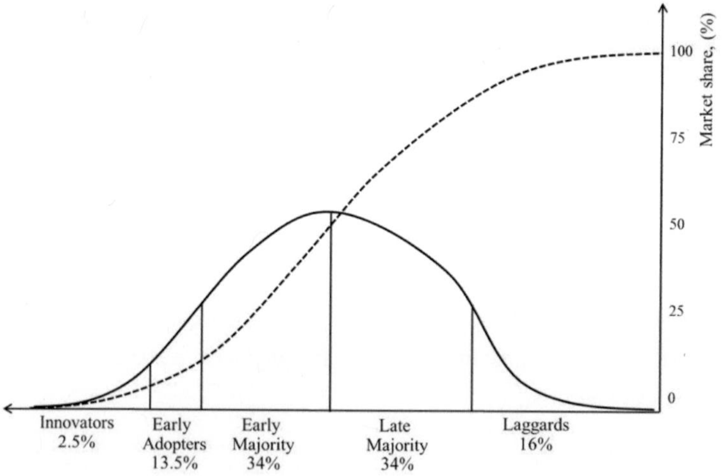

Source: Rogers, (2003), pp. 282-284

---

[575] Cf. Wartenberg, Ziedman, Rickwood (2010), p. 7
[576] For more details and information see: Rogers (2003)
[577] Cf. Bernhard (2010a)

5.3.5 Patients

To be credible and successful in the marketplace, the patient's benefit needs to be in the center of product development and launch decisions.[578]

A quantitative study conducted in Germany in 2010 showed that more than half of the 2,000 patients (53%) interviewed request specific Rx drugs from their physicians. The main driver for this request (35%) was good tolerability of the drug in question.[579]

5.3.5.1 Direct-to-consumer (DTC) Marketing

Promotion is usually directed towards professionals (primarily towards physicians, secondarily towards their staff, at times also towards payers). Marketing prescription drugs to the consumer is illegal in Germany and most other countries.[580] The US and New Zealand are the only countries where direct promotional activities towards to the consumer or patient are allowed.[581] The goal of DTC advertising is to drive the consumer to the physician's office to ask for, and receive, a prescription of the sponsor's product.[582] DTC advertising is estimated at $5 billion in the US and its value is unclear, as studies done on the impact on product usage are inconclusive and do not suggest a measurable impact.[583]

In the US, the only country where promotional expenditure can be tracked rather well, spending has nearly tripled in the past decade (from $11.4 billion in 1996 to $29.9 billion in 2005). Including marketing-related activities (such as e-

---

[578] Cf. BCG (2006), p. 20
[579] Cf. Rademacher (2010), p. 16
[580] Cf. Donahue, Cavasco, Rosenthal (2007), pp. 673-681; Ortwein (2001), pp. 105-106
[581] Cf. Donahue, et al. (2007), p. 681
[582] Cf. Vanderveer (2005), p. 24
[583] Cf. Law, Majumdar, Soumerai (2008); PriceWaterhouseCoopers (2009), p. 3

promotions and meetings) the number might be nearly twice as high ($57.9 billion).[584]

While the IMS and Commercial Accommodation Monitor (CAM) numbers to track these spendings are questioned and believed to underestimate the true spending[585], it is understood that promotional spending in the industry is rather high. Spending the money wisely on the right customers is a key prerequisite for a successful launch. As stated in an IMS study from 2009, above-average impact of the promotional spending is one of the four success factors for launch excellence.[586] In practice, it is advisable to give the physician some lead time to familiarize him- or herself with the drug before doing DTC promotion. After all, doctors do not want to be caught off-balance when a patient requests a prescription for a drug they are not aware of. As a best practice, companies give about 6 months of lead time to physicians before starting the DTC campaigns, such as in the case of Viagra.[587]

While patient communication is limited in most countries, it is crucial to optimize the resources available to a more and more educated patient base. Whether providing general disease state education, providing information to patient forums or doing outright DTC advertising, the customer's satisfaction and buy in remain the ultimate goal.[588] Studies show that in 60% of the cases, patients receive the drug they request from their healthcare provider.[589] Thus ways of addressing the patient needs is part of every launch plan.

Lifestyle drugs, such as for the treatment of erectile dysfunction (e.g. Viagra (sildinafil / PFE)), anti-wrinkles (e.g. Botox (botulinum toxin / Allergan)), and against male baldness (e.g. Propecia (finasteride / Merck)) are becoming more im-

---

[584] Cf. Donahue, et al. (2007), pp. 673-681; PriceWaterhouseCoopers (2009), p. 2
[585] Cf. Gagnon, Lexchin (2009), pp. 29-33
[586] Cf. Seiter, Holz, (2009), pp. 924-930
[587] Cf. Simon, Kotler (2003), pp. 102-103
[588] Cf. PriceWaterhouseCoopers (2009), p. 21
[589] Cf. Fischer, Breitenbach (2010b) p. 266

portant.[590] If they are paid for by the consumer, their marketing is barely different from other consumer products and needs to be addressed as such, talking directly to the patient as much as legally possible.[591]

In the future, it is to be expected that patients will continue to play a more and more important role and need to be addressed and explicitly included in any launch plan to ensure success. One indicator is the increase in ethnographic market research, which is aiming to understand who the patient really is as a person, not just his medical history and prescription needs, to better differentiate one's product, particularly when entering new markets.[592] An ongoing rapport with the patient can happen in form of online forums, patient advisory and advocacy groups, hotlines, educational programs and materials, adherence support etc.[593]

As therapy is becoming more and more individualized, patients have become an important target group in themselves.[594] With this, the required target groups are also becoming more specific, harder to find, and require more concentrated and long-term efforts, as can be provided by online forums and blogs.[595]

5.3.5.2 Patient Adherence

Patient adherence is the overarching concept that a patient does not only take his or her prescription as directed (compliance), but also continues to do so until directed to discontinue by their health care provider (persistence):

Adherence = Compliance x Persistence[596]

---

[590] Cf. Ng (2004), pp. 293-294; Vanderveer, Pines (2003), p. 4
[591] Cf. Fischer, Breitenbach (2010c), p. 303
[592] Cf. Kelly, Gibbons (2008), pp. 279-285
[593] Cf. Fischer, Breitenbach (2010c), p. 304; PriceWaterhouseCoopers (2009), p. 3, 12, 16
[594] Cf. Rademacher (2010), p. 16; Scholtissek (2005), p. 257
[595] Cf. Scholz-Ligma (2010), p. 18
[596] Cf. Vanderveer (2005), pp. 24-25

Compliance in clinical trials is usually better than in everyday situations.[597] A study on long-term compliance published in 'Values in Health' found that merely 33% of patients still took their statins after one year, dropping to 13% after five years.[598]

As figure 5-12 below shows, compliance is a problem in minor and serious diseases alike:

Figure 5- 12: Non-compliance across disease states

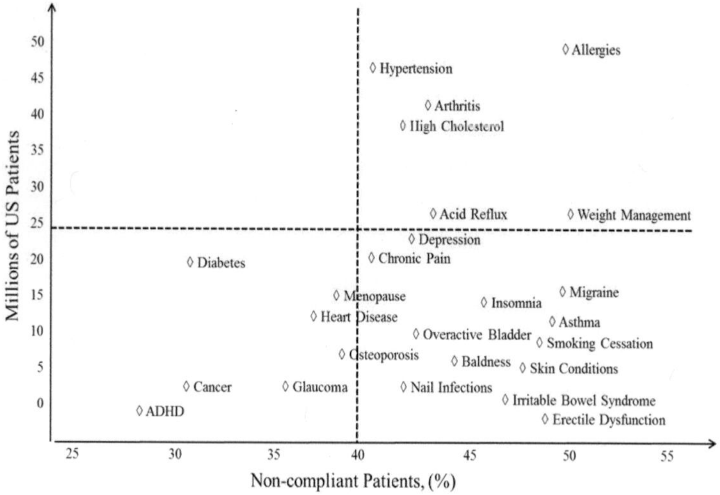

Source: PriceWaterhouseCoopers (2008), p. 21

As additional data becomes available for the efficacy of specific drug, physicians will increasingly be asked to distinguish responders from non-responders, implementing adherence programs for the former (while changing therapy for the latter).[599]

[597] Cf. PriceWaterhouseCoopers (2009), p. 8
[598] Cf. PriceWaterhouseCoopers (2009), p. 8; Catalan, Le Lorier (2000), pp. 417-426
[599] Cf. PriceWaterhouseCoopers (2008), pp. 38-39

Even a script written by a treatment provider, does not mean the patient actually takes the prescribed medication. In Germany, non-compliance is estimated to be between 30-50%, leading to direct costs (hospitalizations, emergency services, and discarded medications) are estimated at around 5.4 billion Euros, indirect cost (such as sick days and premature deaths) are estimated at another 5 billion Euros in Germany alone.[600] In the US, nearly 20% of patients never fill their prescriptions and the ones who do often do not remain compliant.[601] The impact of non-compliance is estimated at up to $300 billion in the US alone.[602] While being long-term or life-long treatment, new hyperlipidemia patients stay on their statins for an average of six months, usually without their health care provider's consult.[603] According to the WHO, the adherence to long-term therapies in developed countries is about 50%, adherence rates for short-term medicines, like antibiotics, is not much better.[604] Improving adherence rates is both in the interest of the pharmaceutical company, selling more drugs, and in the interest of the payer, since patient care is comparably more expensive than the drug cost. In various disease states, each incremental dollar spent on the prescription drug lowered the expense for patient care by $7 for diabetes, about $5 in cholesterol patients and about $4 for patients with hypertension.[605] The root of the adherence problem lies in the initiation of the therapy, as patients are unclear about the drug's benefits and their long-term need of medication, as depicted in figure 5-13.[606]

---

[600] Cf. Erbe, Lauer, Lange (2009), p. 335
[601] Cf. PriceWaterhouseCoopers (2008), pp. 20-21
[602] Cf. Medco Health Solutions (2005); PriceWaterhouseCoopers (2008), p. 22
[603] Cf. Vanderveer (2005), p. 25
[604] Cf. PriceWaterhouseCoopers (2008), p. 22
[605] Cf. Medco Health Solutions (2005); PriceWaterhouseCoopers (2008), pp. 22-23
[606] Cf. Vanderveer (2005), p. 25

Figure 5- 13: Forms of non compliance

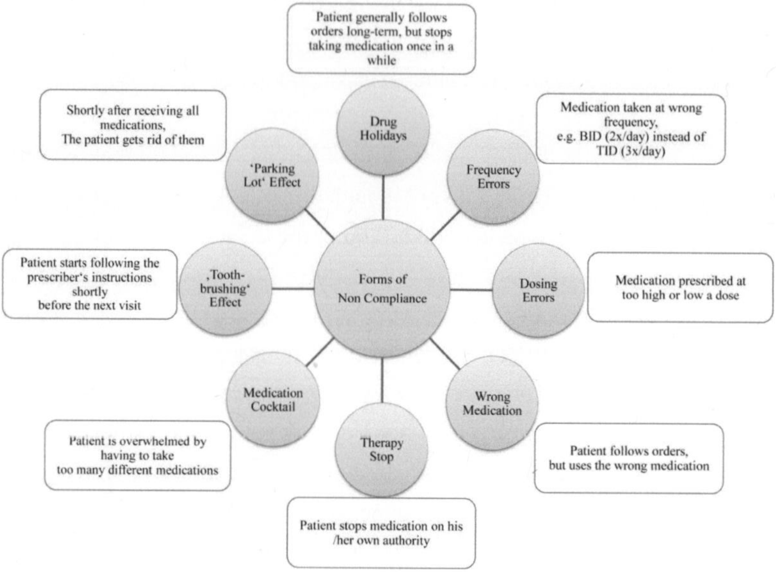

Source: Breitenbach, Fischer (2010c), p. 312

Thus, in addition to the regulatory requirements of efficacy and safety data, providing a functional, maybe even personalized, adherence program might become a key requirement for the bio / pharmaceutical companies trying to launch new drugs in the future.[607] This requires a concerted effort between corporate efforts such as Customer Relationship Management Programs, in-depth market research to fully understand the drivers of adherence in the respective disease state, and potentially DTC initiatives.[608] Targeted compliance programs also need to be the focus of today's pre-launch market research as they also increase revenues while providing a better service to the patient, improving the relationship and the overall reputation of the industry.[609]

---

607 Cf. PriceWaterhouseCoopers (2008), p. 23; Robinson (2010), p. 3; Vanderveer (2005), p. 25
608 Cf. Vanderveer (2005), pp. 25-26
609 Cf. PriceWaterhouseCoopers (2008), p. 24; Vanderveer (2007), p. 131

5.3.5.3 Patient Organizations

Patient organizations become increasingly important players as well, as they form a strong lobby, especially in high-interest medical fields such as HIV / AIDS and oncology, as well as severe chronic diseases.[610] Since DTC advertising is illegal in most countries, the tried approach to reach these groups is by executing relevant and helpful public relations work.[611] In Germany alone, many patients are organized in more than 70,000 patient organizations, in chronic disease fields like diabetes, it is estimated that 70% of patients are participating in patient organizations. Thus, gaining the trust and support of patient organizations is crucial to allow for a good connection to patients and potentially market-relevant on-time information and immediate feedback. In many cases, the bio / pharmaceutical companies provide special services (such as sponsoring disease-related talks by experts) to patient organizations to establish and foster this relationship. Patient organizations are usually careful, or even suspicious, when entering collaborations with the industry, working with them requires interpersonal skills and a lot of tact. To ensure that these relationships are all 'above board' and openly pursue common educational goals of patients, patient organizations and bio / pharmaceutical companies have decided to make all collaborations with and financial support for patient organizations transparent.[612]

5.3.6 Considerations towards General Public and Media

5.3.6.1 Public Relations

Not technically considered a promotional tool, PR needs to be mentioned as a key communication vehicle to the public. Public relations consist of all company ac-

---

[610] Cf. Hermansson (2005), p. 146; Vanderveer, Pines (2003)
[611] Cf. Zeiner, Schiel (2007), p. 1401
[612] Cf. VFA (2011a)

tivities that are geared towards internal and external customers to gain their trust and understanding.[613]

Since the pharmaceutical industry suffers from a poor overall reputation, improved communication regarding new drugs and their impact on the public's health is a worthwhile effort not only for the product in question, but also for the company and the industry as a whole.[614] When it comes to new products in particular, public relations are charged with creating a buzz about the incumbent product launch in the respective marketplace and with the respective stakeholders, particularly through the media.[615] The general media efforts are supported by more clinical efforts in the trade journals and the specialized press. These efforts can be summarized under publication planning.

5.3.6.2 Publication Planning

Also from a clinical side, the use of media needs to be optimized. Pivotal studies, but also other relevant disease state or product research results, need to be optimally placed in key publications, especially the so-called peer-reviewed journals. The process of doing this is called 'publication planning'. Since lead journals, such as the New England Journal of Medicine (NEJM), have extensive review and lead times, publication planning needs to be started and executed on in a timely manner. Oftentimes, next to the corporate researchers, unbiased external KOLs, such as lead investigators in the trials, are mentioned as the authors of these papers. Thus the selection of lead investigators, in addition to their clinical merit and ability to enlist patients in an expedient manner, also needs to take into consideration their public image and clout for the publication of key data in peer-reviewed journals. As a third point, these KOLs also need to be easy to work with and passable writers. Otherwise, companies enlist so-called 'ghostwriters' at

[613] Cf. Bruhn (1995), p. 233
[614] Cf. Terblanche (2008), p. 209
[615] Cf. Vanderveer (2005a), p. 3

times, to help the lead investigators write these crucial papers in a timely and publishable manner.[616]

Publication planning is another key aspect of the use of media. In the case of Singulair, the company decided to publish extensively, but selectively, in the most prestigious peer-reviewed publications in its field. By doing so, Singulair was effectively self-marketed in asthma specialist circles. To ensure Singulair would not lose momentum post launch, Merck had an expansive publication plan, publishing new findings (mainly regarding new formulations and cross indications) up to four years post launch.[617]

5.3.7 Considerations Regarding the Channels

Pharmacists, pharmacy chains, and buying groups become more and more important in the marketing of bio / pharmaceutical drugs. For them, the financial criteria are more in the forefront of the buying decision than medical criteria.[618]

Classic distribution for pharmaceuticals goes from the wholesalers to the pharmacies. In case of biologics, which often require special handling, such as cooling from manufacturing to patient, specialty pharmacies are in place who take the space of specialty distributors, integrating the role of wholesalers and pharmacies into one. Countries differ in this regard, such in the number, size of pharmacies and their distribution and dispensing margins.[619]

In the UK, pharmacists get to keep the difference between a generic product's reimbursement price and their purchasing price, which is a strong incentive for find-

---

[616] Cf. Gagnon, Lexchin (2008), p. 31
[617] Cf. Datamonitor (2004a), p. 10
[618] Cf. Hilleke-Daniel (1989), p. 20; Scholtissek (2005), p. 257
[619] Cf. Kyle (2007), p. 90, Note: In Japan, for example, physicians are allowed to dispense medications themselves, which leads to prescription of lower doses and combination drug prescriptions (Iizuka (2007), pp. 844-847).

ing the cheapest generic possible. Substitution of an original branded prescription with a generic is not allowed.[620]

In Germany, on the contrary, pharmacies have been required by an 'aut idem' regulation passed in February of 2002 to choose the cheapest available product whenever a physician has specified only the active ingredient of a drug or if the ingredients between the product specified and the cheaper option can be seen as identical.[621]

Another new channel are online pharmacies. The European Court of Justice issued a directive allowing online pharmacies to mail prescription drugs EU-wide, which is successively turned into national laws. Thus online channels do not play a key role yet, but are becoming increasingly important. The best-known player in this field is the Dutch mail order pharmacy 'Doc Morris'.[622]

[620] Cf. Hermansson (2005), p. 142
[621] Cf. Fricke (2008), pp. 53-54
[622] Cf. Weißbäcker, Müller (2005), pp. 204-205; Doc Morris (2011)

6. Organizational Considerations

Launch excellence studies suggest that there remains a disconnect between the actual clinical data and its use by the commercial team, which is oftentimes more driven by hope than clear facts. This can be prevented by an early collaboration between the R&D department and the M&S department early in the process, both on global as well as on regional and local levels, as has been widely stated and assessed in the current literature.[623]

Especially in disease states where compounds frequently have multiple indications, such as cancer or CNS treatments, early positioning work can help determine which indication to focus on to eventually lead to most prescriptions based on current needs. For example, GSK's Paxil (paroxetine) was first launched as an antidepressant and subsequently launched for social anxiety disorder and panic disorder indications.[624]

The prerequisites for failure are set well before the in-line R&D efforts are initiated, which is at the moment where the idea for a product is first perceived.[625] Ideally, marketing and sales professionals liaise with their R&D counterparts so early that they have input on which molecules, and eventually which medicines, provide real value to the customers.[626] In reality, this does not happen often enough. Oftentimes, companies are so excited about the prospect of a new promising compound that its commercial viability and the unmet medical need are not adequately assessed.

An example for this is the development of Leptin, a proteo-hormone detected in 1994, as an anti-obesity drug by Amgen with promising results in mice. While further testing results were less promising, the company management kept en-

---

[623] Cf. Brown, Ennew (1995), p. 340; De Luca, et al. (2010), p. 314; Langerak, et al. (2004), pp. 89-90; Robinson (2010), p. 4; Zeiner, Schiel (2007), p. 1402

[624] Cf. Vanderveer (2005a), p. 2

[625] Cf. Hackett (2007), p. 46

[626] Cf. PriceWaterhouseCoopers (2009), p. 21

couraging the scientific team to continue exploring the product's potential irrespective of the cost involved. In the end, this resulted in a lot of wasted resources for Amgen and the admission of its CEO that they needed to learn how to simply say 'stop'.[627]

Ideally, and many companies do so, the manufacturer uses an internal evaluation process of their pipeline compounds to assess its clinical and commercial potential.[628] The success of a product hinges on the seamless interaction between all parts within the company, the project management.[629] As in all businesses, the usual cycle of analysis, planning, implementation and control[630] is also followed in the bio / pharmaceutical business and launch process.

Planning the launch, assessing if these success factors are met, and implementing changes as necessary is usually the job of the product manager (PM). This person is accountable for the profits and losses of his or her product (or product range) and develops the budgets and marketing plans for it.[631] The success of a launch oftentimes hinges on the capabilities of the project leader (such as strength, skill set, commitment) which means that this position needs to be filled prudently.[632] Clear alignment with the strategic direction and decision making of the senior management team is essential to ensure a smooth launch process.[633]

Even if this assessment is done well, questions like reimbursement eligibility cannot be fully addressed or only estimated, as the government agencies in most countries do not give guidance in this regard prior to launch.[634]

---

[627] Cf. Hemp (2004), p. 73
[628] Cf. PriceWaterhouseCoopers (2008), p. 8
[629] Cf. Fischer, Breitenbach (2010a), pp. 37-38; Kiskalt (2010), pp. 199-201; Zeiner, Schiel (2007), p. 1402
[630] Cf. Kotler, Armstrong (1989), pp. 48-50
[631] Cf. Trilling (2008), p. 37
[632] Cf. Ernst (2002), p. 14; Ernst (2007), pp. 434-435
[633] Cf. Spanjol, et al. (2011), p. 637
[634] Cf. PriceWaterhouseCoopers (2008), p. 8

6.1 Organizing a Launch Team

Qualified personnel are one of the deciding factors for a company's success.[635] This refers to the technical skill set and expertise as well as the communication and collaboration skills.[636] Both are imperative to ensure a successful launch. To share information and to get all team members to buy into the same vision for the product, launch teams usually start their joint work in a kick-off meeting, often lasting more than one day, and done offsite, to take all participants out of their everyday work routine.[637] Well-defined rules and responsibilities, as well as the involvement of executives and managers, ensures that strategic questions are addressed and the necessary buy-in.[638] To clearly define these rules and responsibilities, the so-called 'RACI'-Grid, consisting of a clear outline of all necessary tasks as well as the people who are 'Responsible', 'Accountable', 'Consulted' and 'Informed' (see table 6-1) is a helpful tool for everyone to fully understand everyone's, particularly their own responsibilities. It enables everyone to confidently act without any question of overstepping boundaries or unintentionally leaving out relevant players.

---

[635] Cf. BCG (2006), p. 31; Ernst (2002), p. 14
[636] Cf. Chandy, et al. (2006), p. 505
[637] Cf. Hartmann, Skubch, Moll, Fleischer-Hehn (2009), p. 1109
[638] Cf. Aaker (1995), pp. 343-344

Table 6- 1: Sample RACI grid

Task	Responsible	Accountable	Consulted	Informed
Package Insert				
Product Packaging				
Forecasting				
Sales Materials				
Press Releases				
Etc.				

R: Responsible – Person owns the work, decision, or objective.
Several people can be jointly responsible or create or produce the assigned task
A: Accountable – Owner of the work, must sign off or approve when completed.
Only one person is accountable
C: Consulted – These team members give input before work is started, completed, accepted.
I: Informed – People who must be kept informed of progress, but do not need to be consulted.
Source: Own depiction based on Myers (2009)

In general, decisions should be clearly identified, then a full inventory of information relevant for the decision should be taken, followed by a decision making grid, such as the RACI, and an institutionalized process should be put into place that helps make these kinds of decisions on a regular and reliable basis.[639]

In this context, a strong collaboration with a high-quality advertising agency and market research company is imperative as well. Both should be well-versed in the bio / pharmaceutical field, and preferably within disease state, including launch experience. By nature, the launch team leader (product manager in most cases) is a generalist[640] without the in-depth knowledge a good ad agency and market researcher can bring to the table. If chosen wisely with the launch in mind, these two external functions can add valuable input to the launch process, not only on

---

[639] Davenport (2009), p. 118
[640] Cf. Trilling (2008), pp. 37-40

the content level, but also due to their outsider's perspective and insights from other launch experiences outside of the company currently in the launch process.

In the interest of time, some launch teams tend to 'work in the dark' without executive feedback and buy-in until too late, thus risking a change in direction and subsequent delays, in case the executive team does not agree with their assumptions and decisions. Thus it pays off to take the time in the beginning to get the necessary buy-in, and then to be able to execute expediently.[641]

It is up to the team leaders to recruit top talent for the product launch, a skill that requires leadership talent as well as enthusiasm for the new product[642], to potentially convince their colleagues to leave their well-known brand or product range to participate in the launch product, whose future success is yet unknown.

Oftentimes, individual companies (especially smaller ones without a huge international base) do not have the necessary know-how about individual country requirements and guidelines necessary for a product launch in the respective country. In France, for example, it used to be required to establish a factory in France to produce the product or alternatively to give commercial rights to a French company. FDA launch requirements in the US are generally the strictest in the world, often necessitating a US-based and knowledgeable partner for non-US bio / pharmaceutical companies.[643] It has been shown that experience in a country does increase the likelihood of entry, suggesting economies of scope in a familiar market. The probability of a launch is 3.4 times higher in the company's home country than the average likelihood of entry in this country.[644]

A study conducted in the 1990s showed a clear correlation between shorter launch delays in companies with global launch experience, reflecting the advantages of

---

[641] Cf. Brown, Ennew (1995), p. 340
[642] Cf. Falk (2005), p. 250
[643] Cf. Breitenbach, Lewis (2010), pp. 244-247
[644] Cf. Kyle (2006), pp. 613-614

experience and multinational operations, including local subsidiaries and multi-country trials.[645]

Since the launch affects a multitude of areas of the company, it is crucial to include decision makers from all areas involved.[646] The launch plan needs to include the individual country's idiosyncrasies, such as the long summer vacations typical in Southern Europe (not a good time to reach stakeholders or launch a product), as well as specific requirements and restrictions (e.g. cost effectiveness agency involvement, availability of certain stakeholders, such as payers, patients or physicians in certain countries etc.).[647]

To ensure alignment and appropriate talent management in the launch process, it is necessary to adjust performance measures and incentive systems according to the necessary behaviors and focus needed for the product launch.[648] This is an additional step in the already busy schedule that in practice sometimes gets overlooked or downplayed, but it is an instrumental tool to ensure everyone's alignment and appropriate performance review during and after the launch. Typically, this is an area where the HR Team gets involved and can be utterly helpful. It is important to start the integrative HR process in a timely manner, so that the appropriate goals and incentives are already implemented into the individuals' review files, and thus the basis for their performance evaluation, before the launch process begins.

Under the guidance of a top-management steering committee, and managed by the launch project lead (usually the product manager) the key functions need to build a working group[649], consisting of all relevant groups, such as marketing, marketing services, medical affairs, legal, regulatory, manufacturing, pricing, PharmacoEconomics, managed care etc. as depicted in figure 6-1:

---

[645] Cf. Danzon, et al. (2005), p. 290
[646] Cf. Falk (2005), p. 246
[647] Cf. Eleveld, Chui (2010); Weiner, Hull (2006)
[648] Cf. PriceWaterhouseCoopers (2009), p. 16
[649] Cf. Falk (2005), p. 246; Kiskalt (2010), pp. 200-202

Figure 6- 1: Exemplary launch team set-up

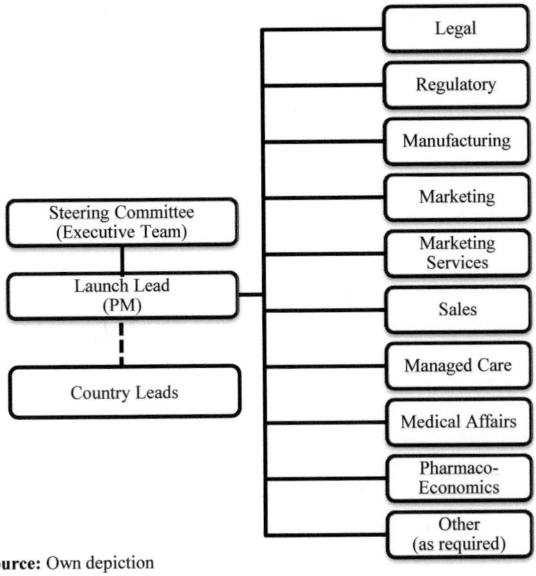

Source: Own depiction

Close collaboration with the country leaders does not only help consider market-relevant information that central functions in headquarters might not be aware of, but also facilitates the understanding and thus acceptance of corporate decisions, leading to a more seamless execution at the time of launch.[650]

Another crucial step is to do plan the implementation in detail, consisting of clear timelines and deliverables, giving everyone enough time and resources to do their job well and thoroughly. A key point is to allow enough time to think through a problem and establish all assumption as valid before jumping into execution mode.[651]

---

[650] Cf. Falk (2005), p. 246

[651] Cf. Hackett (2007), pp. 49-50

6.2 Internal Coordination and Communication

In practice, communication is a key factor and oftentimes a problem in stressful situations such as during a launch.[652] Since the launch of a product involves many departments that do not necessarily work together on a daily basis[653], a clear and concise communication plan is necessary to ensure collaboration and alignment, and to avoid unwelcome surprises.[654] To safeguard full alignment within the launch team and in communications to the outside world, be it customers or colleagues, it is advisable to repeat key goals and messages on a regular basis.[655]

Including Senior Management into the communication process and having their physical presence at key points is helpful to keep the spirits up throughout the launch process in various appropriate settings.[656] One factor to keep in mind is that Senior Management needs to be an ally and not an entity to woe: It is important to professionally, but frankly address issues and to set realistic expectations, e.g. in the forecasts. It does take some strength to stand up to management and show them the information they need to see, not what they want to see.[657]

For a successful launch, the flawless communication and collaboration between all functions involved is necessary. For example, only through a close link between R&D and sales and marketing functions, it is possible to include the payers' views, expectations and requirements (communication partners of the sales and marketing functions) in the development process (the domain of R&D).[658]

[652] Cf. Foldes (2010), p. 4
[653] Cf. Müller (2005a), p. 166
[654] Cf. Ernst (2002), p. 14; Illert, et al. (2007), p. 3
[655] Cf. Falk (2005), p. 253
[656] Cf. Falk (2005), p. 254
[657] Cf. Foldes (2010), p. 9; Stephen (2009)
[658] Cf. PriceWaterhouseCoopers (2009), p. 16

6.3 Pre-launch Activities

Pre-launch activities could be to increase awareness of a certain disease state or factor in the disease's mechanism of action, which then facilitates the product's introduction post-launch, depending on the market entry position and competitive advantage.[659]

Another factor to keep in mind is the necessary units required at launch. Since forecasts are unreliable at this point in time and an approval is not certain yet, the first batches of the product have to be produced and packaged at risk. Usually, the company develops a worst, base, and best case scenario for the necessary product volume at launch and adjusts this (and goes back into production) as soon as the first approvals and orders are coming in. This also necessitates a whole list of site and supplier readiness work that needs to be integrated into the overall launch plan and will be managed by the manufacturing representative in the launch team.[660]

6.3.1 The Global Launch Plan

Seamless process management has been established as a key factor for a successful new product development and launch.[661] To ensure a smooth launch process, a detailed launch plan needs to be established early in the game.[662] Like other formal corporate plans[663], this oftentimes is a concentrated effort executed by the key contributors and decision makers in a short period of time. Of course, the launch plan has to be a living document, meaning that it needs to be reviewed and revisited on a regular basis to reflect all changes.

---

[659] Cf. Hermansson (2005), pp. 144-145; Trilling (2008a), pp. 227-228
[660] Cf. Hartmann, et al. (2009), pp. 1107-1109
[661] Cf. Ernst (2007), p. 423
[662] Cf. Falk (2005), p. 246
[663] Cf. Aaker (1995), pp. 341-345

A few factors to keep in mind are:

- The launch plan has to be established in a timely manner, allowing enough time for all tasks at hand as well as time to make critical decisions along the way.
- The launch plan needs to provide an organizational layout for the launch and ensure that all decision makers are aware of their rules and responsibilities.
- Regular analysis and status tracking of all activities is necessary in all functional and geographical areas. Here, both the quality of the work (based on previously established benchmarks) and the relevance (aligned with strategy and overall direction) are reviewed.[664]

As this is a living document, priorities might have to not only be set, but also to be re-set and communicated.[665]

In general, simple traffic-light colored schemes are a useful way to visualize the status and progress of all parts within a launch plan: green = on target, yellow = slightly off target, can be rectified without escalation, red = significantly off target, warrants escalation. This way, no part is overlooked and all parts need to be constantly supervised and evaluated. There are various ways of visualizing these kinds of dashboards[666], the following table 6-2 is just a simple depiction to demonstrate the idea:

---

[664] Cf. Illert, et al. (2007), p. 3
[665] Cf. Chandy, et al (2006), p. 505; Falk (2005), p. 246; Seiter, Holz (2009), p. 929
[666] Cf. Few (2006)

Table 6- 2: Illustrative launch dashboard

Performance Measure	Objective	Current Status
Distribution	Product in market day 2 post-launch	Product in market day 2 post-launch
Launch Announcement	Sent to all stakeholders on day 1	Sent to all stakeholders on day 1
Sales	$ x	$ x-2
Publication	Article in NEJM on date x	Article turned down
Etc.		

On track
Slightly off track
Off track

Source: Own depiction

It is important to shorten the development time and optimize the diffusion rate of the product by running as many processes in parallel as possible.[667] Too punishing a schedule can be as counterproductive as one that is too slack. Including team members with launch expertise that know the ins and outs might be helpful to strike the right balance.[668] Here it is essential to know what information is necessary to start each process and fine-tune the overall launch schedule accordingly. Usually, the Critical Path Method (CPM) and the Project Evaluation and Review Technique (PERT) are used to manage intricate launch projects. In practice, the software program Microsoft Project is a useful tool to put these into action and to make the process – as well as its current state of execution - accessible and transparent to all participants.[669]

Microsoft Project ensures clear visibility of all tasks, interdependencies, resources and responsibilities – to determine a crucial path and check in on progress (or delays) on a regular basis. Depending on the overall plan, integrating contingency

[667] Cf. Simon (1989), p. 15
[668] Cf. Chandy, et al. (2006), p. 505
[669] Cf. Fischer, Breitenbach (2010a), pp. 36-38; Kiskalt (2010), pp. 210-212

plans and alternate scenarios triggered by certain events (e.g. approval delay, failure of a clinical trial etc.) might be advisable.[670]

While detailed planning is necessary to ensure a smooth launch process[671], it is important to note that this launch plan is a living document, open to relevant and necessary change, adjustment and improvement at any time, otherwise it runs the risk of becoming a straightjacket for the team implementing it[672] – otherwise it might be so stifling that it simply gets ignored in everyday business activities.

6.3.2 Country Plans

While an internationally consistent framework and guidelines are necessary and provided by the global launch plan, and potential synergies should be used, each country needs to develop its own launch plan based on the overall launch plan with a consistent set of KPIs based on best practices and benchmarks. As previously discussed, country plans also need to take into account local legislation, approval processes, payer systems, marketing requirements, as well as country-specific contingency plans. Due to reference pricing schemes (see chapter 4.3.5) these also need to be coordinated with each other. This creates a highly complex process.[673]

In practice, deviations in the countries' timetable, pricing, market expectations etc. from the overall launch plan often result in difficult situations. On the country side, the country managers are using their local market knowledge to adjust the corporate launch plan for their regional needs. On the corporate headquarters' side, any deviation from the overall guideline is viewed with suspicion (e.g. "Does the country manager 'sand bag' their market numbers to look particularly

---

[670] Cf. Aaker (1995), p. 348
[671] Cf. Seiter, Holz (2009), p. 927
[672] Cf. Aaker (1995), pp. 347-348
[673] Cf. Illert, et al. (2007); Müller (2005a), pp. 150-151; PriceWaterhouseCoopers (2009), p. 18; Seiter, Holz (2009), p. 927; Vanderveer (2005a), p. 3; Zeiner, Schiel (2007), p. 1401

good at launch time? Are the goals ambitious enough? Are these changes really necessary of just more comfortable for the country team?"). In these situations, it is of high value to work closely with the country managers and their launch team to fully understand their situation and judge the changes in their respective country plans based on in-depth understanding. At times, bio / pharmaceutical companies consider involving (local) market specialists, such as consultancies and ad agencies, to better understand and manage deviations. Here it is also helpful to carefully plan and execute all pre-launch and launch meetings to ensure alignment and a sense of unity across the board. Also, making the product 'real' by sharing patient stories of even bringing in patients helps establish meaning and a common cause.[674]

Central and local rules and responsibilities need to be clearly defined[675] to avoid unnecessary struggles and lengthy processes in the preparation for the launch. To make launch preparations comparable and transparent, it is important to provide a clear structure for the individual country plans, which could look as follows:

- Overview of the local health system
- Country-specific goals, success factors, strategies and tactics
- Local organizational structure for the launch product's business unit, including development over time
- Background information explaining revenue and expense calculations
- Number and nature of target customer, prioritized communication plan by decile through headquarters as well as sales representatives
- Sales team specifics, such as training plans, territory lists, reach and frequency
- Media plans
- Scientific agenda (local conference presence etc.)
- Marketing plans (sales force materials, advertising etc.)[676]

---

[674] Waldrop-Bay (2004), p. 12
[675] Cf. Müller (2005a), p. 160
[676] Cf. Falk (2005), p. 250-251

6.3.3 Brand Book

To ensure a unified presence of the brand throughout the world, key elements of the design, color and visuals of the product need to be centrally decided and communicated.[677] At times, marketing materials have to be altered to be relevant in the respective markets. Nonetheless, the more coherence is possible, the better as all target groups alike tend to travel across borders, especially within smaller continents with many countries such as Europe.[678]

This is oftentimes done in form of a brand book that contains all necessary design guidelines, key visuals, logos, key messages and color schemes etc. to enable a seamless brand presence.[679] While the brand book used to be a physical book, and sometimes still is, it now is advisable to host it electronically instead, allowing authorized users to log in and browse the website as well as to download all necessary files in required graphics formats. While this means an additional initial cost as well as a maintenance fee this approach does not only simplify the distribution process, but also facilitates any changes, additions, and updates to the overall brand book in an immediate and paperless manner on a global scale. Ad agencies usually offer these services today.

6.3.4 Launch Budget

There is no set formula for establishing a budget for a product launch. Key factors of the product have to be taken into account, specifically its unique advantages over competitive products as well as the size and competitive level within the marketplace.[680]

---

[677] Cf. Falk (2005), p. 247
[678] Cf. Gaston-Breton, Martin (2011), p. 285
[679] Cf. Müller (2005a), p. 158
[680] Cf. Bolesh (2006), p. 17

It is important to remember that positioning the product correctly in the right players' minds (the qualitative aspect of launch planning) is more important than the amount money spent during the launch.[681] Thus, as the launch budget gets planned, it is crucial to factor in sufficient time and funds needed to get the pre-launch activities right and not only to 'save up' funds for promotional activities post-launch. In general, expenses usually exceed profits during the launch phase of a product.[682]

Based on a study by Cutting Edge Information (depicted in figure 6-5), brands spend 10-15% of their launch budget during Phase III (more than half of it is spent on market research), another 25% in the months between FDA submission and launch, and the rest after launch.[683]

Figure 6- 2: Common trends in launch spending

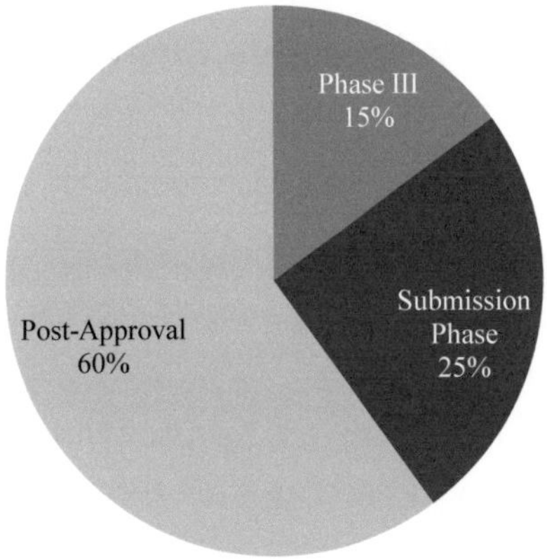

Source: Bolesh, E. (2006), p. 18

[681] Cf. Zeiner, Schiel (2007), p. 1401
[682] Cf. Bruhn (1995), p. 66; Kotler, Armstrong (1989), p. 289
[683] Cf. Bolesh (2006), p. 18

6.3.5 Clinical Studies (Phase IV)

In addition to the pivotal trials, the studies necessary for the approval of a product, there are additional studies that might be relevant post-launch and should be included in a launch plan, as their approval and initiation can be a rather lengthy process.

Post-launch studies are called 'Phase IV', which means that they are not label-enhancing, and often focus on specific questions, such as drug-drug-interactions, side effects, effectiveness in specific patient groups (women, age groups, co-morbidities, racial differences etc.).[684]
First of all, there are strategic studies, initiated by the company, that provide additional relevant information on the product, oftentimes long-term data.[685] These can be post-marketing requirements by the regulatory authorities, which are requiring more information, e.g. a pregnancy registry for a cancer drug. They can also be driven by the company as a potential marketing tool, e.g. in form of a head-to-head trial versus the largest competitor (such as in the Tykerb case previously mentioned).

Studies conducted in this phase should clearly define and align with the product's position as well as take into consideration country-specific needs to influence prescribing behavior and increase market access by providing relevant information to guideline developers, early adopter prescribers, and key patient groups.[686] A good example for excellent network marketing in this context is Fosamax (aledronic acid/Merck) in the 90s where the company worked closely with international policy makers and payers, influencing guidelines to ensure preventative treatment of women with a risk of osteoporosis.[687]

---

[684] Cf. Ortwein (2001), pp. 48-49
[685] Cf. Aigner, et al. (2010), pp. 107-108; Falk (2005), p. 252-253
[686] Cf. Zeiner, Schiel (2007), p. 1399
[687] Cf. Zeiner, Schiel (2007), p. 1399; Zeiner (2008), pp. 437-438

Secondly, Investigator-Sponsored Trials (ISTs) are, as the name indicates, initiated by physicians to test a certain clinical hypothesis. Other than the company, physicians are allowed to use products off-label, for indications that the product is not yet approved.[688] They usually receive free drug and monitoring support from the manufacturer in return for clean protocol data that might be used for additional scientific evaluations within the company.[689]

6.4 Getting the Product on the Road

Up to date, the sales team is the face to the customer and the most personal and thus effective way to interact with the potential product prescribers. According to a Datamonitor study between 1998 and 2001, pharmaceutical companies spend up to four times as much on sales force than on all other promotional activities.[690] Nonetheless, due to regulatory restrictions, for cost effectiveness reasons, changes can be seen in this arena as well, which will be discussed in the following.

Additionally, it is also important to ensure corporate compliance in every country (or even state), meaning that all corporate citizens, and especially the sales force, are acting according to current laws and regulations. Particularly during a launch phase, regulatory as well as competitive eyes are on the new product and the means applied to introduce it into the marketplace. Thus it is crucial to ensure that all measures planned are executed in a compliant way.

6.4.1 Recent Sales Force Developments

Over the past decades, the sales force has become one of the, if not the most important tools for the bio / pharmaceutical industry, doubling in the US alone from

---

688 Cf. Aigner, et al. (2010), p. 107
689 Cf. Falk (2005), p. 252-253
690 Cf. Müller (2005b), p. 211

about 57,500 in 1998 to over 90,000 by 2003.[691] Between 1996 and 2000, Novo Nordisk has increased their sales force by 240%, Roche by 110%, Novartis by 100%.[692]

At this point, it is estimated that about 800,000-900,000 pharmaceutical sales reps work worldwide, with 10% (80,000-90,000) in the US alone[693]. Here, sales force expenses are estimated to be over $7 billion annually.[694] The majority of sales costs are driven by the personnel and their travel & entertainment expenses.[695]

Yet, sales forces differ based on country, product life cycle stage and the company's overall portfolio and one size does not fit all.[696] While in the US the sales team still accounts for about 50% of the post-launch prescription volume and are thus the promotional key driver, their influence in the UK is rather limited due to the nationalized healthcare system with its clear regulations, leading bio / pharmaceutical companies to consider giving up on classical sales representative activities.[697]

Due to regulatory pressures and general cost savings[698], it is no surprise that some companies have downsized their sales force of the past years. This trend became apparent when Pfizer, the leading pharmaceutical company and employer of about 13,000 sales reps, downsized its sales force in 2005 and by another third in 2008.[699] Further industry job cuts took place internationally in 2010, as the industry is adapting to cost pressures and patent expirations, attempting to cut costs across the board.[700]

---

[691] Cf. Hradecky (1999); Robinson (2003), pp. 24-27
[692] Cf. Müller (2005b), p. 210
[693] Cf. Müller (2005b), p. 212; Vanderveer, Pines (2003), p. 3
[694] Cf. Ahearne, Rapp, Hughes, Jindal (2010), p. 765
[695] Cf. Scholtissek (2005), p. 263
[696] Cf. Müller (2005b), p. 224
[697] Cf. Bernhard (2010), p. 2
[698] Cf. Trilling (2008b), p. 233
[699] Cf. Fischer, Breitenbach (2010a), pp. 24-25; Pettypiece, Alesci (2009); Rubenstein (2009)
[700] Cf. Ringler (2010)

It is important to remember that the physician is overloaded with information in the hyper-communicative and hyper-competitive marketplace. Physicians do not necessarily pay attention to the information provided by the sales force anymore, they rely on other, new sources of information (such as the internet), the competition is taking every opportunities to exploit the opponents' weaknesses in their discussions with the physician, and regulations are limiting the use of certain promotional tactics (such as fiscal limits or bans on product-related gadgets provided to the physician).[701]

Thus, the ROI on sales representatives and their calls is diminishing as nearly half the calls end at the receptionist's desk – and never make it to the prescriber – and, in case of a successful call on a prescriber, these interactions last about 2 minutes in prescription-relevant high-volume practices.[702] In general, an average sales call has diminished to about 2-5 minutes.[703] Thus it needs to be used wisely and be targeted to the physician's current needs. The two types of information usually needed are point-of-care information (regarding the treatment of a specific patient) and updates (new information about a product). Sales representatives have to be well-versed in directing their call time into these two categories, where at the point of launch, a general product overview is necessary to lay the baseline.[704] The information needed at that point most likely exceeds the two-five minute call slot and needs to be supplemented with CME or dinner presentation invites.

Pharmaceutical representatives spend up to 75% of their time traveling from office to office and waiting to see their target physician.[705] Here the search for suitable e-tools to support their work becomes more and more relevant. One approach is to render the sales rep more efficient in his work day (e.g. providing him with laptops, pocket PCs etc). The other is to supplement their efforts with alternate ways of communication.

[701] Cf. Vanderveer (2001); Vanderveer, Pines (2003), p. 2
[702] Cf. Vanderveer (2001)
[703] Cf. Vanderveer, Pines (2003), p. 2
[704] Cf. Vanderveer (2006), p. 2
[705] Cf. Vanderveer (2001a), p. 58

6.4.2 Types of Sales Forces

Generally speaking, a larger sales force is needed for general practitioner (GP) products than for specialist products, as more customers make up the relevant customer base. In a survey conducted in 2004, it was assessed that in the more GP-centric cardiovascular field, for example, the sales force makes up 58% of the overall marketing cost, whereas in the clinic and specialist field of oncology, sales made up merely 27%.[706] Since the sales force is an expensive, but important tool for bio / pharmaceutical sales it needs to be fine-tuned prior to launch.

Different countries do have different market requirements, which needs to be addressed in the country plans (see chapter 6.3.2) so one size does not fit all. The UK, for example, is a very GP-centric country and, while sales representatives play a more limited role as described in 6.4.1, more than 80% of them address this customer group. Germany traditionally is a specialist market, thus pharmaceutical companies focus their sales efforts on specialist groups.[707] While general sales forces for GPs are on the decline, specialized sales forces with a deep medical knowledge are still highly successful.[708] Since fewer specialists require fewer specialized sales people, an overall trend towards specialization and focus on key physicians can be observed.

For all sales forces, it is important that they have in-depth knowledge of the product as well as the relevant disease state(s), can provide information on the product use, especially for patients with co-morbidities, and can provide and cite scientific studies that support the product's use.[709] This is even truer in the specialty markets.

The sales and marketing process is expected by experts to change towards a more concentrated effort, focusing on (potentially fewer) sales representatives that take

---

[706] Cf. Müller (2005b), p. 211
[707] Cf. Müller (2005b), p. 216-220
[708] Cf. Hermansson (2005), pp. 146-147
[709] Cf. Müller (2005b), p. 213

on the job of a key account manager. These key account managers need to concentrate on government and payers as they become more involved in the decision making process, taking away some of the attention from the treatment providers and pharmacists, who will be more and more regulated in their decision making by the respective payers.[710]

6.4.3 Sales Force Considerations at Launch

In general, it should not be assumed that the sales force will automatically adopt and sell the new launch product. The sales force adoption of a new product determines their performance to a large degree.[711] Many factors have to be considered, both staffing and training-related.[712]

Thus, a first consideration is the sales force size. While it is tempting to immediately ramp up the sales force for the product launch, a look at other sectors, such as the technology-driven consumer industry, suggests considering other options as well. Analogous to the manufacturing learning curve, every product launch also goes through a sales learning curve, which requires different skills and maybe even different number of sales representatives through its process:[713] In the initiation phase, a 'renaissance rep' is needed, with the ability to resourcefully develop his or her own sales approach. Studies find that many sales people thrive on the volatile market environment of a launch and would thus be well-suited for it.[714] In the transition phase, the 'enlightened rep' is needed who can deal with a still-adapting sales approach but without the analytical skills of a renaissance rep from the previous phase. In the final execution phase, a 'coin-operated rep' is needed, who can execute simply based on a sales plan, territory call list, and adequate marketing materials.[715] While the bio / pharmaceutical industry is far more restric-

---

[710] Cf. PriceWaterhouseCoopers (2008), p. 38-39
[711] Cf. Hultink, Atuahene-Gima (2000), p. 435
[712] Cf. Atuahene-Gima (1997), p. 498
[713] Cf. Leslie, Holloway (2006), pp. 115-120
[714] Cf. Hultink, Atuahene-Gima (2000), p. 447
[715] Cf. Leslie, Holloway (2006), pp. 120-121

tive than other industries, it behooves a company to consider the various sales needs throughout the launch process and adjust its sales training, as well the profile it is hiring to, accordingly.

Based on interviews with pharmaceutical managers in 25 EU-countries, the number of sales reps assigned to a product is usually highest during the product's launch phase. Two years post launch, it is usually reduced to half its size and downsized by another 30% towards the end of its patent life.[716] During a launch phase in a GP market, it happens that up to five different sales reps visit a key physician.[717] The question is how effective this sales technique is and to what extent it only annoys and frustrates the physician, giving every individual sales representative less time and ultimately diminishing the rate of return. While cost increased over that past decade, productivity did not.[718]

6.4.4 Sales Force Training

As mentioned before, the integration of commercial and R&D function is crucial for the new product development and a successful launch.[719] Here, it also needs to be distinguished between the marketing department, which is ideally involved early on, but then also the sales department, which is the key link between the customer (and his or her needs) and the company (and the product) and thus needs to be carefully trained and prepared.[720]

Larger companies have their own sales training and sales team, smaller outfits sometimes take advantage of external training teams and even external sales teams (the so-called 'rent-a-reps').[721] Since their commitment to the product is not always as high as the commitment of a full-time employee, many smaller compa-

---

[716] Cf. Müller (2005b), p. 213
[717] Cf. Müller (2005b), p. 220
[718] Cf. Scholtissek (2005), p. 257
[719] Cf. De Luca, et al. (2010), p. 314
[720] Cf. Ernst, Hoyer, Rübsaamen (2010), pp. 89-90; Ortwein (2001), p. 108
[721] Cf. Ortwein (2001), p. 103

nies decide to partner with larger companies that have their own sales team to ensure better long-term results. As an example for that, Gilead Sciences developed Tamiflu (oseltamivir) during a time in its life cycle where the company did not have a commercial team yet. Thus, commercialization rights were given to Roche. While Gilead now focuses on other disease states, this became quite a hot topic during the flu scare (SARS (Severe Acute Respiratory Syndrome), Avian flu) in the mid 2000's as entire countries were suddenly stockpiling large quantities of Tamiflu.

Due to the increased information overload and the diminishing return on traditional sales methods described above, it is relevant to move from an 'interruption marketing', where the sales representative disrupts the prescribers office work, to 'permission marketing', where the sales representative is invited by the prescriber to share his or her information with him. This can be supported by targeted training, which also includes digital tools, such as handheld POC (Point of Care) devices, web-based services and e-detailing devices. Nonetheless, just transferring previously printed devices into an electronic format does not serve this purpose. Here it is relevant to successfully micro-market by tailoring the presentation and information to the specific customers' needs.[722] This is a task that the bio / pharmaceutical industry – despite substantial expenses - has not yet fully mastered, but that holds large promises for the successful executioner.

Yet, technology alone is not sufficient to ensure success. One interesting example is the iPhysicianNet Initiative (IPNI), where a video conference-enabled computer was installed in a prescriber's home office free of charge. In return, the physician had to participate in one monthly video detail from up to 12 pharmaceutical company sponsors. The physician's advantage of having high-tech audio visual (AV) equipment at home came at the cost of having to spend personal time listening to promotional information from pharmaceutical companies in their home. For the pharmaceutical companies, these 8-minute time slots (usually carried out by the physician's regular sales rep with AV capabilities) meant 4 times the time usually

[722] Cf. Vanderveer (2001)

allowed in a regular sales call. It also allowed for more in-depth discussions and the use of more relevant visuals (as compared to a short detail in a sample closet). Here a fine balance has to be found between the physician's specific needs and limited attention span and the medical message to be provided. A trial done by Novartis provided 13 calls (vs. 8 in the field), lasted 9 minutes (vs. 3) and cost $14 / minute (vs. $58).[723] a day. Attempts such as these are expensive and of questionable scalability, but provide a first glimpse at out-of-the-box promotional activities that, if done well, clearly cut through the clutter for everyday information overflow at a physician's office.[724] Unfortunately, more recent searched for this company did not provide any further or more recent information, leading to the conclusion that this idea, after all, failed and that the personal touch and connection might just be an important factor not to be dismissed.

6.4.4 Sales Force Support

While more and more elaborate sales tracking and reporting systems are available[725], this information is often not optimally used and not linked to other corporate systems and decision making tools.[726] Integrating ground-level sales information in top-level decision making represents a great opportunity for bio / pharmaceutical companies in the future. Currently, the sales force is not seamlessly integrated into the company's information systems.[727] One of the reasons sales data is not as useful as one could hope from the team that is in direct contact with the customer on a daily basis lies in the corporate compliance scare (see chapter 6.4.6). Some companies have limited or removed any 'free flow text' options in the reporting tools to avoid careless entries by their sales staff that might lead to legal issues. Fully understanding the law helps sales representatives be more as-

[723] Cf. Simon, Kotler (2003), pp. 285-287
[724] Cf. Vanderveer (2001a), pp. 58-67
[725] Cf. Fischer, Breitenbach (2010c), pp. 295-297
[726] Cf. PriceWaterhouseCoopers (2009), p. 21
[727] Cf. Scholtissek (2005), p. 264

sured not only about their daily actions, but also makes the sales reporting tools more useful during a launch and after.

Unfortunately, oftentimes senior management does not get actively involved into the sales strategy until things go wrong. Since the sales force is the face to the customer and its success key to the success of the launch, a higher level of involvement is advisable. Setting realistic sales expectations internally, to sales and management as well as externally, to board and investors, is crucial for a sustainable market position.[728] All too often, good launch initiatives are aborted prematurely due to unrealistic expectations and resulting frustrations and disillusionment as well as a perceived lack of commitment from the corporation.[729] In summary, the sales team needs to be committed to the product, accountable, have trust in the organization, receive the right kind of management attention and control, and the sales representatives need to match the required profile for the launch. A good mix of these factors is the ingredients for high performance at launch.[730]

While the returns on detailing have steadily declined over the past years, it still remains the most important promotional launch driver[731], the sales team set-up has to be carefully reviewed and cannot be done in a 'more of the same' fashion. Who are the key stakeholders they need to talk to, and who is qualified to in order to successfully position the new product into their minds? This needs to be answered prior to starting the hiring and training process.

6.4.6 Corporate Compliance

In addition to the previously mentioned sales force considerations, another major factor in the physical product launch is corporate compliance.

---

[728] Cf. Leslie, Holloway (2006), p. 123
[729] Cf. Atuahene-Gima, p. 512; Leslie, Holloway (2006), p. 115
[730] Cf. Fraenkel (2008), pp. 250-253
[731] Cf. PriceWaterhouseCoopers (2009), p. 3; Zeiner, Schiel (2007), p. 1400

The US has probably the strictest set of rules for corporate compliance at the moment, based on the guidelines of the Office of Inspector General of the US Department of Health and Human Services, issued in April 2003 and constantly updated and adjusted.[732] On top of this, most bio / pharmaceutical companies also have a voluntary set of rules and regulations. In the US, this is provided by Pharmaceutical Research and Manufacturers of America (PhRMA).[733] In the UK, the ABPI code of practice for the pharmaceutical industry was instituted in 1958, and updated on an ongoing basis, limiting marketing activities, especially push marketing.[734] In Germany, the VFA (Verband der forschenden Pharma-Unternehmen) prepared its own code of conduct[735] in addition to the German legislation.

These specific corporate compliance measures, both legislative as well as voluntary, need to be taken into account in every country plan and orchestrated internationally, as the markets are getting more and more interdependent, stakeholders (as well as products) travel between borders (if for conferences, work, or pleasure), and even tools like the internet provide ample room for additional information that might not be compliant in some countries, but perfectly fine in others.

6.5 Monitoring the Launch Success

Forecasts for launch products are notoriously unpredictable and can vary widely.[736] It is thus important to carefully track all data and make adjustment, both in forecasts and in actions, as necessary. Oftentimes, launch failures can be traced back to naïve assumptions; or rather assumptions that were true in the past (or for a competitive product) but do not hold water in the current marketplace.[737]

---

[732] Cf. Human and Health Services (HHS) (2011); PriceWaterhouseCoopers (2009), p. 16
[733] For details, please see:PhRMA (2011)
[734] Cf. Association of the British Pharmaceutical Industry (ABPI) (2011); Hermansson (2005), p. 147
[735] Cf. VFA (2010)
[736] Cf. Christopher, McDonald (1995), p. 136
[737] Cf. Christopher, McDonald (1995), p. 137; Foldes (2010), p. 6

Thus, the more clearly all assumptions are spelled out and tracked after launch, the easier it will be to quickly make the necessary adjustments.

Here it is important to define the right lead indicators, such as market share in new prescriptions or switches from old products onto the launch product. These are indicative of the product's future success. The classic overall market share takes time to develop and thus is more of a lag indicator that is not helpful to assess the product's success over the first crucial months that it is in the market. A few months after launch, revisiting incidence and prevalence data to reassess the epidemiological potential of the drug, as well as patient compliance data become more relevant and have moved more into the focus.[738] Using a dashboard to visualize the status of these indicators is a common best practice (also see table 6-2).[739]

While the focus is usually on numbers of Rx written, a more detailed look at patient retention and new patient gain (naïve and switches, depending on the line of treatment) is a valuable target to include in the launch tracker to better understand the success in the marketplace.[740]

A study reviewing 56 ethical drug launches derived that within the first three quarters post-launch the future success of a drug is detectable. A drug that is not successful by then is highly unlikely to become so even with strong promotional measures.[741]

6.5.1 Post-launch Market Research Tools

To test for sales force effectiveness, a variety of market research tools can be put into place. Most commonly these are unaided and aided message recall (what the

[738] Cf. Seiter, Holz (2009), pp. 928-929; Vanderveer (2007), p. 131; Zeiner, Schiel (2007), p. 1401
[739] Cf. Seiter, Holz (2009), pp. 930
[740] Cf. Terblanche (2008), pp. 209-210
[741] Cf. Corstjens, et al. (2005), p. 327

customer things the representative said and if the rep delivered the intended message), response to the message (was the message believable in relevant to the physician), as well as specific behavior recollection (did the rep use sales aids, other materials, ask for business etc.). These tests can help establish if the sales force is doing what they are asked to do and if these actions – in combination with sales data – lead to the desired results. Used correctly and implemented swiftly, this market research can help quickly course correct (e.g. refine a message that is not relevant to the physician as currently stated, or retrain the sales force to effectively use their new materials etc.).[742]

One specific way to derive relevant market information is Awareness, Trial & Usage (ATU) market research: As the name implies, in this research the customer's (both physicians and patients) familiarity, perceptions and usage of the brand are examined. Customers are asked first unaided, then aided questions about the brand and its competition to establish their knowledge and perception at a point in time, as well as over time, as ATUs are generally repeated on a regular basis. In a launch setting, the first ATU is usually done prior to launch as a baseline. Post-launch, they are usually repeated in quarterly intervals. To get actionable quick interim 'early indicator' results, these ATUs may be repeated in shorter intervals and with a smaller sample. It is important to know what to ask for and also how to address potential deviations from the hoped-for results (e.g. what to do if the physicians do not attribute the desired key attributes with the product, what if the patients do not recall any of the DTC efforts etc.). Also, an analysis of the differences between users and non-users might offer additional insights.[743]

In the interest of time, ATUs are often done online or in computer-based phone interviews.[744] For more detailed information and insights, qualitative tracking studies are conducted as personal IDI with a smaller sample of users and non-users.[745]

---

742 Cf. Kelly, Liftin, Vaughn (2009), p. 2
743 Cf. Pines (2008), pp. 1-2
744 Cf. Pines (2008), p. 1
745 Cf. Pines (2008), p. 3

In general, there is a plethora of market research tools, both qualitative and quantitative, available to the launch team and it is essential to determine the type and number of market research to be done during launch early on to allow for ample testing, fine-tuning, and potentially some baseline market research to better understand the impact the product launch has on the marketplace.[746]

6.5.2 Post-launch Analysis

While every launch is different and all external, product-specific, and organizational factors have to be evaluated anew every time, every launch also contains a few lessons. Both in regard to the successful mastering of challenges and best practices, as well as oversights and last-minute fire drills that can be anticipated and avoided the next time around. Thus, one important exercise is the post-launch analysis of the launch, even though the time never seems right and the teams are busy working on new projects or finalizing the launch work on the current one. Timeliness of the post-launch analysis is of the essence, because with the next set of challenges and projects, the details of the launch are easily put in the back of one's mind and forgotten. Since it is likely that another set of individuals will be in charge of the next corporate launch, it is essential to capture these learnings, make them part of the corporate memory of a learning organization, and make them accessible to the individuals who would benefit within the company.[747] One helpful tool to get started on the specifics of the launch experience is to use the presentations, dashboards, timelines, RACI grids etc. that were developed during the launch process, assessing their usefulness as well as accuracy in predicting how things actually worked out in the end. The focus here lies on how to improve processes and the way the organization adapts to change and masters unexpected events, not the specifics of a previous launch.

---

[746] Cf. Kelly, Rupert (2009), pp. 3-9
[747] Cf. Fischer, Breitenbach (2010b), pp. 278-279; Illert, et al. (2007), p. 3; Senge (2006)

6.5.3 Course Correction

Feedback during the launch phase is crucial in all areas. After the findings of the analysis and planning phases have been implemented, they now need to be controlled and continuously assessed.[748] Using decision support systems, previously established decisions and strategies can be adjusted.[749] It is important to note, though, that due to the strict regulatory requirements, re-launches and course corrections are significantly more cumbersome, time-intensive, and potentially impossible in this marketplace. Thus it is key to stay flexible throughout the process, not to lose sight of the target and thus to get it right the first time.

For every lead indicator and KPI, there should also be an action plan in place in case these indicators do not show the desired results. E.g. should the message recall be below expectations post-launch, a plan to get the sales team on message should be in place, such as an additional sales training.[750]

Organizationally speaking, it might make sense to set up a hotline for all colleagues to address issues, questions, concerns, as well as positive customer feedback. This voicemail system is usually checked by the launch team leader, who evaluates the incoming information and shares it with the launch team on a regular basis to derive appropriate action steps.

[748] Cf. Ernst (2002), p. 9; Kotler, Armstrong (1989), p. 48
[749] Cf. Riemenschneider, Sprandel (2007), p. 167
[750] Cf. Seiter, Holz (2009), pp. 929-930; Trilling (2008a), p. 230

7. Summary and Outlook on Bio / Pharmaceutical Product Launches

While a few attempts have been made to characterize the key success factors for product launches, the practice shows that these are moving targets, determined by external factors, such as the legal, regulatory and competitive environment, as well as product-inherent factors, and corporate factors.

This dissertation first defined the product launch itself and then proceeded to categorize the product types, and quantified the market size and growth as well as its therapeutic areas and particularities, before discussing current trends and specific considerations. After the basis had been set, the critical importance of the launch, both from a temporal as well as a content-driven perspective were presented to subsequently derive the three levels where key considerations of a product launch take place, namely: market-based, product-based, and organizational. Here the main themes and results in current literature and reviews were categorized into these three areas to ensure that all these points were addressed in the subsequent sections.

Key considerations on the market-based level were reviewed on three levels. First as part of the marketplace assessment, regarding its size and structure, particularly blockbuster and niche markets. Secondly, the implications of market entry (first-to-market vs. follow-on products) as well as treatment lines (first or second line). As a third aspect, the competitive assessment of the marketplace selection was discussed, including the influence of regulations on launch timing and pricing strategies.

Product-based considerations were illuminated from three angles. The first aspect was based on R&D considerations, including clinical trials set up, decision making, and product profiles. Secondly, the marketing-centric considerations were illuminated, with a special focus on the necessary market research, as well as a review of the 7Ps of Bio / Pharmaceutical marketing and branding. The third, important perspective was the stakeholders' points-of-view of the product, which are traditionally more numerous due to the previously discussed nature of this market place, but who are also becoming increasingly more important as of late. Regulatory authorities, payers, cost effectiveness agencies, prescribers, patients and the general public and media were all identified and discussed based on up-to-date information.

On the third level, the organizational considerations were discussed, with a focus on the launch team as a whole, communication and coordination needs within the corporation, or amongst partners in an alliance. Starting out with pre-launch activities, such as the launch plan, country plans, brand books, budgets and phase IV study considerations, the launch requirements of the sales force and regarding compliance and ends with ways to monitor the launch success and course correct, if necessary, were discussed.

From the information derived from this dissertation it becomes clear that to successfully launch products in today's market, it behooves the launching company to assess these factors freshly and step-by-step during the course of the product launch, making the necessary grids, templates, timelines, and charts living documents that can be used as a reference tool and adjusted as needed. This dissertation illustrated these necessary steps and thought processes along the lines of the three areas (external, product-inherent, and corporate considerations) while keeping in mind and addressing the key success factors established in studies, meta-studies and evaluations up to this point. These key considerations were substantiated by examples from real life to make them more palpable and actionable. Due to its open structure and the tools provided to structure processes and do further research, if necessary, it aims to remain a meaningful resource in years to come, as the market changes and morphs due to new pressures, such as regulatory changes, pricing considerations, and pipeline issues.

As a next step, it might be interesting to assess the usefulness of these tools in future product launches as discussed in 6.5.2 (post-launch analysis), and to continuously adapt the individual part as the landscape and the requirements of product launches. Potential adaptations and additions may be due to external factors, such as stricter regulatory requirements, as much as product-inherent ones, such as through increased use of biomarkers and nano-biosensors pre-emptively, which allows for more individualized therapy.[751] In the future, side effects thus might be mitigated and the drug the patient is most likely to respond favorably to can be chosen. A subsequent review might also regard the organizational structure, as increasing co-operations, particularly in new markets, necessitate different and novel team and communication structures.

Finally, every plan is only as good as its execution. In this, current and future launch leaders and executioners must prove themselves – for their own sake, as much as the sake of the many patients and families touched by medical advances and new product launches.

---

[751] Cf. Sakamoto, et al. (2010), pp. 63-64

List of References

105th Congress of the United States of America (1997)
Food and Drug Administration Modernization Act of 1997,
URL: http://www.fda.gov/downloads/RegulatoryInformation/
Legisla-
tion/FederalFoodDrugandCosmeticActFDCAct/SignificantAmendmentstotheFDCAct/FD
AMA/FullTextofFDAMAlaw/UCM089145.pdf [accessed May 24, 2011]

1A Pharma (2011)
URL: http://www.1apharma.de [accessed November 14, 2011]

Aaker, D. (1995)
Strategic Market Management, 4th edition, Hoboken, NJ

Aaker, D. (2007)
Innovation: Brand It Or Lose It, in: California Management Review, Vol. 50, No. 1, pp. 8-24

Accenture (2007)
Achieving High Performance in Pharmaceuticals – Reversing the R&D Productivity Decline, URL: https://microsite.accenture.com/
rdtransfor-
mation/Documents/Accenture_Achieving_High_Performance_in_Pharmaceuticals-
Reversing_the_RD_Productivity_Decline.pdf [accessed March 3, 2011]

Adams, D. (2009)
Prospect-Driven Launch, in: Sales & Service Excellence, Vol. 9, No. 9, p. 16

Ahearne, M., Rapp, A., Hughes, D., Jindal, R. (2010)
Managing Sales Force Product Perceptions and Control Systems in the Success of New Product Introductions, in: Journal of Marketing Research, Vol. 47, pp. 764-776

Aigner, A., Czubayko, F., Klebe, G., Stubbs, M. (2010)
Das Nadelöhr – Von der Forschung zur Entwicklung, in: Fischer, D., Breitenbach, J. (ed.): Die Pharmaindustrie. Einblick – Durchblick – Perspektiven, 3rd edition, München, pp. 47-108

Albers. S., Herrmann, A. (ed.) (2007)
Handbuch Produktmanagement – Strategieentwicklung, Produktplanung, Organisation, Kontrolle, 3rd revised and updated edition, Wiesbaden

Albiez, P., Danielsohn-Weil, P., Scholl, M. (2007)
Segmentierung für ein systematisches Kundenmanagement, in: Pharmind - die pharmazeutische industrie, Vol. 69, No. 10, pp. 1133-1137

Amelung, V., Sydow, J., Windeler, A. (ed.) (2009)
Vernetzung im Gesundheitswesen – Wettbewerb und Kooperationen, Stuttgart

Anashkina, V. (2005)
Russland – Europa und doch so anders, in: Müller, M. (ed.): Europäisches Pharmamarketing – Ein Leitfaden für Manager der pharmazeutischen Industrie und Beteiligte des europäischen Gesundheitswesens, Wiesbaden, pp. 121-132

Association of the British Pharmaceutical Industry (2011)
URL:
http://www.patientsorganizations.org/iapo_media/Toolkits/current/resources/ABPI_Code_2011.pdf [accessed October 20, 2011]

Astebro, T., Michela, J. (2005)
A Longitudinal Study of the Impact of R&D, Patents, and Product Innovation of Firm Performance, in: Journal of Product Innovation Management, Vol. 22, No. 5, pp. 725-740

Atuahene-Gima, K. (1997)
Adoption of New Products by the Sales Force: The Construct, Research Propositions, and Managerial Implications, in: Journal of Product Innovation Management, Vol. 14, No. 6, pp. 498-514

Avitabile, D. (2006)
Marketing Strategies for Clinical Trial Recruitment and Patient Retention: Behind Every New Medicine are the Volunteers Who Take Part in Clinical Research Studies, However, the Number of People who Participate in Clinical Trials is Quite Small, in: Product Management Today, URL: http://findarticles.com/p/articles/mi_hb6148/is_2006_Dec/ai_n29332644/pg_5/ [accessed February 24, 2011]

Baraclude Website (2011)
URL: http://www.baraclude.com/index.aspx [accessed October 20, 2011]

Barnett, K. (2009)
Plan Early Or Pay The Price, in: Medical Marketing & Media, Vol. 44, No. 3, pp. 55-57

Barclay, I. (1992a)
The New Product Development Process - Past Improving the Process of New Product Development, in: R&D Management, Vol. 22, No. 3, pp. 255-263

Barclay, I. (1992b)
The New Product Development Process - Part 2. Evidence and Future Practical Application - Part 1, in: R&D Management, Vol. 22; No. 4, pp. 307-317

Barclay, I. (1992b)
The New Product Development Process - Part 2. Evidence and Future Practical Application - Part 1, in: R&D Management, Vol. 22; No. 4, pp. 307-317

BBC News (2008)
Deal reached on NHS drug prices, URL: http://news.bbc.co.uk/2/hi/health/7737027.stm [accessed June 18, 2010]

Becker, R. (2010):
Dem Arzneistoff eine Chance – die Arzneiform, in: Fischer, D., Breitenbach, J. (ed.): Die Pharmaindustrie. Einblick – Durchblick – Perspektiven, 3rd edition, München, pp. 109-134

Bernhard, B. (2010)
Launch Excellence I, IMS Health, URL: http://www.presseportal.ch/de/pm/100018940/100600262/ims_health_gmbh [accessed March 10, 2011]

Bernhard, B. (2010a)
Launch Excellence II, IMS Health, URL: http://www.presseportal.ch/de/pm/100018940/100605749/ims_health_gmbh [accessed March 10, 2011]

Birkner, C. (2011)
What's In A Name?, in: Marketing News, Vol. 45, No. 4, p. 6

Bolesh, E. (2006)
Launch on a Budget, in: Supplement to Pharmaceutical Executive, Vol. 6, No. 3, pp. 16-22

Bolesh, E. (2008)
Defusing the Time Bomb, in: Pharmaceutical Executive, Vol. 29, No. 3, pp. 22-30

Bonney, M. (2008)
Specialty Sales Gets No Resistance, in: Pharmaceutical Executive, Vol. 29, No. 10, pp. 34-37

Boulding, W., Christen, M. (2008)
Pioneering Plus a Broad Product Line Strategy: Higher Profits or Deeper Losses, Additional contact information, in: Management Science, 2009, vol. 55, issue 6, pages 958-967

Boston Consulting Group (2006)
Medizinische Biotechnologie in Deutschland 2006 - Wirtschaftliche Bedeutung und Erfolgsfaktoren

Breitenbach, J., Lewis, J. (2010):
Business Development – Geschäftsentwicklung und Lizenzgeschäft, in: Fischer, D., Breitenbach, J. (ed.): Die Pharmaindustrie. Einblick – Durchblick – Perspektiven, 3rd edition, München, pp. 243-257

Brettel, M., Sattler, M. (2009)
What Drives Firms to Excellence in Innovation Management, in: AMA Winter Educators' Conference Proceedings, Vol. 20, pp. 217-219

Brown, A., Ennew, C. (1995)
Market Research and the Product Politics of New Product Development, in: Journal of Marketing Management, Vol. 11, No. 4, pp. 339-353

Bruhn, M. (1995)
Marketing – Grundlagen für Studium und Praxis, 2nd revised edition, Wiesbaden

Bundesgesetzblatt (2010)
Gesetz zur Neuordnung des Arzneimittelmarktes in der gesetzlichen Krankenversicherung (Arzneimittelmarktneuordnungsgesetz – AMNOG), December 22, 2010, Part I, No. 67, Bonn, URL: http://www.bgbl.de/Xaver/start.xav?startbk=Bundesanzeiger_BGBl&bk=Bundesanzeiger_BGBl&start=//*[@attr_id=%27bgbl110s2262.pdf%27] [accessed March 15, 2011]

Bundesministerium für Gesundheit (2011)
Das Gesetz zur Neuordnung des Arzneimittelmarktes, March 3, 2011,
URL: http://www.bmg.bund.de/krankenversicherung/arzneimittelversorgung/amnog/amnog.html [accessed March 15, 2011]

Buono, D. (2007)
Launches boom as branded drugs lose patents, in: Drug Store News, pp. 36 and 39, URL: http://findarticles.com/p/articles/mi_m3374/is_12_29/ai_n21053491/] [accessed November 9, 2011]

Bureth, A., Penin, J., Wolff, S. (2010)
Start-Up Creating in Biotechnology: Lessons From the Case of Four New Ventures in the Upper Rhine Biovalley, in: International Journal of Innovation Management, Vol. 14, No. 2, pp. 253-283

Burton, T., Adams, C. (2001)
New Government Cholesterol Standards Would Triple Number of Prescriptions, in: The Wall Street Journal, Vol. 237, No. 96

Business Insights (2011):
Drug Approval Trends at the FDA and EMEA – Process improvements, heightened scrutiny and industry response,
URL: http://www.globalbusinessinsights.com/content/rbhc0200m.pdf [accessed February 1, 2011]

Buzzell, R. (2004)
The PIMS Program of Strategy Research – A Retrospective Appraisal, in: Journal of Business Research, Vol. 57, No. 5, pp. 478-483

Cacciotti, J., Clinton, P. (2011)
12th Annual Pharm Exec 50, URL: http://pharmexec.findpharma.com/pharmexec/article/articleDetail.jsp?id=719596&sk=&date=&pageID=3 [accessed May 16, 2011]

Calantone, R., Griffith, D. (2007)
Challenges and Opportunities in the Field of Global Product Launch, in: Journal of Product Innovation Management, Vol. 24, pp. 414-418

Call, G. (1997)
Entstehung und Markteinführung von Produktneueinheiten – Entwicklung eines prozess-orientierten Konzepts, Wiesbaden

Cameron, D. (2007)
A slow saga of success, in: Paradigm Research – Whitehead Institute for Biomedical Research, URL: http://www.wi.mit.edu/news/paradigm/spring_2007/Gleevec/Glivec.html [accessed May 18, 2011]

Campbell, D., Chui, M. (2010)
Pharmerging Shake-Up – The Imperatives in a Redefined World, IMS Health, URL: http://www.imshealth.com/deployedfiles/imshealth/Global/Content/StaticFile/Pharma_Shake-up_Imperatives_3_10.pdf [accessed July 26, 2011]

Carpenter, D., Rynbrandt R. (2003)
Early Entrant Protection in the U.S. Pharmaceutical Regulation, URL: http://www.hks.harvard.edu/inequality/Seminar/Papers/Carpenter.pdf [accessed May 31. 2011]

Carbonell, P., Rodriguez, A. (2006)
The Impact of Market Characteristics and Innovation Speed on Perceptions of Positional Advantage and New Product Performance, in: International Journal of Research in Marketing, Vol. 23; No. 1, pp. 1-12

Carbonell, P., Rodriguez-Escuerdo, A. (2010)
The Effect of Market Orientation on Innovation Speed and New Product Performance, in: Journal of Business & Industrial Marketing, Vol. 25; No. 5, pp. 501-513

Carr, D., Cone, E. (2004)
Merck Seeks A Cure, in: Baseline, No. 31, pp. 38-54

Carroll, J. (2011)
2010: Another blah year at FDA as new drug approvals slip, in: FierceBiotech, URL: http://www.fiercebiotech.com/story/2010-another-blah-year-fda-new-drug-approvals-slip/2011-01-03 [accessed January 14, 2011]

Catalan, V., Le Lorier, J. (2000)
Predictors of long-term persistence on statins in a subsidized clinical population, in: Value in Health, Vol. 3, No. 6, pp. 417-426

Chakravorti, B. (2004)
The New Rules for Bringing Innovations to Market, in: Harvard Business Review, Vol. 82, No.3, pp. 59-67

Chandy, R., Hopstaken, B., Narasimhan, O., Prabhu, J. (2006)
From Invention to Innovation - Conversion Ability in Product Development, in: Journal of Marketing Research, Vol. 42, pp. 494-508

Christopher, M., McDonald, M. (1995)
Marketing – An Introductory Text, London

Center for Drug Evaluation and Research (1998)
The CDER Handbook, FDA, URL: http://www.fda.gov/downloads/AboutFDA/CentersOffices/CDER/UCM198415.pdf [accessed January 13, 2011]

ClinicalTrials.gov (2011)
Chemotherapy and Lapatinib or Trastuzumab, in: Treating Women with HER2 – Neu-Positive Metastatic Breast Cancer,
URL: http://clinicaltrials.gov/ct2/results?term=EGF108919 [accessed January 28, 2011]

Clinton, P., Mozeson, M. (2010)
The Pharm Exec 50, in: Pharmaceutical Executive, Vol. 30, No. 5, pp. 68-80

CMR International (2001)
Profile of Performance: Review Times – Is There Still Room for Improvement?, in: R&D Briefing, No. 31 http://cirsci.org/sites/default/files/RD31Feb01RegRevTimes.pdf [accessed June 14, 2011]

Code of Federal Regulations Title 21, Part 312 (2010)
Subpart E- Drugs Intended to Treat Life-Threatening or Severely-debilitating Illnesses, April 1, 2010, URL: http://www.accessdata.fda.gov/scripts/cdrh/cfdocs/cfcfr/CFRSearch.cfm?CFRPart=312&showFR=1&subpartNode=21:5.0.1.1.3.5 [accessed February 10, 2011]

Code of Federal Regulations Title 21, Part 601 (2010)
Subpart E- Accelerated Approval of Biologic al Products for Serious or Life-Threatening Illnesses, April 1, 2010, URL: http://www.accessdata.fda.gov/scripts/cdrh/cfdocs/cfcfr/cfrsearch.cfm?cfrpart=601&showfr=1&subpartnode=21:7.0.1.1.2.5 [accessed February 10, 2011]

Cohen, F. (2006)
Entry order as a consideration for innovation strategies, in: Nature Reviews Drug Discovery, Vol. 5, No. 4, pp. 285-294

Comiteau, Fahey (1996)
Eli Lilly Ponders Corporate Image, in: Adweek Eastern Edition, Vol. 37, No. 51, p. 2

Commission of the European Communities (2008)
Guideline on aspects of the application of Article 8(2) of Regulation (EC) No. 141/2000: Review of the period of market exclusivity of orphan medicinal products. Brussels 17.9.2008, URL: http://ec.europa.eu/health/files/orphanmp/doc/c_2008_4051_en.pdf [accessed February 7, 2011]

Congress of the Congressional Budget Office (2005)
Prices for Brand-Name Drugs Under Selected Federal Programs,
URL: http://www.cbo.gov/showdoc.cfm?index6481&sequence=0 [accessed July 29, 2011]

Cook, J., Vermon, J., Manning, R. (2008)
Pharmaceutical Risk-Sharing Agreements, in: PharmacoEconomics, Vol. 26, No. 7, pp. 551-555

Cooper, R., Kleinschmidt, E. (1993)
Screening New Products for Potential Winners, in: Long Range Planning, Vol. 26, No. 6, pp. 74-81

Cooper, R., Kleinschmidt, E. (1995)
New Product Performance: Keys to Success, Profitability & Cycle Time Reduction, in: Journal of Marketing Management, Vol. 11, No. 4, pp. 315-337

Council of the European Communities (1993)
Regulation (EEC) No 2309/93 – Council Regulation (EEC) No 2309/93 of 22 July 1993 laying down Community procedures for the authorization and supervision of medicinal products for human and veterinary use and establishing a European Agency for the Evaluation of Medicinal Products, URL: http://ec.europa.eu/health/files/eudralex/vol-1/reg_1993_2309/reg_1993_2309_en.pdf [accessed January 16, 2011]

Corstjens, M., Demeire, E., Horowitz, I. (2005)
New-product Success in the Pharmaceutical Industry. How Many Bites at the Cherry?, in: Economics of Innovation and New Technology, Vol. 14, No.4, pp. 319-331

Cox, W. (1967)
Life Cycles as Marketing Models, in: The Journal of Business, Vol. 40, No. 4, pp. 375-384

Dagher, R., Johnson, J., Williams, G., Keegan, P., Pazdur, R. (2004)
Accelerated Approval of Oncology Products - A Decade of Experience, in: Journal of the National Cancer Institute, Vol. 96, No. 20, pp. 1500-1509

Danzon, P., Epstein, A. (2009)
Effects of Regulation on Drug Launch and Pricing in Interdependent Markets, University of Pennsylvania, Yale University (script provided by authors)

Danzon, P., Wang, R., Wang, L. (2005)
The impact of price regulation on the launch delay of new drugs – evidence from twenty-five major markets in the 1990s, in: Health Economics, Vol. 14, pp. 269-292

Darba, J., Rovira, J. (1998)
Parallel Imports of Pharmaceuticals in the European Union, in: PharmacoEconomics, Vol. 14, Supplement 1, pp. 129-136

Datamonitor (2004)
Gleevac Case Study – The benefits of aggressive pre-launch marketing in an immature market, Reference Code: BPCS15, London

Datamonitor (2004a)
Singulair Case Study – Building a successful launch strategy through clinical differentiation, Reference Code: BPCS04, London

Datamonitor (2004b)
Pfizer Case Study – How Celebrex became class leader within a year of launch, Reference Code: BPCS09, London

Datamonitor (2005)
GlaxoSmithKline Case Study – Launching a follow-up to Zovirax in the herpes antiviral market, Reference Code: BPCS114, London

Datamonitor (2008)
MarketWatch-Pharmaceuticals - Pharmaceutical companies must adapt to changing market dynamics in 2008, May 2008, pp. 24-25

Datamonitor (2008a)
Lyrica Case Study – Building a successful drug launch strategy, Reference Code: BPCS337, London

Datamonitor (2008b)
Combination Products Case Study (Novartis, GSK; Abbott, Merck/Schering/Plough), Reference Code: BPCS303, London

Davenport, T. (2009)
Make Better Decisions, in: Harvard Business Review, Vol. 87, No. 11, pp. 117-123

David, E., Tramontin, T., Zemmel, R. (2009)
Pharmaceutical R&D - the Road to Positive Returns, in: Nature Reviews, Vol. 8, No. 8, pp. 609-610

De Luca, L., Verona, G., Vicari, S. (2010)
Market Orientation and R&D Effectiveness in High-Technology Firms: An Empirical Investigation in the Biotechnology Industry, in: Journal of Product Innovation Management, Vol. 27, No. 3, pp. 299-320

Demeire, E. (2011)
What it takes to get your pharma brand's positioning right!,
URL: http://www.celforpharma.com/pharma-management/knowledge-centre/pearls-of-wisdom/pow-pharma-brands-positioning.html [accessed May 19, 2011]

Di Benedetto, C. (1999)
Identifying the Key Success Factors in New Product Launch, in: Journal of Product Innovation Management, Vol. 16, pp. 530-544

Dietrich, E. (2003)
"Vierte Hürde" im Gesundheitswesen - Auf Kosten und Nutzen geprüft. In: Deutsches Ärzteblatt, Vol. 100, No. 9 URL: http://www.aerzteblatt.de/v4/archiv/artikeldruck.asp?id=35775 [accessed January 27, 2011]

DiMasi, J. (1995)
Success rates for new drugs entering clinical testing in the United States, in: Clinical Pharmacology & Therapeutics, Vol. 58, No. 1, pp. 1-14

DiMasi, J. (2001)
Risks in new drug development - Approval success rates for investigational drugs, in: Clinical Pharmacology & Therapeutics, Vol. 69, No. 5, pp. 297-307

DiMasi, J., Grabowski, H. (2007)
Economies of New Oncology Drug Development, in: Journal of Clinical Medicine, Vol. 25, No. 2, pp. 209-216

DiMasi, J., Parquette, C. (2004)
The Economics of Follow-on Drug Research and Development - Trends in Entry Rates and Timing of Development, in: PharmacoEconomics, Vol. 22, Supplement 2, pp. 1-14

Dobni, D., Zinkhan, G. (1990)
In Search of Brand Image - A Foundation Analysis, in: Advances in Consumer Research, Vol. 17, pp. 110-119

DocMorris (2011)
URL: http:// http://www.docmorris.de/ [accessed November 14, 2011]

Donahue, J., Cevasco, M., Rosenthal, M. (2007)
A Decade of Direct-to-Consumer Advertising of Prescription Drugs, in: New England Journal of Medicine, Vol. 357, pp. 673-681

Dooren, J. (2010)
Drug Approvals Slipped in 2010 – Some potential blockbusters suffered delays amid FDA's tougher safety stance, in: The Wall Street Journal, December 31, 2010, URL: http://online.wsj.com/article/ SB10001424052748704543004576052170335871018.html [accessed January 14, 2011]

Drugs.com (2011)
Bextra, URL: http://www.drugs.com/bextra.html, [accessed October 27, 2011]

Drugs.com (2011a)
Celebrex, URL: http://www.drugs.com/celebrex.html, [accessed June 14, 2011]

Dubey, R., Dubey, J. (2009)
Pharmaceutical product differentiation - A strategy for strengthening product pipeline and life cycle management, in: Journal of Medical Marketing, Vol. 9, No. 2, pp. 104-118

Dyckerhoff, G., Weber, B. (1989)
Wachstum durch Internationale Joint Ventures, in: Simon, H., Kucher, E., Hilleke-Daniel, K. (ed.): Wettbewerbsstrategien im Pharmamarkt, Stuttgart, pp. 177-185

Eleveld, J., Chui, M. (2010)
Markteinführung in China - So gelingt ein Blockbuster, IMS Health, URL: http://www.presseportal.ch/de/pm/100018940/100607182/ims_ health_gmbh [accessed February 14, 2011]

Eli Lilly Press Release (2002)
Lilly Given OK to Make Alimta Available on Expanded Access Basis,
URL: http://www.stayinvest.com/stayinvestcom/
Mesothelioma/alimta-compassionate.htm [accessed March 9, 2011]

Emerton, D. (2006)
Patent expiries in the US statin market - Generics to slash market size by 80 per cent over the next ten years, in: Journal of Generic Medicines, Vol. 4, No. 1, pp. 73-78

Enbrel Website (2011)
URL: http://www.enbrel.com/index.jspx [accessed November 9, 2011]

Erbe, B., Lauer, C., Lange, S. (2009)
Compliance Assistenten im Gesundheitswesen – Therapietreue von Patienten verbessern, in: Amelung, V., Sydow, J., Windeler, A. (ed.): Vernetzung im Gesundheitswesen – Wettbewerb und Kooperationen, Stuttgart

Ernst, H. (2002)
Success Factors of New Product Development - A Review of the Empirical Literature, in: International Journal of Management Reviews, Vol. 4, No. 1, pp. 1-40

Ernst, H. (2007)
Management der Neuproduktentwicklung, in: Albers. S., Herrmann, A. (ed.): Handbuch Produktmanagement – Strategieentwicklung, Produktplanung, Organisation, Kontrolle, 3rd revised and updated edition, Wiesbaden

Ernst, H., Hoyer, W., Rübsaamen, C. (2010)
Sales, Marketing, and Research-and-Development Cooperation Across New Product Development Stages: Implications for Success, in: Journal of Marketing, Vol. 74, No. 5, pp. 82-90

Ernst & Young (2005)
Beyond Borders – The Global Biotechnology Report 2005

European Medicines Agency (EMA) (2005)
Guideline on Similar Biological Medicinal Products,
URL: http://www.ema.europa.eu/docs/en_GB/document_library/
Scientific_guideline/2009/09/WC500003517.pdf [accessed January 12, 2011]

European Medicines Agency (EMA) (2007)
Guideline on the Acceptability of Names for Human Medicinal Products processed Through the Centralised Procedure, CMPM/328/98, Revision 5,
URL: http://www.ema.europa.eu/docs/en_GB/document_library/
Regulatory_and_procedural_guideline/2009/10/WC500004142.pdf [accessed February 1, 2011)

European Medicines Agency (EMA) (2007a)
Guideline on Compassionate Use of Medicinal Products, Pursuant to Article 83 of Regulation (EC) No 726/20004, EMEA/27170/2006,
URL: http://www.ema.europa.eu/docs/en_GB/document_library/
Regulatory_and_procedural_guideline/2009/10/WC500004075.pdf [accessed February 1, 2011]

European Medicines Agency (EMA) (2007b)
Guideline of Compassionate Use of Medicinal Products, Pursuant to Article 83 of Regulation (EC) No 726/2004, 19 July 2007,
URL: http://www.ema.europa.eu/docs/en_GB/document_library/
Regulatory_and_procedural_guideline/2009/10/WC500004075.pdf [accessed February 7, 2011]

European Medicines Agency (EMA) (2011)
Pharmaceuticals in the European Union, URL: http://ec.europa.eu/
enter-
prise/newsroom/cf/document.cfm?action=display&doc_id=1684&userservice_id=1&requ
est [accessed January 14, 2011]

European Medicines Agency (EMA) (2011a)
Orphan designation, URL: http://www.ema.europa.eu/ema/index.
jsp?curl=pages/regulation/general/general_content_000029.jsp&murl=menus/regulations/
regulations.jsp&mid=WC0b01ac05800240ce&jsenabled=true [accessed February 1, 2011]

European Parliament (2004)
Regulation (EC) No726/2004 of the European Parliament and of the Council of 31 March 2004, URL: http://ec.europa.eu/health/files/
eudralex/vol-1/reg_2004_726_cons/reg_2004_726_cons_en.pdf [accessed January 12, 2011]

EvaluatePharma (2011)
World Preview 2016, URL: http://www.evaluatepharma.com/
EvaluatePharma_World_Preview_2016.aspx [accessed June 5, 2011]

Falk, K. (2005)
Erfolgsfaktoren für das Management einer Produktneueinführung in Europa, in: Müller, M. (ed.): Europäisches Pharmamarketing - Ein Leitfaden für Manager der pharmazeutischen Industrie und Beteiligte des europäischen Gesundheitswesens. Wiesbaden

Favole, J., Mundy, A. (2008)
U.S. Drug Ban Hits Ranbaxy - Indian Maker of Generics,
URL: http://online.wsj.com/article/SB122158892271844021.html [accessed May 20, 2011]

Few, S. (2006)
Information Dashboard Design - The Effective Visual Communication of Data, Sebastopol, CA

Fischer, D., Breitenbach, J. (2010a)
Wandel und Herausforderung – die pharmazeutische Industrie, in: Fischer, D., Breitenbach, J. (ed.): Die Pharmaindustrie. Einblick – Durchblick – Perspektiven, 3rd edition, München, pp. 1-45

Fischer, D., Breitenbach, J. (2010b)
Pharma-Marketing. Sozioökonomische Trends bestimmen die Zukunft, in: Fischer, D., Breitenbach, J. (ed.): Die Pharmaindustrie. Einblick – Durchblick – Perspektiven, 3rd edition, München, pp. 259-279

Fischer, D., Breitenbach, J. (2010c)
Quo vadis? Versuch eines Ausblicks, in: Fischer, D., Breitenbach, J. (ed.): Die Pharmaindustrie. Einblick – Durchblick – Perspektiven, 3rd edition, München, pp. 281-314

Fischer, D., Breitenbach, J. (ed.) (2010d): Die Pharmaindustrie. Einblick – Durchblick – Perspektiven, 3rd edition, München

Foldes, G. (2010)
New Product Forecasting in the Pharmaceutical Industry, in: Journal of Business Forecasting and Marketing Intelligence, Vol.29, No.4, pp. 4-11

Food and Drug Administration (FDA) (2003)
Briefing Document on Safety (BLA STN 1030976/0) for Omalizumab (Xolair), April 18, 2003, URL: http://www.fda.gov/ohrms/dockets/ac/03/briefing/3952B1_02_FDA-Xolair-Safety.pdf [accessed January 28, 2011]

Food and Drug Administration (FDA) (2007)
PDA Proposed to Strengthen Label Warming for Xolair, URL: http://www.fda.gov/NewsEvents/Newsroom/Press Announcements/2007/ucm108850.htm [accessed January 12, 2011]

Food and Drug Administration (FDA) (2009a)
Expanded Access and Expedited Approval of New Therapies Related to HIV / AIDS, URL: http://www.fda.gov/ForConsumers/ByAudience/ForPatientAdvocates/HIVandAIDSActivities/ucm134331.htm [accessed February 7, 2011]

Food and Drug Administration (FDA) (2010)
Guidance for Industry – Contents of a Complete Submission for the Evaluation of Proprietary Names, February 2010, URL: http://www.fda.gov/downloads/Drugs/GuidanceComplianceRegulatoryInformation/Guidances/ucm075068.pdf [accessed February 1, 2011]

Food and Drug Administration (FDA) (2010a)
Fast Track, Accelerated Approval and Priority Review, URL: http://www.fda.gov/forconsumers/byaudience/forpatientadvocates/speedingaccesstoimportantnewtherapies/ucm128291.htm#accelerated [accessed February 1, 2011]

Food and Drug Administration (FDA) (2010b)
The FDA's Drug Review Process - Ensuring Drugs Are Safe and Effective,
URL: http://www.fda.gov/Drugs/ResourcesForYou/
Consumers/ucm143534.htm [accessed May 25, 2011]

Food and Drug Administration Website (FDA) (2011),
URL: http://www.fda.gov/ [accessed June 14, 2011]

Fraenkel, S. (2008)
A Proposed Model for Key Success Factors for Sales Force Management Strategy During the Launch of Pharmaceutical Products in Sweden, in: Society for Marketing Advances Proceedings, pp. 250-253

Freeman, R. (1984)
Strategic Management: A Stakeholder Approach. Boston

Fricke, F.-U. (2008)
Steuerungsinstrumente in der Arzneimittelversorgung, in: Schöffski, O., Fricke, F., Guminski, W. (ed.): Pharmabetriebslehre, 2nd, fully revised and expanded edition, Heidelberg, pp. 47-72

Gagnon, M.-A., Lexchin, J. (2008)
The Cost of Pushing Pills - A New Estimate of Pharmaceutical Promotion Expenditures in the United States, in: PLoS Medicine, Vol. 5, No. 1, pp. 29-33

Gal, A.; Chou, T. ; Chari, N. (2008)
Evaluating the Patent Risk of Specialty Pharmaceutical Companies, in: Black Book – Small Cap Strategy, pp. 111-117

Gaston-Breton, C., Martin, O. (2011)
International Market Selection and Segmentation: A Two-Stage Model, in: International Market Review, Vol. 28, No. 3, pp. 267-290

Gilbert, J., Henske, P., Singh, A. (2003)
Rebuilding Big Pharma's Business Model, in: In Vivo – The Business & Medicine Report, Vol. 21, No.10, also available at URL: http://www.bain.com/
bainweb/PDFs/cms/Marketing/rebuilding_big_pharma.pdf [accessed February 24, 2011]

Glaeske, G., Klauber, J., Lankers, C., Selke, G. (2003)
Stärkung des Wettbewerbs der Arzneimittelversorgung zur Steigerung von Konsumentennutzen, Effizienz und Qualität,
URL: http://www.gesundheitspolitik.net/01_gesundheitssystem/reformkonzepte/arzneimittelversorgung/Gutachten-BMGS-kurz_20030416.pdf [accessed January 27, 2011]

Global Insight (2008)
NICE Endorses Pioneering Lucentis Reimbursement Scheme - Rejects Macugen in Wet AMD, URL: http://www.globalinsight.com/SDA/
SDADetail12103.htm [accessed June 18, 2010]

Golder, P. (2000)
Insights from Senior Executives about Innovation in International Markets, in: Journal of Product Innovation Management, Vol. 17, No. 5, pp. 326-340

Grabowski, H. (1989)
An Analysis of US International Competitiveness in Pharmaceuticals, in: Managerial and Decision Economics, Vol. 10, pp. 27-33

Grabowski, H. (2002)
Patents, Innovation and Access to New Pharmaceuticals, Duke University July 2002, URL: http://levine.sscnet.ucla.edu/archive/ grabow-patents_innov.pdf [accessed March 3, 2011]

Grabowski, H. (2005)
Increasing R&D Incentives for neglected diseases - Lessons from the Orphan Drug Act, in: Maskus, K, Reichman, J. (ed.): International Public Goods and Transfer of Technology under a Globalized Intellectual Property Regime, Cambridge, pp. 457-480

Grabowski, H., Vernon, J., DiMasi J. (2002)
Returns on Research and Development for 1990s New Drug Introductions, in: Pharmaco-Economics, Vol. 20, No.3, pp. 11-29

Grabowski, H., Wang, R. (2006)
The Quantity and Quality of Worldwide New Drug Introductions 1982-2003, in: Health Affairs, Vol. 25, No. 2, pp. 452-460

Green, P., Krieger, A. (1991)
Segmenting Markets with Conjoint Analysis, in: Journal of Marketing, Vol. 55, No. 4, pp. 20-31

Green, P., Krieger, A. (1992)
An Application of a Product Positioning Model to Pharmaceutical Products, in: Marketing Science, Vol. 11, No. 2, pp. 117-132

Gudiksen, M., Fleming, E., Furstenthal, L., Ma, P. (2008)
What Drives Success for Specialty Pharmaceuticals?, in: Nature Reviews, Vol. 7, No.7, pp. 563-567

Günzel, P., Bass, R. (1991)
Considerations Regarding the Development of Individual Non-Clinical Test Strategies in the European Community, in: Human & Experimental Toxicology, Vol. 10, No. 5, pp. 297-304

Hackett, J. (2007)
Preparing for the Perfect Product Launch, in: Harvard Business Review, Vol.85, No.4, pp. 45-50

Haffner, M. (2006)
Adopting Orphan Drugs – Two Dozen Years of Treating Rare Diseses, in: New England Journal of Medicine, Vol. 354, pp. 445-447

Harms, F., Drüner, M. (2003)
Pharma-Marketing - Innovationsmanagement im 21. Jahrhundert, Stuttgart

Hart, S., Hultink, E., Tzokas, N., Commandeur, H. (2003)
Industrial Companies' Evaluation Criteria in New Produce Development Gates, in: Journal of Product Innovation Management, Vol. 20, No. 1, pp. 22-36

Hartmann, V., Skubch, N., Moll, T., Fleischer-Hehn, J. (2009)
Launch Readiness Check – ein Instrument für das Projektmanagement globaler Produkteinführungen, in: Pharmind - die pharmazeutische industrie, Vol. 71, No. 7, pp. 1106-1110

Hauser, J., Tellis, G., Griffin, A. (2006)
Research on Innovation: A Review and Agenda for Marketing Science, in: Marketing Science, Vol. 25, No. 6, pp. 687-717

Healy, E., Kaitin, K. (1999)
The European Agency for the Evaluation of Medicinal Products' Centralized Procedure for Product Approvals - Current Status, in: Drug Information Journal, Vol. 33, pp. 969-978

Heavner, B., Harlan, S. (2010)
New Guide for the Journey to Drug Name Approval,
URL: http://www.dddmag.com/news-A-New-Guide-for-the-Journey-to-Drug-Name-Approval-101810.aspx [accessed February 1, 2011]

Hemp, P. (2004)
A Time for Growth – An Interview with Amgen CEO Kevin Sharer, Harvard Business Review, Vol.82, No.7, pp. 67-74

Henard, D., Szymanski, D. (2001)
Why Some New Products Are More Successful Than Others, in: Journal of Marketing Research, Vol. 38, pp-362-375

Henderson, B. (1994)
Die wirklichen Ziele, in: Oetinger, B. von (ed.): Das Boston Consulting Group Strategie-Buch, Düsseldorf

Hepsera Website (2011)
URL: http://www.hepsera.com/ [accessed November 9, 2011]

Herceptin Development Timeline (2011)
URL: http://www.gene.com/gene/products/information/oncology/herceptin/timeline.html [accessed June 18, 2011]

Hermannson, S. (2005)
Großbritannien – Evidenz basierte Medizin setzt sich durch, in: Müller, M. (ed.): Europäisches Pharmamarketing – Ein Leitfaden für Manager der pharmazeutischen Industrie und Beteiligte des europäischen Gesundheitswesens, Wiesbaden, pp. 133-147

Hilleke-Daniel, K. (1989)
Wettbewerbsdynamik und Konkurrenzanalyse im Pharmamarkt, in: Simon, H., Kucher,E., Hilleke-Daniel, K. (ed.): Wettbewerbsstrategien im Pharmamarkt, Stuttgart, pp. 16-28

Honig, P. (2011)
Comparative Effectiveness - The Fourth Hurdle in Drug Development and a Role for Clinical Pharmacology, in: Clinical Pharmacology & Therapeutics, Vol. 89, No. 2, pp. 151-156

Hoyle, M. (2008)
Future Drug Prices and Cost-Effectiveness Analyses, in: PharmacoEconomics, Vol. 26, No. 7, pp. 589-602

Hradecky, G. (1999)
Trend - Shift in Marketing, in: Pharmaceutical Representative, Vol.29, No. 1, also available at URL: http://pharmrep. findpharma.com/pharmrep/Trend-shift-in-marketing/articlestandard/article/detail/112994?searchstring=shiftinmarketing [accessed June 9, 2011]

Hull, B., Ramakrishan, V. (2006)
Maximising Market Research Data for Early-Stage Product Development, in: Product Management Today
URL: http://www.gfk.com/imperia/md/content/gfkv2/product_management_today_-_april__2006.pdf [accessed January 31, 2011]

Hultink, E., Atuahene-Gima, K. (2000)
The Effect of Sales Force Adoption on New Product Selling Performance, in: Journal of Product Innovation Management, Vol. 17, No. 6, pp. 453-450

Hultink, E., Griffin, A., Hart, S., Robben, H. (1997)
Industrial New Product Launch Strategies and Product Development Performance, in: Journal of Product Innovation Management, Vol. 14, No. 4, pp. 243-257

Hultink, E., Robben, H. (1999)
Launch strategy and new product performance - An empirical examination in The Netherlands, in: Journal of Product Innovation Management, Vol. 16, No. 6, pp. 545-556

Human and Health Services (2011)
Compliance Guidance, URL: http://oig.hhs.gov/compliance/ compliance-guidance/index.asp [accessed June 5, 2011]

Humira Website (2011)
URL: http://www.humira.com/ [accessed November, 14, 2011]

IBM Global Business Services (2006)
The Perfect Product Launch

Iizuka, T. (2007)
Experts' agency problems - Evidence from the prescription drug market in Japan, in: RAND Journal of Economics, Vol. 38, No. 3, pp. 844-862

Illert, G., Betz, G., Schlumberger, C. (2007)
Striving for Product Launch Excellence, URL: http://www.capgemini.com/insights-and-resources/by-publication/striving_for_product_launch_excellence/ [accessed November 3, 2011]

Jack, A. (2008)
GSK Varies Price to Raise Sales, in: Financial Times Online, URL: http://www.ft.com/cms/s/4dc2b3bc-f380-11dc-b6bc-0000779fd2ac,dwp_uuid=d7e814a8-3012-11da-ba9f-00000e2511c8,print=yes.html [accessed March 3, 2011]

Jørgensen, J. (2008)
From blockbuster medicine to personalized medicine, in: Future Medicine, Vol. 5, No. 1, pp. 55-63

Johne, F.; Snelson, P. (1988)
Success Factors in Product Innovation: A Selective Review of the Literature, in: Journal of Product Innovation Management, Vol. 5, No. 2, pp. 114-128

Karakaya, F, Yannopoulos, P. (2011)
Market Entrant Characteristics and Incumbent Reactions to Market Entry, Vol. 19, No. 2, pp. 171-185

Karst, K. (2011)
Orphan Drug Designations and Applications Took Off in 2010 While Orphan Drug Approvals Tapered Off, FDA Law Blog Hyman, Phelps & McNamara, URL: http://www.fdalawblog.net/fda_law_blog_hyman_phelps/orphan-drugs/ [accessed February 10, 2011]

Kavanaugh, S. (2008)
Product Launch. Take five steps to succeed, in: Sales & Service Excellence, Vol. 8, No. 12, p. 8

Kelly, D., Garcia, M. (2009)
Resisting persuasion - Building defenses against competitors' persuasive attacks in the context of war-gaming methodology, in: Journal of Medical Marketing, Vol. 9, No. 2, pp. 83-88

Kelly, D., Gibbons, M. (2008)
Market Analysis. Marketing Methodologies. Ethnography - The good, the bad and the ugly, in: Journal of Medical Marketing, Vol. 8, No. 4, pp. 279-285

Kelly, D., Liftin, A., Vaughn, S. (2009)
6 Steps to a Dynamic Message, in: Medical Marketing & Media, Vol. 44, No. 3, URL: http://www.gfk.com/imperia/md/content/gfkv2/mmm_6_steps_to_messaging_03-09.pdf [accessed January 31. 2011]

Kelly, D., Rupert, E. (2009)
Professional emotions and persuasion - Tapping non-rational drivers in health-care market research, in: Journal of Medical Marketing, Vol. 9, No. 1, pp. 3-9

Kesic, D., Bertoncelj, A. (2008)
Importance of Marketing Management in the World Pharmaceutical Industry, in: Trziste / Market, Vol. 20, No. 1, pp. 79-93

Kotzian, P. (2004)
Pharmaceutical R&D in the Setting of Incomplete European Integration, in: International Journal of Economics of Business, Vol. 11, No. 2, pp. 175-195

Khurana, A.; Rosenthal, S. R. (1998): Towards Holistic "Front Ends", in: New Product Development; The Journal of Product Innovation Management 15; 1: 57-74

Kiskalt, U. (2010)
Konzert der Vielfalt – Projektmanagement, in: Fischer, D., Breitenbach, J. (ed.): Die Pharmaindustrie. Einblick – Durchblick – Perspektiven, 3rd edition, München, pp. 197-215

Knoke, C. (2008)
Marketing aus betriebswirtschaftlicher Sicht – wichtige Aspekte, in: Trilling, T. (ed.): Pharmamarketing – Ein Leitfaden für die tägliche Praxis, 2nd, revised edition, Berlin, Heidelberg, pp. 1-46

Köstlin, U. (2005)
Möglichkeiten für eine europäische Preisstrategie und deren Anforderungen, in: Müller, M. (ed.): Europäisches Pharmamarketing – Ein Leitfaden für Manager der pharmazeutischen Industrie und Beteiligte des europäischen Gesundheitswesens, Wiesbaden, pp. 225-242

Kotler, P. (1972)
Marketing Management - Analysis, Planning, and Control, 2nd edition, London

Kotler, P., Armstrong, G. (1989)
Principles of Marketing, 4th edition, London

Kucher, E. (1989)
Pharma-Preismanagement für Innovationen, in: Simon, H., Kucher, E., Hilleke-Daniel, K. (ed.): Wettbewerbsstrategien im Pharmamarkt, Stuttgart, pp. 102-123

Kucher, E., Hilleke, K. (1993)
Value Pricing through Conjoint Measurement - A Practical Approach, in: European Management Journal, Vol. 11, No. 3, pp. 283-290

Kucher, E., Janssen, V. (2004)
Strategies for success, in: Scrip Magazine, No.4, also available at: http://www.simon-ku-cher.com/PROJEKTE/Publication.nsf/233a7777fcff90dbc1256f70005c3ba3/cbbb45dde22fc6f0c1256e8200454e0d/$FILE/Scrip_Strategies%20for%20success_04-2004.pdf [accessed June 14, 2011]

Kuhn, J. (2007)
Markteinführung neuer Produkte, first edition, Wiesbaden

Kyle, M. (2006)
The Role of Firm Characteristics in Pharmaceutical Product Launches, in: The RAND Journal of Economics, Vol. 37, No. 3, pp. 602-618

Kyle, M. (2007)
Pharmaceutical Price Controls and Entry Strategies, in: The Review of Economics and Statistics, Vol. 89, No. 1, pp. 88-99

Lach, C. (2001)
Gestaltungsempfehlungen zur Einführung komplexer Neuprodukte, Aachen

Lai, C., Gane, E., Liaw, Y., Hsu. C., Thongsawat, S., Want, Y., Chen, Y., Heathcote, E., Rasenack, J., Bzowej, N., Naoumov, N., Di Disceglie, A., Zeuzem, S., Moon, Y., Goodman, Z., Chao, G., Constance, B., Brown, N. (2007)
Telbivudine versus Lamivudine in Patients with Chronic Hepatitis B, in: New England Journal of Medicine, Vol. 357, No. 25, pp. 2576-2588

Lam, P., Chin, K. (2005)
Identifying and Prioritizing Critical Success Factors for Conflict Management in Collaborative New Product Development, in: Industrial Marketing Management, Vol. 34, No. 8, pp. 761-772

Langerak, F., Hultink, E., Robben, H. (2004)
The Impact of Market Orientation, Product Advantage, and Launch Proficiency on New Product Performance and Organizational Performance, in: Journal of Product Innovation Management, Vol. 21, pp. 74-94

Lanjouw, J. (2005)
Patents, Price Controls and Access to New Drugs - How Policy Affects Global Market Entry, Center for Global Development, Working Paper Number 61, URL: http://www.nber.org/papers/w11321.pdf [accessed June 14, 2011]

Larkin, C. (2010)
New Drug Approvals Fall in 2010 as Safety Concerns Slow U.S. FDA Decisions, in: Bloomberg Online, URL: http://www.bloomberg.com/news/2010-12-30/new-drug-approvals-fell-in-2010-as-safety-concerns-slow-u-s-fda-decisions.html [accessed January 14, 2011]

Law, J. (2010)
Blockbusters – Alive and well, Jacky Laws reports that news of the blockbuster's death has been greatly exaggerated. But it may no longer be the preserve of Big Pharma, in: Pharmaceutical Executive. Blockbusters, Vol. 30, No.5, also available at http://digital.findpharma.com/nxtbooks/advanstaruk/pee_digest_20100526/#/4 [accessed June 16, 2011]

Law, M., Majumdar, S., Soumerai, S. (2008)
Effect of illicit direct to consumer advertising on use of etanercept, momentasone, and tegaserod in Canada - A controlled longitudinal study, in: British Medical Journal, Vol. 337, also available at http://www10.gencat.net/catsalut/rsb/farmacia/efarma/arxius/efectes_transfronterers.pdf [accessed June 14, 2011]

Leslie, M., Holloway, C. (2006)
The Sales Learning Curve, in: Harvard Business Review, Vol.84, No.7, pp. 115-123

Lichtenberg, F. (2005)
The Impact of New Drug Launches on Longevity - Evidence from Longitudinal - Disease-level Data from 52 Countries 1982-2001, in: International Journal of Health Care Finance and Economics, Vol. 5, pp. 47-73

Light, D. (2007)
Misleading Congress about Drug Development, in: Journal of Health Politics, Policy and Law, Vol. 32, No. 5, pp. 895-913

Lin, C.; Chen, C. (2004)
New Product Go/No-Go Evaluation at the Front End: A Fuzzy Linguistic Approach, in: IEEE Transactions on Engineering Management, Vol. 51, No. 2, pp. 197-207

Mahlich, J. (2007)
The Japanese Pharmaceutical Industry in Transition - Has Higher Research Value Orientation Resulted in Higher Market Value?, in: Asian Business & Management, Vol. 6, pp. 75-94

Maskus, K, Reichman, J. (ed.) (2005)
International Public Goods and Transfer of Technology under a Globalized Intellectual Property Regime, Cambridge

McCarthy, J. (1964)
Basic Marketing - A Managerial Approach, Homewood

McGuire, S. (2007)
IMS Reveals How to Avoid Common Launch Miscues, in: Medical Marketing & Media, July issue, p. 26

Medco Health Solutions (2005)
New study finds lack of medication compliance leads to high medical costs, URL: http://www.redorbit.com/news/health/154583/new_study_finds_lack_of_medication_compliance_leads_to_high/index.html [accessed January 31, 2011]

MedTRACK (2011)
http://www.medtrack.com/research/Istats.asp#list3 [accessed November 8, 2011]

Milne, C.-P., Bergman, E. (2001)
Fast Track Product Designation under the Food and Drug Administration Modernization Act - The Industry Experience, in: Drug Information Journal, Vol. 35, pp. 71-83

Mirasol, F. (2008)
Pharma taps biologics, ICIS.com, URL: http://www.icis.com/Articles/2008/09/29/9158479/pharma-firms-bolster-pipelines-with-biologics.html [accessed May 20, 2010]

Müller, M. (2005)
Europa im Überblick, in: Müller, M. (ed.): Europäisches Pharmamarketing – Ein Leitfaden für Manager der pharmazeutischen Industrie und Beteiligte des europäischen Gesundheitswesens, Wiesbaden, pp. 17-29

Müller, M. (2005a)
Anforderungen an ein zentrales, europäisches Pharmamarketing, in: Müller, M. (ed.): Europäisches Pharmamarketing – Ein Leitfaden für Manager der pharmazeutischen Industrie und Beteiligte des europäischen Gesundheitswesens, Wiesbaden, pp. 149-166

Müller, M. (2005b)
Außendienststruktur abhängig von Portfolio, Produkt-Lebenszyklus und Markt, in: Müller, M. (ed.): Europäisches Pharmamarketing – Ein Leitfaden für Manager der pharmazeutischen Industrie und Beteiligte des europäischen Gesundheitswesens, Wiesbaden, pp. 209-223

Müller, M. (ed.) (2005c): Europäisches Pharmamarketing – Ein Leitfaden für Manager der pharmazeutischen Industrie und Beteiligte des europäischen Gesundheitswesens, Wiesbaden

Myers, R. (2009)
RACI Matrix, URL: http://www.articlesbase.com/management-articles/raci-matrix-1447548.html [accessed February 14, 2011]

Naderer, G., Balzer, E. (ed.) (2007)
Qualitative Marktforschung in Theorie und Praxis, Wiesbaden
National Cancer Institute (2001)
FDA Approves Important New Leukemia Drug,
URL: http://www.cancer.gov/newscenter/pressreleases/2001/Gleevec/Glivecpressrelease [accessed May 18, 2011]

National Cancer Institute (2011)
Chemotherapy and Lapatinib or Trastuzumab in Treating Women With HER2/neu-Positive Metastatic Breast Cancer,
URL: http://www.cancer.gov/search/viewclinicaltrials.aspx?cdrid=594764&version=healthprofessional&print=1 [accessed January 28, 2011]

National Institute for Clinical Excellence (NICE) (2003)
Guidance on the use of imatinib for chronic myeloid leukaemia, URL: http://www.nice.org.uk/nicemedia/live/11516/32754/32754.pdf [accessed May 18, 2011]

N.a. (1992)
New Product Development Research Factors Differentiating Studies into NPD, in: European Journal of Marketing, Vol. 26, No. 11, pp. 6-12

N.a. (2005)
Herceptin and Early Breast Cancer. A Moment for Caution, in: The Lancet, Vol. 366, p. 1673

Ng, R. (2004)
Drugs - From Discovery to Approval, Hoboken, NJ

Oetinger, B. von (ed.) (1994)
Das Boston Consulting Group Strategie-Buch, Düsseldorf,

Official Journal of the European Communities (2000)
Regulation (EC) No 141/2000 of the European Parliament and of the Council of 16 December 1999 on Orphan Medicinal Products,
URL: http://ec.europa.eu/health/files/eudralex/vol-1/reg_2000_141/reg_2000_141_en.pdf [accessed February 1, 2011]

Official Journal of the European Union (2006)
Commission Regulation (EC) No 507/2006 of 29 March 2006 on the conditional marketing authorisation for medicinal products for human use falling within the scope of Regulation (EC) No 726/2004 of the European Parliament and of the Council,
URL: http://ec.europa.eu/health/files/eudralex/vol-1/reg_2006_507/reg_2006_507_en.pdf [accessed February 1, 2011]

Orphanet Report Series (2011)
Lists of Orphan Drugs in Europe,January 2011,
URL: http://www.orpha.net/orphacom/cahiers/docs/GB/list_of_orphan_drugs_in_europe.pdf [accessed February10, 2011]

Ortwein, I. (2001)
Das Arzneimittel - Eine Einführung in die Entwicklung, Herstellung und Vertrieb, 4th edition, Aulendorf

Pettypiece, S., Alesci, C. (2009)
Pfizer May Fire 2,400, One-Third of US Sales Force, Bloomberg Online, January 15, 2009. URL: http://www.bloomberg.com/apps/news?pid=newsarchive&sid=agblRsSlsicY [accessed February 23, 2011]

Pfister, G. (2010)
Hervorragende Markteinführung - Härtere Zeiten Erfordern Weltweit Neue Prioritäten, IMS Health, Intelligence. Applied, URL: http://www.imshealth.ch/Uploads/N381.pdf [accessed January 31, 2011]

Pfizer (2011)
Celebrex Website, URL: http://www.celebrex.com [accessed October 27, 2010]

PhRMA Website (2011)
URL: http://www.phrma.org/ [accessed October 20, 2011]

Pines, N. (2008)
Standard and Innovative Methods for Tracking Pharmaceutical Brand Performance, in: Topline – News & Views on Pharmaceutical Market Research. URL: http://gfk-pipeline.com/pipeline/2008/may/
topline_05_08_tracking.html [accessed October 22, 2011]

Pisano, G. (2006)
Can Science be a Business? Lessons from Biotech, in: Harvard Business Review, Vol. 84; No.10, pp. 114-125

Pleschak, F., Sabisch, H. (1996)
Innovationsmanagement, Stuttgart

Pollack, A. (2007)
Pricing Pills by the Results, The New York Times,
URL: http://www.nytimes.com/2007/07/14/business/14drugprice.html?scp=1&sq=pollack+pricing+pills&st=nyt [accessed June 18, 2010]

Porter, M. (2008)
The Five Competitive Forces That Shape Strategy, in: Harvard Business Review, Vol. 86, No.1, also available at http://www.asec-sldi.org/dotAsset/292822.pdf [accessed June 22, 2011]

Pray, L. (2008)
Gleevec/Glivec - the Breakthrough Cancer Treatment, in: Nature Education, Vol. 1, No. 1, URL: http://www.nature.com/scitable/
topicpage/Gleevec/Glivec-the-breakthrough-in-cancer-treatment-565 [accessed May 18, 2011]

PriceWaterhouseCoopers (2008)
Pharma 2020 - The Vision, URL: http://www.pwc.com/extweb/
pwcpublications.nsf/docid/91BF330647FFA402852572F2005ECC22 [accessed July 7, 2011]

PriceWaterhouseCoopers (2009)
Pharma 2020 - Marketing the future, URL: http://www.pwc.com/
pharma [accessed March 6, 2011]

PriceWaterhouseCoopers (2010)
Pharma 2020 - Taxing times ahead, URL: http://www.pwc.com/pharma [accessed February 12, 2011]

Prounis, C. (2007)
Positive Positioning - 10 Steps to Achieving Standout, in: Medical Marketing & Media, Vol. 7, No. 2, pp. 55-61

Rademacher, U. (2010)
Pharmamarktforschung - Der mündige Patient – Herausforderung für Ärzte und Markforscher?, in: Planung & Analyse, Vol. 3, p. 16

Raje, N., Anderson, K. (1999)
Thalidomide – A Revival Story, in: The New England Journal of Medicine, Vol. 341, No. 21, pp. 1606-1609

Rao, S. (2008)
Market Access – An innovative approach to developing and managing biopharmaceutical pricing strategy, in: Journal of Medical Marketing, Vol. 8, No. 2, pp. 94-100

Raptiva Website (2011)
URL: http://www.raptiva.com [accessed November 9, 2011]

Riedl, P. (2010)
Intellectual Property – Patente und Marken, in: Fischer, D., Breitenbach, J. (ed.): Die Pharmaindustrie. Einblick – Durchblick – Perspektiven, 3rd edition, München, pp. 217-241

Riemenschneider, F., Sprandel, U. (2007)
Zukunftsorientiertes Pharma-Marketing – Ansätze zur erfolgreichen Optimierung, in: Fischer, D., Breitenbach, J. (ed.): Die Pharmaindustrie. Einblick – Durchblick – Perspektiven, 2nd edition, München, pp. 153-169

Ries, A., Trout, J. (2001)
Positioning - The Battle for Your Mind, New York

Ringler, J. (2010)
2010 - A Year of Big Layoffs for Big Pharma, Pharm Exec Blog, URL: http://blog.pharmexec.com/2010/10/19/2010-a-year-of-big-layoffs-for-big-pharma/ [accessed February 23, 2011]

Roberts, R., Lynch, T., Chabner, B. (2003)
The Phase III Trial in the Era of Targeted Therapy - Unraveling the “Go or No Go” Decision, in: Journal of Clinical Oncology, Vol 21, No 19, pp. 3683-3695

Robinson, J. (2003)
Changing the Face of Detailing by Motivating Physicians to See Pharmaceutical Sales Representatives, in: Product Management Today, Vol. 13, No.11, pp. 24-27

Robinson, R. (2010)
Nichebusters vs. Blockbusters, in: PharmaVoice.com,
URL: http://www.pharmavoice.com/archives/article.esiml?id=2087 [accessed June 14, 2011]

Rodriguez-Pinto, J., Rodriguez-Escudero, S., Gutierrez-Cillan, J. (2008)
Order, Positioning, Scope and Outcomes of Market Entry, in: Industrial Marketing Management, Vol.37, No.2, pp. 154-166

Rogers, E. (2003)
Diffusion of Innovations, 5th edition, New York

Ropp, K. (1993)
Just what is a biologic, anyway?; in: FDA Consumer, Vol. 27, No.4,
URL: http://findarticles.com/p/articles/mi_m1370/is_n3_v27/ai_13608896/ [accessed January 31, 2011]

Rubenstein, S. (2009)
Report - Pfizer May Cut Sales Force by Nearly a Third, in: Wall Street Journal Blog,
URL: http://blogs.wsj.com/health/2009/01/15/report-pfizer-may-cut-sales-force-by-nearly-a-third/ [accessed February 23, 2011]

Sakamoto, J.; van de Ven, A.; Godin, B.; Blanco, E.; Serda, R. E.; Grattoni, A.; Ziemys, A.; Bouamrani, A.; Hu, T.; Ranganathan, S.; Rosa, E. de; Martinez, J.; Smid, C.; Buchanan, R. M.; Lee, S.; Srinivasan, S.; Landry, M.; Meyn, A.; Tasciotti, E.; Liu, X.; Decuzzi, P.; Ferrari, M. (2010)
Enabling Individualized Therapy Through Nanotechnology, in: Pharmacological Research, Vol. 62, No. 2, pp. 57-89

Santhera Website (2011)
URL: http://www.santhera.com/ [accessed November 14, 2011]

Schilsky, R. (2004)
Accelerated Approval Seen as Triumph and Roadblock for Cancer Drugs, in: Journal of the National Cancer Institute, Vol. 96, No. 20, pp. 1495-1496

Schlemminger, M. (2010)
The proof of the pudding – die Zulassung, in: Fischer, D., Breitenbach, J. (ed.): Die Pharmaindustrie. Einblick – Durchblick – Perspektiven, 3rd edition, München, pp. 135-147

Schöffski, O. (2007)
Grundformen gesundheitsökonomischer Evaluationen, in: Schöffski, O., Schulenburg, J.-M. Graf v. d. (ed.): Gesundheitsökonomische Evaluationen, Third, fully revised edition, Heidelberg, pp. 65-94

Schöffski, O. (2010)
Der Fall Lantus - Wozu brauchen wir die Gesundheitsökonomie?, in: Deutsche Medizinische Wochenschrift, Vol. 135, pp. 1033-1035

Schöffski, O., Fricke, F.-U. (2008)
Evaluationsforschung, in: Schöffski, O., Fricke, F., Guminski, W. (ed.): Pharmabetriebslehre, 2nd, fully revised and expanded edition, Heidelberg, pp. 73-87

Schöffski, O., Fricke, F.-U., Guminski, W. (ed.) (2008)
Pharmabetriebslehre, 2nd, fully revised and expanded edition, Heidelberg,

Schöffski, O., Schulenburg, J.-M. Graf v. d. (ed.) (2007)
Gesundheitsökonomische Evaluationen, Third, fully revised edition, Heidelberg,

Scholtissek, S. (2005)
Innovationspartnerschaften in Forschung & Entwicklung und Marketing & Vertrieb der Pharmaindustrie, in: Müller, M. (ed.): Europäisches Pharmamarketing – Ein Leitfaden für Manager der pharmazeutischen Industrie und Beteiligte des europäischen Gesundheitswesens, Wiesbaden

Scholz-Ligma, J. (2010)
Es wird weniger Massenprodukte in der Pharmabranche geben, in: Planung & Analyse, Vol. 3, p. 18

Schulz, E. (2001)
Laws of Branding, in: Executive Excellence, Vol. 18, No. 11, pp. 12-13

Schweitzer, A., Siewert, M. (2007)
Der Pharmamarkt – Forschen im Extremen, in: Naderer, G., Balzer, E. (ed.): Qualitative Marktforschung in Theorie und Praxis, Wiesbaden, pp. 625-632

Scott Morton, F. (1999)
Entry Decisions in the Generic Pharmaceutical Industry, in: RAND Journal of Economics, Vol. 30, No. 3, pp. 421-440

Sebivo Package Insert (2010)
URL: http://www.novartis.com.au/PI_PDF/seb.pdf [accessed January 28, 2011]

Seiter, S., Holz, B. (2009)
Launch Excellence aktuell – Anforderungen an Produktneueinführungen im veränderten Marktumfeld, in: pharmind – die pharmazeutische industrie, Vol. 71, No. 6, pp. 924-930

Senge, P. (2006)
The Fifth Discipline – The Art and Practice of the Learning Organization, 2nd edition, New York

Simon, F., Kotler, P. (2003)
Building Global Biobrands – Taking Biotechnology to Market, New York

Simon, H. (1989)
Strategie als Herausforderung im Pharmaunternehmen, in: Simon, H., Kucher, E., Hilleke-Daniel, K. (ed.): Wettbewerbsstrategien im Pharmamarkt, Stuttgart, pp. 1-15

Simon, H., Kucher, E., Hilleke-Daniel, K. (ed.) (1989)
Wettbewerbsstrategien im Pharmamarkt, Stuttgart

Simon, W. (1989)
Die Japanische Bedrohung – Japanische Pharmaunternehmen auf dem Vormarsch, in: Simon, H., Kucher, E., Hilleke-Daniel, K. (ed.): Wettbewerbsstrategien im Pharmamarkt, Stuttgart, pp. 241-252

Spanjol, J., Tam, L., Qualls, W., Bohlmann, J. (2011)
New Product Team Decision Making: Regulatory Focus Effects on Number, Type, and Timing Decisions, in: Journal of Product Innovation Management, Vol. 28, No. 5, pp. 623-640

Stephen, K. (2009)
Retooling the Pharma Marketing Model, in: Pharmaceutical Executive, Vol. 29, No. 4, also available at URL: http://pharmexec.findpharma.com/pharmexec/Marketing/Retooling-the-Pharma-Marketing-Model/ArticleStandard/Article/detail/592063 [accessed May 25, 2011]

Suh, D., Manning, W., Schondelmeyer, S., Hadsall, R. (2000)
Effect of multiple-source entry on price competition after patent expiration in the pharmaceutical industry, in: Health Services Research, Vol. 25, No. 2, pp. 529-547

Sullivan, U, Coughlan, A.. (2007)
The Detail of Drugs: Horizontal Distribution Alliances in the Global Pharmaceutical Industry, in: AMA Winter Educators' Conference Proceedings, Vol. 18, p. 203

Swissmedic Website (2011)
URL: http://www.swissmedic.ch/ [accessed September 11, 2011]

Taenzler, J. (2006)
Delivering New Insights for Product Managers by Studying the Patient's Symptom Presentation, in: Product Management Today, No.1,
URL: http://www.entrepreneur.com/tradejournals/article/160641721.html [accessed June 14, 2011]

Talke, K., Hultink, E. (2010)
Managing Diffusion Barriers When Launching New Products, in: Journal of Product Innovation Management, Vol. 27, No. 4, pp. 537-553

Teichmann, G., Twelsiek, O. (2008)
Portfolio-Management-Strategien für Pharmaunternehmen,
URL: http://www.pwc.de/de/gesundheitswesen-und-pharma/portfolio-management-strategien-fuer-pharmaunternehmen.jhtml [accessed January 31, 2011]

Terblanche, N. (2008)
New pharmaceutical product development - Barriers to overcome and opportunities to exploit, in: Journal of Commercial Biotechnology, Vol. 14, No. 3, pp. 201-212

Teva Pharmaceuticals (2011)
URL: http://www.tevapharm.com/ [accessed May 16, 2011]

Thölke, J., Hultink, E., Robben, H. (2001)
Launching New Product Features - A Multiple Case Examination, in: Journal of Product Innovation Management, Vol. 18, No. 1, pp. 3-14

Thomson Compumark (2011)
Pharmaceutical Services – Specialized Industry Solutions,
URL: http://thenewsaegis.com/PDF/TCMTR_PharmaServices_Final.pdf [accessed February 1, 2011]

Thumm, N.(2004)
Strategic Patenting in Biotechnology, in: Technology Analysis & Strategic Management, Vol. 16, No. 4, pp. 529-538

Towse, A., Garrison, L. (2010)
Can't Get No Satisfaction? Will Pay for Performance Help? Toward an Economic Framework for Understanding Performance-Based Risk-Sharing Agreements for Innovative Medical Products, in: PharmacoEconomics, Vol. 28, No. 2, pp. 93-102

Trilling, T. (2008)
Anforderungen an einen Produktmanager der pharmazeutischen Industrie, in: Trilling, T. (ed.): Pharmamarketing – Ein Leitfaden für die tägliche Praxis, 2nd, revised edition, Berlin, Heidelberg, pp. 37-40

Trilling, T. (2008a)
Besonderheiten bei der Neueinführung eines Arzneimittels, in: Trilling, T. (ed.): Pharmamarketing – Ein Leitfaden für die tägliche Praxis, 2nd, revised edition, Berlin, Heidelberg, pp. 219-232

Trilling, T. (2008b)
Die Zukunft des pharmazeutischen Marktes, in: Trilling, T. (ed.): Pharmamarketing – Ein Leitfaden für die tägliche Praxis, 2nd, revised edition, Berlin, Heidelberg, pp. 233-238

Trilling, T. (ed.) (2008c)
Pharmamarketing – Ein Leitfaden für die tägliche Praxis, 2nd, revised edition, Berlin, Heidelberg

Troll, K. (1989)
Marketingorientiertes Innovationsmanagement im Pharmamarkt, in: Simon, H., Kucher, E., Hilleke-Daniel, K. (ed.): Wettbewerbsstrategien im Pharmamarkt, Stuttgart, pp. 89-101

Tufts Center for the Study of Drug Development (2009)
URL: http://csdd.tufts.edu/_documents/www/Outlook2010.pdf [accessed May 24, 2011]

Tufts Center for the Study of Drug Development (2010)
U.S. Orphan Product Designations More than Doubled During Last Decade, URL: http://csdd.tufts.edu/news/complete_story/pr_jan-feb_2010 [accessed February 10, 2011]

UK Department of Health (2006)
Pharmaceutical Price Regulation Scheme, Ninth Report to Parliament

Vahs, D., Burmester, R. (2005)
Informationsmanagement - Von der Produktidee zur erfolgreichen Vermarktung, third edition, Stuttgart

Vanderveer, R. (2001)
Pharmaceutical Marketing is Going to be Different, and Very Soon, in: Medical Marketing & Media, Vol. 26, No. 1 URL: http://www.gfk.com/imperia/md/content/gfkv2/mm_m_volume_36__1_january_2001.pdf [accessed October 20, 2011]

Vanderveer, R. (2001a)
Building the Bridge between 'e' and the Sales Force, in: Medical Marketing & Media, Vol. 26, No. 11, pp. 58-67

Vanderveer, R. (2005)
The Doctor and the DTC, in: DTC Perspectives, Vol. 3, No. 4, pp. 24-28

Vanderveer, R. (2005a)
Position, Position, Position, in: Pharmaceutical Executive.com, URL: http://pharmexec.findpharma.com/pharmexec/PE+Features/Position-position-position/ArticleStandard/Article/detail/175701 [accessed June 7, 2011]

Vanderveer, R. (2006)
The Information Diet – How, when and why physicians consume information, in: Pharmaceutical Executive, Vol.26, No.9, also available at http://pharmexec.findpharma.com/pharmexec/Articles/The-Information-Diet/ArticleStandard/Article/detail/369278 [accessed June 14, 2011]

Vanderveer, R. (2007)
Revolutionary Marketing Research for and Evolutionary Pharmaceutical Market, in: Next Generation Pharmaceutical, No.10, pp. 130-131

Vanderveer, R. (2009)
Exploring the Impact of Health Care Reform on the Role of Marketing Research, in: PBIRG Perspectives, pp. 27-28, reprint on GfK website at URL: http://www.gfk.com/imperia/md/content/gfkv2/productinserts/hc_reform_pbirg_perspectives_fall_2009.pdf [accessed January 31, 2011]

Vanderveer, R., Heasley, J. (2005)
War Gaming – Exercises in defending brand territory, in: Medical Marketing & Media, May 2005 URL: http://www.gfk.com/imperia/md/content/gfkv2/medical_marketing___media__may_2005.pdf [accessed January 31, 2011]

Vanderveer, R., Pines, N. (2003)
A Marketer's Cure for Attention Deficit Disorder, in: Medical Marketing & Media, URL: http://www.gfk.com/imperia/md/content/gfkv2/pharmaceutical_representative_magazine__october_2003.pdf [accessed January 31, 2011]

Vanderveer, R., Pines, N. (2003a)
Where do Sales Aids come from?, reprint on GfK website of: Pharmaceutical Representative, Vol.33, No.10,
URL: http://www.gfk.com/imperia/md/content/gfkv2/pharmaceutical_representative_magazine__october_2003.pdf [accessed January 31, 2011]

Vanderveer, R., Pines, N. (2007)
Customer-Driven Positioning - The next generation approach to pharmaceutical product positioning, in: Journal of Medical Marketing, Vol. 7, No. 1, pp. 71-76

Vaughn, S., Gruber, S. (2009)
Examining Physician Segments – Understanding doctors' attitudes can drive better sales, in: Pharmaceutical Representative, Vol. 39, No.4, pp. 12-15

VFA – Verband der forschenden Pharma-Unternehmen (2010)
Verhaltensempfehlungen, URL: http://www.vfa.de/de/verband-mitglieder/verhaltensempfehlungen [accessed June 5, 2011]

VFA – Verband der forschenden Pharma-Unternehmen (2011)
Orphan Drugs, URL: http://www.vfa.de/de/wirtschaft-politik/positionen/pos-orphan-drugs.html [accessed February 11, 2011]

VFA – Verband der forschenden Pharma-Unternehmen (2011a)
Zusammenarbeit der vfa-Mitgliedsunternehmen mit Patientenorganisationen, URL: http://www.vfa.de/de/patienten/zusammenarbeit-mit-patientenselbsthilfegruppen/zusammenarbeit-vfa-mitgliedsunternehmen-patientenorganisationen.html [accessed June 5, 2011]

Viread Website (2012)
URL: http://www.viread.com [accessed November 14, 2011]

Waknine, Y. (2007)
FDA Adds Black Box Warning to Xolair Label, Medscape Today, URL: http://www.medscape.com/viewarticle/559244 [accessed October 27, 2010]

Waldrop-Bay, H. (2004)
Global Launch Meetings: How to Avoid Disaster and Build the Brand, in: Pharmaceutical Executive, Vol. 24, pp. 12-19

Wartenberg, F., Ziedman, D., Rickwood, S. (2010)
Launch Excellence - Facing Different Challenges,
URL: http://www.imshealth.com/imshealth/Global/Content/Document/Intelligence.360%20Documents/Launch_Excellence_Facing_Different_Challenges.pdf [accessed March 8, 2011]

Whalen, J. (2008)
Glaxo Seeks Guidance from Health Systems, in: Wall Street Journal, Vol. 243, No.188, p. B1

Weiner, B., Hull, B. (2007)
Global Marketing Research, in: Medical Marketing & Media, Vol. 42, No.7, pp. 55-65

Weißbäcker, S., Müller, M. (2005)
Vertriebsstrukturen in Europa, pp. 189-207, in: Müller, M. (ed.): Europäisches Pharmamarketing – Ein Leitfaden für Manager der pharmazeutischen Industrie und Beteiligte des europäischen Gesundheitswesens, Wiesbaden

Wolf Sussman, J. (2008)
Pharmamarketing, in: Schöffski, O., Fricke, F., Guminski, W. (ed.): Pharmabetriebslehre, 2nd, fully revised and expanded edition, Heidelberg, pp. 232-248

World Health Organization (WHO) (2011)
General principle for guidance devising international nonproprietary names for pharmaceutical substances, URL: http://www.who.int/medicines/services/inn/GeneralprinciplesEn.pdf [accessed May 24, 2011]

World Health Organization (WHO) (2011a)
WHO International Nonproprietary Names – Business Model Process,
URL: http://www.who.int/medicines/services/inn/inn_b_proc_simplified_Nov2005.jpg [accessed May 24, 2011]

World Intellectual Property Organization (2011)
URL: http://www.wipo.int/pct/en/ [accessed May 19. 2011]

World Intellectual Property Organization (2011a)
URL: http://www.wipo.int/madrid/en [accessed June 9, 2011]

Xolair Package Insert (2010)
URL: http://www.gene.com/gene/products/information/pdf/xolair-prescribing.pdf [accessed January 28, 2011]

Zeiner, R. (2008)
Erfolgsfaktoren der Neuprodukteinführung, in: Schöffski, O., Fricke, F., Guminski, W. (ed.): Pharmabetriebslehre, 2nd, fully revised and expanded edition, Heidelberg, pp. 429-441

Zeiner, R., Schiel, D. (2007)
Launch Excellence, in: pharmind – die pharmazeutische industrie , No. 12, pp. 1396-1402

Zollondz, H.-D. (2008)
Marketing-Mix - Die sieben P des Marketings, 3rd edition, Berlin

Appendix

Overview of Key Success Factor Study Data used in this dissertation

General Literature and Studies	
Barclay (1992)	• Meta-Analysis of numerous new product success studies conducted, namely: o Hopkins (1981): 91 medium and large sized US companies; o Booz Allen & Hamilton (1982): Comprehensive best practices study on new product development in Fortune 1000 companies as reported by product managers and executives o Stanford Innovation Project (1982): List of new product success factors in the technology field o Peters and Waterman (1982): Study of successful US companies and their characteristic attributes o Coopers (1983): Meta-analysis and synthesis of previous research studies o Lin (1986): Tangible and intangible reasons for product failure o Souder (1987): study searching for common characteristics in 289 new product development innovations o Barclay and Benson (1987): Literature review o Johne and Snelson (1988): R&D checklist for successful product development based on McKinsey '7S' model o Barclay and Benson (1990): Questionnaire survey of 149 companies • 140 factors associated with new product success identified, digitally analyzed and summarized
Brettel, Sattler (2009)	• Meta-analysis of previous analysis on a project- and organizational level • 293 effects from 48 independent samples and 45 studies were identified and reviewed

Di Benedetto (1999)	• Product launch success data collected from 183 Product Development & Management Association (PDMA) practitioner members (11% response rate on the initial mailing and follow up mailing) using retrospective perceptions on recent new product launches • Perceptual data provided for 7 skills and resources, 14 strategic activities, and 17 tactical activities, and 8 marketing information-gathering activities, previously identified in scant launch literature
Ernst (2002)	• Meta-analysis of review articles and other meta-analyses in the general field of new product development over the course of the past 30 years. • Focused on works that empirically analyze the relationship between potential success factors and the actual success with large samples and statistical significance information on the empirical results (excluded are studies that simply ask for success factors and case studies).
Henard, Szymanski (2001)	• Meta-analysis of 60 studies with the goal to present insights on determinants of new product performance. • Using the correlation matrixes of the original studies, the data was entered into a database and analyzed for correlations across all models.
Langerak, et al. (2004)	• Study to determine the importance of new product development for market-oriented firms, using data from 126 firms in the Netherlands • Questions generated using available literature and expert interviews in academia and practice, then pretested in multiple rounds
Kuhn (2007)	• Dissertation on key success factors for product launches (marketing focus) • Extensive review of studies done on sequencing, competitive reactions, pre-marketing, product-specific, market-specific, and marketing success factors, all integrated into questionnaire for the empirical part of the dissertation • Starting in 2004, 178 surveys were filled out by highest-ranking marketing & sales executives responsible for new product launches in 62 companies (8% by the pharmaceutical industry) in Germany and Austria

Bio / Pharmaceutical Literature and Studies	
Gudiksen, et al. (2008)	• McKinsey study rating all specialty pharmaceutical launches between 1994 and 2003 across various dimensions and using regression analysis to establish the critical factors.
Illert, et al. (2007)	• Capgemini Consulting Paper based on experience in international projects with biopharmaceutical companies
Seiter, Holz (2009)	• IMS Management Consulting quantitative evaluation of 3081 pharmaceutical launches in 64 therapeutic areas within 8 key markets (Canada, Germany, France, Italy, Japan, Spain, United Kingdom, United States) between 2000-2005 • 3 evaluation criteria (early market leadership, promotional effectiveness, and quick market penetration) were selected by IMS
Simon, Kotler (2003), p. 115	• Experience-based expert overview of the triple process necessary to address the innovated nature of the market and its therapies. Derived from consulting efforts and experiences by SDC Group, partially adapted from McKinsey (Achieving World-Class Performance in Pharmaceutical Product Launches, April 2002)
Zeiner, Schiel (2007), pp. 1396-1402	• Launch Excellence Study, reviews quantitative market data of 4225 product launches (77% primary care, 23% specialty) in 8 countries (Canada, Germany, France, Italy, Japan, Spain, United Kingdom, United States) over 8 years (1995-2004) • Three success criteria (medical competence, promotional effectiveness, and market penetration) are statistically proven

Schriften zur Gesundheitsökonomie

HERZ

Health Economics Research Zentrum
Buchweizenfeld 27
31303 Burgdorf
Fax: +49(0)5136/976187
email: herz@schoeffski.de

Bisher erschienen:

Band 1 *Steininger-Niederleitner, M., Sohn, S., Schöffski, O. (2003)*
Managed Care in der Schweiz und Übertragungsmöglichkeiten nach Deutschland
ISBN 3-936863-00-8, 172 S., 18 Abb., Geb. EUR 19,90

Band 2 *Esslinger, A. S. (2003)*
Qualitätsorientierte strategische Planung und Steuerung in einem sozialen Dienstleistungsunternehmen mit Hilfe der Balanced Scorecard
ISBN 3-936863-01-6, 276 S., 36 Abb., 50 Tab., Geb. EUR 29,90

Band 3 *Lindenthal, J., Sohn, S., Schöffski, O. (2004)*
Praxisnetze der nächsten Generation: Ziele, Mittelverteilung und Steuerungsmechanismen
ISBN 3-936863-02-4, 216 S., 16 Abb., 19 Tab., Geb. EUR 24,90

Band 4 *Steinbach, H., Sohn, S., Schöffski, O. (2004)*
Möglichkeiten der Kalkulation von sektorenübergreifenden Kopfpauschalen (Capitation)
ISBN 3-936863-03-2, 312 S., 22 Abb., 28 Tab., Geb. EUR 29,90

Band 5 *Glock, G., Sohn, S., Schöffski, O. (2004)*
IT-Unterstützung für den medizinischen Prozess in der integrierten Versorgung
ISBN 3-936863-04-0, 208 S., 22 Abb., Geb. EUR 24,90

Band 6 *Hagn, D., Schöffski, O. (2005)*
Orphan Drugs. A Challenge for the Pharmaceutical Industry in Europe
ISBN 3-936863-05-9, 160 S., 37 Abb., 20 Tab., Geb. EUR 19,90

Band 7 *Pelleter, J., Sohn, S., Schöffski, O. (2004)*
Medizinische Versorgungszentren. Grundlagen, Chancen und Risiken einer neuen Versorgungsform
ISBN 3-936863-06-7, 196 S., 18 Abb., Geb. EUR 24,90

Band 8 *Sohn, S. (2006)*
Integration und Effizienz im Gesundheitswesen. Instrumente und ihre Evidenz für die integrierte Versorgung
ISBN 3-936863-07-5, 288 S., 26 Abb., 28 Tab., Geb. EUR 29,90

Band 9 *Hämmerle, P., Estelmann, A., Schwandt, M., Schöffski, O. (2006)*
Moderne Verfahren der Qualitätsberichterstattung im Krankenhaus
ISBN 3-936863-08-3, 140 S., 33 Abb., Geb. EUR 19,90

Band 10 *Marschall, D. (2007)*
Positionierung einer erfolgreichen Arzneimittelmarke
ISBN 978-3-936863-09-3, 244 S., 54 Abb., 24 Tab., Geb. EUR 24,90

Band 11 *Haarländer, S., Bühner, A., Schwandt, M., Schöffski, O. (2007)*
Public Private Partnership (PPP) im Krankenhausbereich
ISBN 978-3-936863-10-9, 192 S., 32 Abb., 3 Tab., Geb. EUR 24,90

Band 12 *Schmitt-Rüth, S., Esslinger, A. S., Schöffski, O. (2007)*
Der Markt für Medizintechnik – Analyse der Entwicklungen im Wandel der Zeit
ISBN 978-3-936863-11-6, 172 S., 20 Abb., 6 Tab., Geb. EUR 19,90

Band 13 *Sauer, F. (2007)*
Erfolgsfaktoren für das marktorientierte Management patentgeschützter Arzneimittel
ISBN 978-3-936863-12-3, 388 S., 54 Abb., 29 Tab., Geb. EUR 34,90

Band 14 *Emmert, M. (2008)*
Pay for Performance (P4P) im Gesundheitswesen – Ein Ansatz zur Verbesserung der Gesundheitsversorgung?
ISBN 978-3-936863-12-3, 460 S., 41 Abb., 77 Tab., Geb. EUR 39,90

Band 15 *Patzak, M. (2009)*
Alternative Finanzierungsinstrumente für Krankenhäuser
ISBN 978-3-936863-14-7, 320 S., 340 Abb., 28 Tab., Geb. EUR 39,90

Band 16 *Heil, A., Schwandt, M., Schöffski, O. (2009)*
Darstellung ärztlicher Weiterbildungskosten im Krankenhaus
ISBN 978-3-936863-15-4, 156 S., 9 Abb., 8 Tab., Geb. EUR 24,90

Band 17 *Held, S., Bolte, C., Bierbaum, M., Schöffski, O. (2009)*
Impact of Big Pharma organizational structure on R&D productivity
ISBN 978-3-936863-16-1, 160 S., 22 Abb., 29 Tab., Geb. EUR 24,90

Band 18 *Lauerer, M., Emmert, M., Schöffski, O. (2011)*
Die Qualität des deutschen Gesundheitswesens im internationalen Vergleich
ISBN 978-3-936863-17-8, 204 S., 14 Abb., 27 Tab., Geb. EUR 24,90

Band 19 *Scheppach, M., Emmert, M., Schöffski, O. (2011)*
Pay for Performance (P4P) im Gesundheitswesen: Leitfaden für eine erfolgreiche Einführung
ISBN 978-3-936863-18-5, 184 S., 23 Abb., 18 Tab., Geb. EUR 24,90

Band 20 *Pelleter, J. (2012)*
Organisatorische und institutionelle Herausforderungen bei der Implementierung von Integrierten Versorgungskonzepten am Beispiel der Telemedizin
ISBN 978-3-936863-19-2, 675 S., 67 Abb., 10 Tab., Geb. EUR 49,90

Band 21 *Kloep, M. (2012)*
Managed Equipment Services as a Conceptual Business Opportunity Model for the GCC with Focus on UAE - An Institutional and Economic Analysis.
ISBN 978-3-936863-20-8, 212 S., 17 Abb., 22 Tab., Geb. EUR 24,90

Band 22 *Wolf Sussman, J. (2013)*
Key Considerations for Successful Biotechnological and Pharmaceutical Product Launches
ISBN 978-3-936863-21-5, 268 S., 47 Abb., 26 Tab., Geb. EUR 29,90